Thinking Clearly About Death

Thinking Clearly About Death

Jay F. Rosenberg

University of North Carolina at Chapel Hill

Prentice-Hall, Inc., Englewood Cliffs, New Jersey 07632

Library of Congress Cataloging in Publication Data

Rosenberg, Jay F.
    Thinking clearly about death.

    Includes bibliographical references.
    1. Death.   2. Euthanasia.   3. Suicide.
4. Death—Psychological aspects.   I. Title.
HQ1073.R67 1983   306.9   82-12189
ISBN   0-13-917559-8

Printed in the United States of America

10   9   8   7   6   5   4   3   2   1

Editorial/production supervision and design by Patricia V. Amoroso
Cover design by Ray Lundgren
Manufacturing buyer: Harry P. Baisley

ISBN 0-13-917559-8

Prentice-Hall International, Inc., *London*
Prentice-Hall of Australia Pty. Limited, *Sydney*
Prentice-Hall Canada Inc., *Toronto*
Prentice-Hall of India Private Limited, *New Delhi*
Prentice-Hall of Japan, Inc., *Tokyo*
Prentice-Hall of Southeast Asia Pte. Ltd., *Singapore*
Whitehall Books Limited, *Wellington, New Zealand*

For Regina

Zweiter Versuch; erster Erfolg.
Übung macht den Meister

For Regina

Zweiter Versuch; erster Erfolg.
Übung macht den Meister

MOTTO

Of all the wonders that I yet have heard,
It seems to me most strange that men should fear;
Seeing that death, a necessary end,
Will come when it will come.

—William Shakespeare
JULIUS CAESAR
II, ii, 34–7

Contents

Preface

This is a book of a species largely unfamiliar to the general public. It is a philosophical treatise. More particularly, it is a work of what one might call "hard-core" analytic philosophy, written by someone whose full-time business is being a professor of such philosophy. A few words of explanation—and reassurance—are consequently in order.

The book is chock full of arguments. That is, definite theses are advanced, definite claims are made, and then reasons are offered—at length and in detail—in support of them, reasons for accepting the theses or believing the claims. The book, therefore, presupposes that its readers have the ability and, more importantly, the inclination to think and that they have the desire to think clearly, specifically about death. But I have tried very hard to make sure that the book presupposes nothing else, and, in particular, to ensure that it does not presuppose any prior encounter or acquaintance with "academic" philosophy, whether of my "analytic" variety or of any other.

To this end, I have delayed, for the length of one chapter, the business of finally getting down to talking about death. Instead, I have begun with a chapter—Chapter 0—in which I have tried to explain my methods, to make clear the sort of enterprise which I will be up to when I finally do, in succeeding chapters, get down to talking about death. Chapter 0, then, is not essential to the theses, claims, and arguments which comprise the body of this work. If I have done my job right, however, Chapter 0 will nevertheless be useful. For it should help the reader to understand what sorts of theses and what kinds of claims I shall be defending in my succeeding chapters, and by what variety of arguments I shall attempt to establish those claims and theses. Chapter 0, in other words, is an introduction to what I mean by "thinking clearly." I would consequently encourage the reader to spend some time on it, however impatiently.

The remainder of the book can be roughly divided into two parts: Chapters 1 through 4 are devoted to what could be called "The Metaphysics of Death"; Chapters 5 through 9, to "The Ethics of Death." Under the heading "The Metaphysics of Death," what I chiefly discuss is the question of "survival"—that is, the question of an "afterlife"—together with such kindred subjects as the nature of persons and the matter of "minds" or "souls," although I have attempted to say something useful as well about the nature of death itself and about its recognition as an empirical phenomenon. Under the heading "The Ethics of Death," I devote my arguments primarily to three topics: euthanasia or "mercy killing," artificially prolonged life versus "letting die," and the morality and rationality of suicide and of various first-person attitudes and expectations with regard to death. The book as a whole, then, constitutes a fairly comprehensive study of those questions about death to which philosophers have traditionally addressed their attentions. Where I have been forced to leave something dangling in the text, I have tried to tie off the loose ends in the footnotes which are collected as an Appendix.

This is not a book to jump around in or to skim. Its arguments are to a large extent cumulative. That is, in defending some claim or thesis, I will frequently rely in an essential way on some other claim or thesis which I have argued for and established earlier in the investigation. Part of what goes into "thinking clearly" about death—or anything else, for that matter—is this deliberate, cumulative, step-by-step sort of reasoning, and so I make no apologies for it. I have tried, however, to ease the tedium of this procedure a bit by dividing each chapter into a series of sections or "bite-sized chunks"—each of which is intended, given what has gone before it, to be a relatively self-contained piece of argumentation which advances the discussion one manageable step. The book thus contains some ninety points at which the reader can safely put it down and go drink a cup of coffee without running a serious risk of losing track of what is going on.

The theses, claims, and arguments constituting this book are, of course, not all the spontaneous creations of my solitary ruminations (although some of them are). Many of them, obviously, first saw light in the works of other philosophers, and appropriate references to those works may be found in the footnotes of the Appendix. In addition, I have been chatting about these matters with my colleagues off and on for some fifteen years now, and those conversations have not been without their effects. In particular, I should acknowledge the influences of Steve Darwall and especially of W. D. Falk on my views in moral and social philosophy, and that of Douglas Long on my thinking about persons. The debt owed my own teachers in philosophy also has a good number of years yet to run. Kurt Baier, Jerome Schneewind, and (as always) Wilfrid Sellars are particularly implicated in the thought-processes which led up to the writing of this book. Responsibility for any errors, fallacies, mistakes, blunders, aberrations, misconstructions, lapses, oversights, distortions, omissions, inaccuracies, misinterpretations, indiscretions, or outright falsehoods which the book may yet contain remains, needless to say, my very own.

There is no typist to thank. I did it all myself—on a TRS-80 Model III Microcomputer with two mini-diskette drives, a line printer, and word-processing software. It seems silly to thank a machine, but my appreciation of the extent to which the electronic beast has eased the annoying process of manuscript preparation is real enough in any event.

My wife, Regina, very patiently tolerated my extended disappearances into my study to commune with my semi-automated electronic muse. My gratitude then, finally, to her—and to Leslie and Glen, who fed the cats and kept out of the way.

JAY F. ROSENBERG

Chapel Hill, NC
1982

PRELUDE

Death as a Problem for Philosophy

According to Socrates, the true philosopher welcomes death. It is not an end, but a transition. It carries the philosopher out of the world of sensory appearances and into a realm of immutable realities, the Forms, which, knowingly or unknowingly, have always been his proper concern.

Socrates' final conversation, brilliantly recounted by Plato in the *Phaedo,* addressed itself precisely to this theme of the nature of death and the prospects for survival.[1] Socrates was also the first to claim the title of philosopher, a "lover of wisdom." The question of death, then, was built into the heart of the philosophical enterprise at its very origins. It belongs to the core of our enduring problematic.

The theme of death has entered historically into the ongoing philosophical conversation in a variety of ways. During the mediaeval period, when philosophy was largely "the handmaiden of theology," philosophical efforts were centrally dedicated to harmonizing the revealed teachings of the Church, accepted as doctrinal truths, with the dictates of reason. This enterprise found perhaps its final flowering, however, in the work of the first post-Mediaeval philosopher, René Descartes. His famous attempt[2] to demonstrate "the real distinctness of the mind from the body" was, at least in part, an effort to secure the possibility of that survival taught by the Church as dogma, a possibility which, at least implicitly, was threatened by the claims to truth of an emerging natural science, experiencing its birth-pangs in the trial and condemnation of Galileo.

Immanuel Kant, in contrast, argued that the possibility of immortality—the survival of death—could not be established by theoretical reasoning at all.[3] Instead, he assigned to immortality, along with God and freedom-of-the-will, the role of a necessary "postulate of practical reason"—something, that is, which we must posit as a condition of the possibility of the moral life. And, closer to our own time, Martin Heidegger of-

1

fered our unique awareness of our own mortality as an essential feature of our distinctive personhood.[4] Unlike other organisms, he argued, we live toward our deaths ("das Leben zum Tod"), and all of our life-projects are thus necessarily conditioned by a consciousness of our own finitude and limitation.

Nowadays, the topic of death and the question of survival are very much in the public eye.[5] An advancing medical technology has given rise to acute, often legal, questions regarding the nature of death: Just what is it? Why does it happen? When can we justifiably conclude that it has happened? Psychologists and sociologists are exploring both personal and public attitudes toward death—the acceptance or denial of impending death by the dying, the struggle for dignity in death, and the strategies for coping with grief and loss pursued among the living. At the same time, researchers have been vigorously gathering evidence and testimony which they, at least, conclude supports the hypothesis of an "afterlife"—not now as an article of Church doctrine but as a matter of "scientific fact." And we are even being treated to a spate of accounts by people who claim in one way or another to have visited "the world beyond the grave" and who, like explorers returned from remote lands, are anxious to share with us their impressions of its climate and topography.

Throughout this recent period, philosophy in the English-speaking world—by which I mean predominantly what is called "linguistic" or "analytic" philosophy—has not remained silent on the topic of death. Its conclusions, however, have made curiously little impact on anyone outside the academy. They have, in fact, not quite made their way into the public debates and discussions at all. This is partly, of course, because there is barely enough unanimity among the views of contemporary analytic philosophers today to allow one to speak of "conclusions" in the first place, but also, and more importantly, because "philosophical analysis" pursues its investigations by methods which are, at best, only tenuously understood outside of the academic world and which yield results that, especially to the untrained public eye, unfortunately give every impression of being sterile and, worse, of being totally removed from any matters of real human concern.

Now I am myself an analytic philosopher, and I have become convinced that this sense of sterility and irrelevance is in fact an illusion—one hopes, a correctable illusion. I do not believe, that is, that my methods, such as they are, are sterile. It is, alas, the case, however, that those methods are rather austere—and, more importantly, sufficiently unlike the methods of, for example, the natural and social sciences to engender justifiable puzzlement in those who encounter them in operation for the first time without any prior explanations. Nor do I believe that our philosophical results, such as they are, are irrelevant to the medical, legal, psychological, sociological, and even theological questions which understandably occupy the forefront of public attention to the topic of death and the question of survival. The relevance of those results, however, does lie at one remove, so to speak, from those questions—for I, at least, do not purport to offer answers to most of them, but rather aspire to a certain kind of clarity about what is being asked

and about what sorts of answers, given this clarity, one can reasonably and rationally expect to be able to find.

I propose in this book to take the topic of death and the question of survival as case studies for the fruitfulness and relevance of today's analytic philosophy. (Or rather, for safety's sake, of my analytic philosophy—for my experiences in academic life have taught me how little straightforward un-qualified agreement I am likely to receive from my colleagues.) My aim is to proceed as directly as possible to a coherent philosophical understanding of the nature of death—one which will allow us to draw some conclusions concerning the prospects for survival and the possibilities regarding an "afterlife"—and then to use the insights won to address, first, some of the key moral questions centering on the theme of death and, finally, the inescapable first-person question: What expectations and attitudes can one reasonably have about the fact of one's own inevitable mortality?

"As directly as possible," however, means different things in different contexts, and in the present instance, I fear, a straight line turns out not to be the shortest distance between my point of departure and my conclusions. It will not be as bad as the Supreme Court's "with all deliberate speed" turned out to be, but we will, I suspect, unavoidably be ranging rather widely over a complicated terrain, and our wanderings will take us down some remote and little-used byways of thought and language. When this happens, I shall try to erect a few signposts to remind us, at least, of our intended destination.

Our first order of business, however, must be to see to our means of conveyance. What I need to talk about next, then, is method—the sorts of questions which I shall be asking and the sorts of considerations which I shall bring to bear in attempting to answer them. Let me first turn briefly, therefore, to the topic of analytic philosophy as I shall understand it—and be practicing it—at least for the balance of this book.

CHAPTER 0

Some Methodological Preliminaries

0.1: ANALYTIC METHOD IN PHILOSOPHY—
FOUR THESES

There is no unanimity among academic philosophers today about what is or should be meant by "analytic philosophy." Since its emergence into methodological self-consciousness with the work of Bertrand Russell and G. E. Moore in the early years of this century,[1] analytic philosophy has meant different things to its different adherents—so much so that nowadays it is not even remotely a unitary school of philosophical thought but rather what is best characterized as a shared style of philosophical practice.[2] Looked at simply as a genre of philosophical prose, the analytic style of philosophizing is distinguished, negatively, by a marked aversion to the advocacy of sweeping metaphysical theses in the grand classical style and to system-building in general and, positively, by a seemingly obsessive attention to niceties and nuances of language and (often with the aid of mathematical symbolisms) to fine points of logic as well.

These appearances are accurate as far as they go, but they are also, of course, only appearances. The analytic style of philosophizing has that look to it for reasons, and we need to locate these reasons in order to appreciate the strengths and weaknesses of its underlying methods. So I want next to offer four methodological theses which capture my understanding of what analytic philosophy is, in general, up to and which, I think, would be acceptable (at least in some qualified form) to most of its practitioners.[3] I shall first simply state the theses, and then I shall comment on them.

> Thesis 1: Analytic philosophy does not attempt to advance a particular vision of the world but rather addresses itself to the conditions of thinking sensibly about the world.

Thesis 2:   The conditions of thinking sensibly are identical to the conditions of speaking sensibly.

Thesis 3:   There is appearance and reality with respect to language.

Thesis 4:   The language in which philosophy itself is practiced is not exempt.

Thesis 1 explains the general absence of traditional "philosophical systems" within the analytic tradition. While an analytic philosopher may be an advocate of some grand world-conception, he is not concerned in his professional capacity so much with articulating and defending this or that world-view, as with articulating and defending criteria according to which the intelligibility, clarity, coherence, rationality, cogency, or plausibility of various theses and systems ought properly to be assessed. This aim puts his questions "at one remove from the facts." Rather than asking "Is this or that thesis true?" or "What evidence is there in favor of this or that belief?", an analytic philosopher will more likely pose such questions as "How are we to understand this thesis?", "What is meant by it?", and "What sorts of grounds or reasons could there be for believing it?"

Thesis 2 captures what has been called "the linguistic turn" of analytic philosophy. It amounts to a denial of "inexpressible thoughts." Whatever can be thought can be said. But Thesis 2 should not be interpreted as saying more than it does. In particular, we should not make the mistake of concluding that the thesis aims to rule out the inexhaustible richness of lived experience. There is much that can be seen or felt or sensed which cannot be said—the pain of an injured tooth, the love of a parent for a child, the diffuse anxieties of adolescence, the beauty of a sunset, the grief at the loss of a dear friend. Thesis 2 denies the reality of none of this. But Thesis 2 does insist that one can think sensibly about such—or any—realities only to the extent that one can speak sensibly about them. Sensitivity, depth of feeling, empathy, and appreciation may remain wordless and inarticulate, but our understanding of any matter extends no further than our abilities to intelligibly formulate what we supposedly understand in words which another could, in principle, equally understand.

Thesis 3 is the very heart of analytic philosophizing. Theses 1 and 2 refocus attention from conceptions of the world onto the words in which such conceptions are expressed. Thesis 3 explains the point of this refocusing. Not only are things not always what they seem, but words, too, are not always what they seem. Sometimes what is being said is not the same as what appears to be being said. And sometimes, when it appears that something is being said, nothing at all is being said.

This distinction between linguistic appearance and linguistic reality is enshrined in the history of analytic philosophizing under a variety of names: "grammatical form" versus "logical form," "surface grammar" versus "depth grammar," and even Ludwig Wittgenstein's famous contrast between "the picture which holds us captive" (This picture, he wrote, "lay in our language and language seemed to repeat it to us inexorably") and "the language game which is actually played."[4] But however the contrast has from time to time been formulated, one central aim of analytic philosophizing has always been to penetrate the superficial appearances of our language and command a clear view of its realities—thereby to command a clear view of what can sensibly be thought about our nonlinguistic realities as well.

Thesis 4, finally, explains our fussiness. Language is not only an object of analytic philosophizing but its medium as well. Obviously this poses a problem for the practitioner. Superficial linguistic appearances can muddy the thinking of philosophers as readily as that of nonphilosophers. How, then, can we claim any confidence in our results?

Well, we can—but it will have to be a guarded confidence. We can at least see to it that the positive theses which we advocate are intelligible according to the standards of intelligibility which we defend. That is, we can apply the results of our investigations reflexively to the contents of those investigations themselves. This will at least protect us against advocacies which are internally incoherent. While that does not guarantee the correctness of our results with certainty, it does warrant a suitably guarded confidence in those results, for (as we shall see) such internally coherent points of view are not all that easy to arrive at.

The upshot of the constraint implied by Thesis 4, however, is that we analytic philosophers wind up spending a lot of time talking about our own talking. This accounts for a large part of the feeling of sterility that can accompany the casual reading of analytic philosophy, I think—and the criticism has a point. But so do we. It is surely exciting to encounter a metaphysical world-view boldly being sketched in broad brushstrokes. But when the excitement dies down, there may well remain the question "But what actually is being said here?"—and that is where my kind of drudgery begins.

Well, I have been using a rather broad brush myself to sketch out these methodological remarks, and one may well be tempted to ask "What actually is being said here." What does all this talk about linguistic appearance and linguistic reality amount to anyway? It is high time, in other words, that we got down to cases. Let me therefore offer a few examples of the sort of thing I will be up to when I turn to the topic of death—and, while I am at it, collect some notions and principles which will prove useful to us later on.

0.2: A MOTLEY OF MODIFIERS

Let's begin with something quite simple:

(A1) The thing on the table is a red book.

Adjectives, as any standard grammar book will tell you, stand for properties. In a sentence such as (A1), for example, the noun 'book' stands for an object or thing (the thing on the table, in fact, if what the sentence says is true) and the adjective 'red' stands for a property of that thing. Properties, on the received account, may be shared by many things. Thus there are red roses, red shirts, red automobiles, red sails in the sunset, and so on, all of which share with the book on the table the property of being red. Still hewing to traditional accounts, properties are distinct from the things whose properties they are. A thing can change its properties—lose some and gain others—and still remain the thing one began with. We can paint or dye the cover of the book on the table, making it a green book or a yellow book, and it will still be the same book we started with. Only its color will have changed.

All this is, so far, rather straightforward. But it contains the seeds of a muddle. Our standard grammar books elevate the muddle into a doctrine, the doctrine with which we began: Adjectives stand for properties. That's wrong. If what it means for some word to stand for a property is for it to behave the way that 'red' behaves in (A1), then it turns out that precious few adjectives indeed stand for properties. For example, (A1) can be paraphrased as

(A2) The thing on the table is a book which is red.

But try the same transformation on

(A3) The woman on the sofa is a nuclear physicist.

What you get is a piece of plain nonsense:

(A4) The woman on the sofa is a physicist who is nuclear.

Or, again,

(A5) The man in the corner is an utter fool.

gives us

(A6) The man in the corner is a fool who is utter.

Nonsense again. Neither 'nuclear' in (A3) nor 'utter' in (A5) is doing the same job as 'red' in (A1). If that job is standing for a property, then neither 'nuclear' nor 'utter' stands for a property.

Consider, in contrast,

(A7) The figure on page six is an equilateral triangle.

Does the word 'equilateral' in (A7) stand for a property of a triangle (the property of being equilateral) as the word 'red' in (A1) stands for a property of a book (the property of being red)? It is tempting to think so. (A7), at least, passes the paraphrasing test which disqualified 'nuclear' and 'utter'. There is nothing wrong with

(A8) The figure on page six is a triangle which is equilateral.

But, according to our traditional account, a thing can change its properties and still remain the thing one began with. Suppose we altered the figure on page six by making it a right triangle. Shall we say that we still have the same triangle with which we began, that only its shape has changed? Surely not. Change the shape and you change the triangle. But why? Well, here's a clue: A book *has* a color, but a triangle *is* a shape.

Or again, consider

(A9) The document in the drawer is a counterfeit passport.

Here the test of paraphrase will be failed again—but for quite a different reason.

(A10) The document in the drawer is a passport which is counterfeit,

is less obviously a bit of nonsense that (A4) or (A6)—but it will not do as a paraphrase of (A9) all the same. The reason is that (A10) claims there to be a passport in the drawer. But if (A9) is true, there is no passport in the drawer. A counterfeit passport is not a kind of passport. This is different from all of our earlier examples. A red book is one kind of book; a nuclear physicist, one kind of physicist; an equilateral triangle, one kind of triangle; and an utter fool, one kind of fool. But a counterfeit passport is merely a document which purports to be a passport. It is not one kind of passport among others. It looks like a passport, perhaps. But it isn't one.

The phenomenon is not just limited to adjectives, of course. Modifiers in general are not all of a piece. An oil stain is a stain caused by oil, but an oil lamp is not a lamp caused by oil. An oil lamp is a lamp which burns oil. But an oil well is not a well which burns oil. An oil well is a well which produces oil. An oil painting, however, is not a painting which produces oil, nor one which burns oil, nor one caused by oil. It is a painting painted with oil-based paints. Nor have we reached an end here. For there are oil stocks, oil tycoons, oil tanks, oil trucks, ...[5] Examples could be multiplied indefinitely.

The thing on the table is a red book.

The woman on the sofa is a nuclear physicist.

The man in the corner is an utter fool.

The figure on page six is an equilateral triangle.

The document in the drawer is a counterfeit passport.

The picture on the wall is an oil painting.

Grammar books tell the same story about all of these. They all have the same look to them:

The X located at Y is a MODIFIER + NOUN.

That is what is meant by linguistic appearances, by "surface grammar" or "grammatical form." But they are all quite different—and different in different ways. And that is what is meant by linguistic realities, by "depth grammar" or "logical form."

Not all adjectives stand for properties. Modifiers in general are not all of a piece. These are the limited morals which I want to carry away from this example. They will, in fact, prove useful when we come to look at death. They would have proved useful at various points in the history of philosophy as well. Philosophers have spent a lot of time trying to figure out what kind of property goodness is, for instance. It is only lately that we have learned to ask "Does the word 'good' stand for a property at all?" And the answer turns out to be: probably not.

0.3: THINGS AND "THINGS"

Let us continue to challenge those cherished principles that we all learned so diligently in our elementary school English classes. The next example will have a somewhat more subtle moral than the first one. I saw my friend Mary today and noticed that

(B1) Mary wore a warm cotton overcoat,

and

(B2) Mary wore a warm welcoming smile.

What shall we say about (B1) and (B2)?

A noun is the name of a person, place, or thing. Everybody knows that. In (B1), for example, the noun 'Mary' is the name of Mary and the noun 'overcoat' stands for her overcoat. And in (B2), the noun 'Mary' is again the name of Mary and the noun 'smile' presumably stands for a smile. So far, everything is again quite straightforward. But let's think about smiles for a minute.

Smiles are really very mysterious things—not just the Mona Lisa's, but all of them. They don't seem to be detachable. Mary can take off her warm cotton overcoat and hang it in the closet, drape it over the back of a chair, lend it to her roommate Sally, send it to the dry cleaner, and so on. But she can't do any of those things with her warm welcoming smile. Indeed, she can't do very much at all with her warm welcoming smile. (Perhaps she could "wipe it off her face," but that's about all.) Now why not? Why can't Mary lend her warm welcoming smile to Sally? Why can't the warm welcoming smile which Sally was wearing tonight be the same warm welcoming smile which Mary wore this morning? The warm cotton overcoat which Sally was wearing tonight certainly could be the same warm cotton overcoat which Mary wore this morning.

So smiles, unlike overcoats, seem to be very private property. They are also elusive, rather thin, things. Consider the relation between Mary's warm welcoming smile and Mary's curved lips, for instance. Are they two things or one thing? Neither answer satisfies. If we say that they are two things, then we seem to be thinking of the smile as a sort of ghostly entity which hovers about Mary's lips or is somehow pasted over them like a decal—and that surely won't do. So perhaps we should say that Mary's warm welcoming smile just is her lips curved in that particular fashion. But suppose that Mary is a subject in a medical experiment. Electrodes are implanted in her face and, when they are energized, the current causes her lips to curve in just that fashion. Would Mary then be wearing a warm welcoming smile? Well, she might look like she was—but it's pretty clear, I think, that she wouldn't be. And that shows that her warm welcoming smile can't just be her curved lips.

Finally, if we think about it for a minute, we'll realize that we have no idea how to count smiles. We can count overcoats easily enough—determine how many Mary owns and how many she wears on a given day. But how many smiles does Mary have? Was the warm welcoming smile she wore when I saw her this morning the same one as the warm welcoming smile she wore when I ran into her last week? Or was it another warm welcoming smile, just like the other one? These questions just don't have any answers.

So smiles seem to be very mysterious things—or we are confused about something. Well, we are indeed confused about something. We think that there are such things as smiles. But there aren't any smiles. That sounds absurd, so let me put it in a different way: Not every noun is the name of a person, place, or thing.

Sentences (B1) and (B2) look alike. Grammar books tell us the same stories about both of them. But this is another case of linguistic appearance. The linguistic reality is something quite different. The quickest way to see this is to notice that we can paraphrase (B2) as

(B3) Mary smiled warmly and welcomingly.

But there is no analogous trick which we can pull off with (B1). Sentences (B2) and (B3) say the same thing—but in (B3) the mysterious smile has vanished. What we are left with is only Mary doing something. That is what I meant when I said that there aren't any smiles. What there are are smiling people. If we were making an inventory of all the kinds of things there are in the universe, in other words, while we would need to list both people and overcoats, we would not need to list smiles. We would only need to make sure that smiling people appeared as one of the subdivisions of the general group of people.

Smiles are what I shall call "nominal objects." A nominal object is not, of course, a kind of object—any more than a counterfeit passport is a kind of passport. A nominal object is an object "in name only." It is an object which we are tempted to believe in only because we think that every noun is the name of a person, place, or thing. But some nouns are just manners of speaking. 'Smile' is like that. It is a transformation of the verb 'to smile'—but that sort of fiddling with our manner of speaking does not create new, mysterious things in the world.

There is a philosophical slogan which runs: No entity without identity.[6] What this means is that a thing, an entity, a genuine object is something there might be one of or two of or three of, and so on. There should be principles, then, for counting such entities and for identifying them, for determining when we have met the same one again and when we have rather encountered another, different one, however similar it might appear. In the absence of such principles, we are not dealing with any genuine object, with some real thing, at all.

This slogan corresponds to our moral: Not every noun is the name of a person, place, or thing. When we encounter something mysterious in the way that smiles seemed mysterious, in other words, we should look to our language. For perhaps what we are dealing with is not a mysterious something at all. Perhaps it is only a nominal object, that is, a manner of speaking.

This moral will also prove useful when we come to look at death. And it, too, would have been handy to philosophers in the past. Pains, for example, have given rise to much spilled philosophical ink. Some philosophers have been inclined to worry, for instance, about how an amputee can have a pain in his foot when he lacks a foot. The pain seems to float mysteriously in space where the foot would be if the unfortunate man still had one. Brooding on this and similar puzzles can engender the same sense of mystery that our earlier ruminations on smiles gave rise to. What is called for is more linguistic therapy. Let us refrain from populating the universe with pains which snuggle in wounded feet or float free in space. Let us instead simply recognize that a person who feels a pain his foot is a person whose foot hurts (or, to include our poor amputee, a person to whom it seems that it is his foot which hurts). The noun 'pain' is not the name of a person, place, or thing. It is merely a manner of speaking. Pains are not mysterious objects; they are nominal objects. What are all too real are suffering people.

0.4: ONE WAY OF TALKING NONSENSE

In each of the preceding examples, we found that we were saying something rather different from what we appeared to be saying. Now let's look at a case in which we appear to be saying something, but are actually not saying anything at all. Suppose I report to you the astonishing fact that

(C1) An undetectable gremlin lives in my refrigerator.

Your first instinct will probably be to ask me "But how do you know?" What I want to convince you of now is that this is the wrong question.

What makes this the wrong question is its presupposition that what I said might be true even if I could never know it. Your question presumes that I have said something significant, that there is no problem about what I said but only about why (for what reason, on what grounds, on the basis of what evidence) I said it.

But let's contrast (C1) with a few other peculiar things I might have said:

(C2) An undetectable demon lives in my refrigerator.

(C3) Two undetectable gremlins live in my refrigerator.

(C4) An undetectable mouse lives in my refrigerator.

(C5) An undetectable mouse lives in my pantry.

When Alice first read Jabberwocky, she remarked "Somehow it seems to fill my head with ideas—only I don't know exactly what they are!" (C1)–(C5) are rather like that. Each of them might very well fill your head with ideas. It is quite easy to imagine something in connection with each of them. (C1) might lead you to picture a small, benign-looking, green creature perched upon a butter dish, for example, while (C2) could lead you to visualize a leather-winged, red grotesque snarling behind a bottle of white wine. A moment's thought, however, will reveal that whatever you are imagining can't be what I said. The reason is very simple. A green creature perched on a butter dish, for instance, would be something that one could see; a snarling grotesque behind a wine bottle, something that one could hear. In neither case would what you are imagining be undetectable. But (C1) speaks of an undetectable gremlin and (C2) of an undetectable demon. So what you are imagining is not what I said.

Notice that this has nothing to do with the peculiarities of gremlins and demons. To imagine a small, furry, brown rodent shivering as it nibbles the cheddar, in connection with (C4), or a squeak and rustle emerging from a box of cornflakes, in connection with (C5), is to encounter the same difficulties. In either case, what you are imagining is something detectable—but each of (C4) and (C5) speaks of an undetectable mouse. So in neither case can what you are imagining be what I said.

The next thing to notice is that this will continue to be the case whatever you imagine in connection with (C1)–(C5). In no case will what you are imagining, picturing, or visualizing be what I said. Suppose you began with some picture that you associated with, say, (C3) and proceeded ruthlessly to eliminate from your imaginings everything which would allow two gremlins living in my refrigerator to be detected—for, after all, they are said to be undetectable gremlins. So you must eliminate anything gremlinesque that you might see or hear or feel or taste or smell. If you imagined that the gremlins in the refrigerator affected the taste or appearance of the contents of the refrigerator—made the bread moldy or the milk sour, for instance—then you'll need to eliminate that, too. For that, after all, would be something by means of which we might detect that the gremlins had moved in. Nor are you allowed to imagine them affecting the way in which the refrigerator operates—making the motor run roughly, for example, or shortening the time of the defrost cycle—for one could detect gremlins in these ways too. And, of course, you are not allowed to import any form of gremlin-detector—meters, geiger counters, thermometers, or the like. For (C3) speaks of undetectable gremlins.

Now if you do all of this, if you are successful in purging from your initial imaginings everything by means of which the two gremlins said to be living in my refrigerator might be detected, what are you left imagining? You are left imagining my refrigerator, of course, for if you had added anything at all to that picture, you would have inadvertently rendered the reportedly undetectable gremlins detectable after all. And now try the same experiment with (C1) and (C2) and (C4). At least (C5) gives you a moment of relief. In that case you get to imagine my pantry instead.

Very well, in (C1) I have mentioned my refrigerator. But what did I say about it? Of course, it is easy enough to repeat (C1), but one can also imitate animal cries and grunts. That is not enough to show that anything is being said. (C2), (C3), and (C4) all also mention my refrigerator. On the face of it, each of them says something different about it. But what is the difference between there being one undetectable gremlin in my refrigerator, two undetectable gremlins in my refrigerator, an undetectable demon in my refrigerator, and an undetectable mouse in my refrigerator? Come to think of it, what is the difference between any these and there being nothing at all (unusual) in my refrigerator? There is no difference at all.

And now I think we can understand why "But how do you know?" was the wrong question to ask about (C1). Each of (C1) through (C4) looks like it says something about my refrigerator, and each of them looks like it says something different about my refrigerator. But these, once again, are linguistic appearances. If (C1) were the sort of sentence which could say anything true at all, then there would be conceivable conditions under which what it said was true, while what (C2), (C3), and (C4) said, in contrast, were all false. But there are no such conditions. If each of (C1) through (C4) said anything at all about my refrigerator, then each would say something different about my refrigerator. But all of (C1)–(C4) have the same conditions of application—namely, none at all. They cannot, therefore, say anything different about my refrigerator—and it follows that, despite appearances, they cannot say anything about my refrigerator at all.

The moral of this example is that good grammar is not enough to make sense out of nonsense. All of (C1) through (C5) are "nonsense" only in a particular way, of course. They are not, after all, gibberish. They are well-constructed, grammatical sentences of the English language, and they do (or could) "fill one's head with ideas." What they lack is any conditions of application. They are, as I shall put it, empty.[7]

(C1)–(C5) look like the sorts of sentences which could be used to say something true or false. But that is linguistic appearance. The linguistic reality, however, is something different. An empty sentence is precisely one which cannot be used to say something true or false. It is not, so to speak, in that line of work. One can, of course, do other things with such sentences—write poems, tell stories, practice one's pronunciation, or even give examples of empty sentences. What one cannot do with them is use them to state truths or falsehoods about the world.

Linguistic appearances alone do not settle the question of whether a sentence has any conditions of application. Grammar is a guide to admissible combinations of linguistic units, but grammatical admissibility is not a guarantee of nonemptiness. Grammar allows us "It is high noon in Calcutta" and "It is very hot on the surface of the sun," and both of these are perfectly in order. Grammar also allows us "It is very hot in Calcutta" and "It is high noon on the surface of the sun," but only the first of these is in order. For high noon, of course, is that time of day when the sun stands directly overhead—a concept which simply has no conditions of application when one is on the sun.[8]

Our grammar books are in trouble again: Some declarative sentences cannot be used to state facts. That is the moral I want to carry away from this third set of examples. Like the first two, it will come in handy again when we get around to talking about death.

0.5: A TRUTH ABOUT "TRUTH"

Before turning finally to the topic of death, there is one last bit of preliminary methodological business to dispose of. A moment ago, I mentioned Jabberwocky. It will do as our last example:

(D)   'Twas brillig, and the slithy toves
      Did gyre and gimble in the wabe;
   All mimsy were the borogoves,
      And the mome raths outgrabe.

Jabberwocky, of course, is nonsense—an inspired piece of manifest nonsense. Unlike the empty sentences of our last example, it does not create (nor was it meant to create) the illusion of formulating truths about the world. Its raison d'être is, in essence, to be appreciated. There is no truth or falsehood in it. The point I want to make now, however, is that there is something like truth and falsehood with respect to it. As I shall put it, Jabberwocky creates a standard of correctness.

To see the point, consider

(D1)   The toves were slithy.

(D2)   The borogoves were mimsy.

(D3)   The toves were mimsy.

(D4)   The borogoves were slithy.

What shall we say about (D1) through (D4)? Well, (D1) and (D2) are at least somehow better off than (D3) and (D4). Whether or not we want, in the end, to say that they are true, (D1) and (D2) are at least right. (D3) and (D4), in contrast, are wrong. Someone who speaks about mimsy toves and slithy borogoves has clearly gotten it wrong. That's not how it goes. It's the toves that were slithy and the borogoves that were mimsy, and not the other way around. On the other hand, someone who speaks about slithy toves and mimsy borogoves has surely gotten it right. That's how it goes. So why not simply say that (D1) and (D2) are true, (D3) and (D4) false? Well, I think that there are some good reasons to resist the suggestion.

Contrast the following examples:

(D5)   The planets move in circles.

(D6)   The planets move in (rough) ellipses.

(D5) records a key tenet of astronomy before Kepler. Kepler advanced (D6) as part of his new theory of planetary motions, and (D6) has remained a tenet of astronomy to this day. As we now understand matters, in other words, (D5) is wrong and (D6) is right.

Here, I think, we need have no qualms about going on to say that (D5) is false and (D6) true as well. In fact, we can say a good deal more. (D5), for example, turned out to be false. Kepler discovered, and later astronomers confirmed, that (D6) was true. According to pre-Keplerian astronomy, to be sure, the planets moved in circles, but now we know that the planets don't really move in circles—although the rough ellipses in which they evidently do move are so nearly circles as understandably to have appeared to have been circles.

The point about withholding the terms 'true' and 'false' from, say, (D1) and (D3) turns on the availability of such additional remarks. Notice how peculiarly the parallel discussion would read:

> (D1) has turned out to be false. It has been discovered and confirmed that (D3) is true, that is, that the toves were (actually?) mimsy. According to Jabberwocky, to be sure, the toves were slithy, but now we know that the toves weren't really slithy—although the particular way in which they were mimsy might understandably have made them appear to be slithy.

It is pretty clear that there are simply no circumstances in which that would be the right, or even a sensible, thing to say. And that is one of the marks which separates mere correctness from full-fledged truth. But there are a few pitfalls to watch out for.

It is very easy, for instance, to confuse (D1) with

> (D7) According to Jabberwocky, the toves were slithy.

But (D1) and (D7) say quite different things. To see the difference, contrast (D5) with

> (D8) According to Ptolemaic astronomy, the planets move in circles.

Now we've discovered that (D5) isn't true. But we haven't thereby discovered that (D8) isn't true. (D8) remains correct—and true—whatever the actual motions of the planets turn out to be. For (D8) doesn't say anything about the actual motions of the planets. (D8) merely reports what Ptolemaic astronomy said about the motions of the planets. So (D5) and (D8) are different—and (D1) and (D7) are different in the same way. (D1) purports, at least, to say something about the characteristics of toves. (D7), however, says nothing about toves. Rather, (D7) says something about Jabberwocky, about a piece of nonsense poetry.

(D7), of course, is not merely correct. It is (as far as we know) true. The authenticity of a text is something about which there can be truth and falsehood. It could be the case, for instance, that the text of Jabberwocky somehow got garbled and mistranscribed between Lewis Carroll's day and our own, and that what Carroll actually wrote was not (D) but, say,

(D*) 'Twas brillig, and the mimsy toves
       Did gyre and gimble in the wabe;
      All slithy were the borogoves,
      And the mome raths outgrabe.

Indeed, were some literary historian to discover this, we might perhaps come to say that (D1) and (D2) were wrong, (D3) and (D4) right. But would this count as its turning out that the toves weren't really slithy? I don't think so. For what we would have made a discovery about would not be toves but texts.

In the case of astronomical theories, we have two questions: How does the theory describe the motion of the planets? How do the planets in fact move? But in the case of Jabberwocky, there is only one question: Is this an authoritative version of the text? Once we have an authoritative version of the text in hand, however, there is no further question about the right thing to say about toves and borogoves. That matter is settled.

We can distinguish, then, between correctness according to a text and what we might call correctness according to the world, that is, the adequacy of some account to some nontextual phenomenon. The term 'truth' is best reserved for such correctness according to the world, for that special kind of correctness which hooks up with the notions of discovery and confirmation and of actually being versus merely seeming.

I shall say that (D1) and (D2) are merely correct. Their correctness is correctness according to a text—the text of Jabberwocky. (D6) is also, of course, correct according to a text—the text of Kepler's astronomical theory, for example. But having settled that, there remains some work to do. We can go on to say that (D6) is (as far as we know) also correct according to the world. That is, Kepler's theory is (at least in this respect) a good theory, one which is adequate to the phenomena which it purports to record and explain. (D6) is not merely correct, in other words. As far as we now know, it is also true.

Truth is not the only sort of correctness. That is the moral of this fourth set of examples. Whether some claim is merely correct or incorrect, or rather true or false, is again not something which can be determined from its linguistic appearance alone, just as whether some sentence was empty could not be determined solely from linguistic appearances. And even nonsense—plain, patent nonsense—can be correct or incorrect.

In the case of emptiness, what proved decisive was the question of conditions of application. In the case of correctness, what counts in the same way is the source or ground or correctness, or (and this amounts to the same thing) the conditions of revisability for a particular claim. A claim which is merely correct can be revised—modified or abandoned—only if the text from which it derives its correctness is revised. There is no procedure for revising (D1), in other words, which does not rest upon our first revising (D7). We can be wrong about toves only by being wrong about Jabberwocky. But (D5) was abandoned in favor of (D6) without affecting (D8) at all. Whether or not the planets actually move in circles, it was and remains true that Ptolemaic astronomy said they do. (D5) and (D6) are claims to be accepted or revised on the basis of what we from time to time observe in the world. The accompanying theoretical texts, to be sure, become outmoded—but they do not need to be rewritten. These conditions of revisability, however, can no more be read off the linguistic appearances than could conditions of application.

Our moral is: Truth is not the only sort of correctness. Before passing on to the next step, let me turn the moral around and make a critical tool out of it: The fact that what someone says is correct doesn't establish that he's said anything true. Indeed, it does not even establish that he's said anything intelligible, for, as we have noticed, even plain, patent nonsense can be correct or incorrect.

0.6: RETROSPECT—
AND WHAT NEXT?

We have now looked at four examples of my peculiar analytic methods in action, and we have collected four morals:

Not all adjectives stand for properties.

Not every noun is the name of a person, place, or thing.

Not every declarative sentence can be used to state a fact.

Truth is not the only sort of correctness.

It is high time, surely, that we got down to business. It is time, in other words, to apply these methods and these morals to our talk about death and survival. As we shall see, we will need to apply them to other sorts of talk besides. But if we are successful, we will know when we have finished how to talk sensibly about death—and thereby how to think clearly about death as well.

It will turn out, in fact, that many of the things that some people (including some philosophers) purport to think about death cannot be sensibly said—and therefore cannot be coherently thought—at all. It will turn out, that is, that much of what passes for thought about death and dying, about survival and "afterlife," is just so much conceptual muck, one form or another of disguised nonsense. And showing that, I think, is the peculiar contribution that today's analytic philosophy can make toward answering the questions about death which were built into the heart of our enterprise and the core of its problematic at its very origin.

CHAPTER 1

"Life After Death": In Search of the Question

1.1: ABOUT WHY IT ISN'T OBVIOUS

Probably the leading "philosophical" question concerning death has always been

> (1) Does a person survive his death?

Socrates, we recall, claimed to argue that the answer is "Yes." Descartes argued that it is at least possibly "Yes," but that a definite answer cannot be given by philosophical reasoning but only through religious revelation. And Kant argued that, while we cannot demonstrate even its possibility, we must suppose that the answer is "Yes" for morality to have a point.

What all of these answers have in common is that they take it for granted that the question makes sense. But does it? What I want to convince you of, first, is that it does not—at least, it does not if it is interpreted straightforwardly. We are dealing with a very peculiar question here. Perhaps it can be given a sense, but, if so, there is a great deal of work that will need to be done first. To see what it is, however, we need to appreciate the genuine oddity of the original question. It will be easier to do that if we replace (1) by a slightly different—actually a prior—question:

> (2) Could a person survive his death?

(2) is every bit as peculiar as (1). Let's see why.
Consider what appears to be the same sort of question:

> (3) Could a person survive the midair collision of two SSTs?

Here, I think, there is no problem about the question or its answer. We understand all too well what the midair collision of two supersonic aircraft would amount to and what sort of horrible consequences it would have. It is, in fact, highly unlikely that anyone could survive such a collision. Most probably, everyone on both planes would be killed. We also understand very well, however, what it would be to survive such a catastrophe. A survivor would be someone who somehow managed to come through it alive.

Now what this example shows is that our ordinary, everyday use of 'survive' excludes death. 'Dead' and 'surviving' are, as the logicians put it, contraries. The survivors of such an accident are just those people who don't die in it. The newspapers' lists of "Dead" and "Surviving" are exhaustive and exclusive lists. The name of everyone involved in the accident must appear on one or the other of them, but no name can appear on both lists.

This "exclusionary" use of 'survive' is, indeed, the only straightforward and customary use. A person who survives a massive head injury is precisely one who does not die from it. Conversely, injuries which one does not survive are fatal injuries, that is, injuries which result in death. Again, an obituary notice may report that the deceased is survived by his wife and children, but it could not correctly report that the deceased was himself also among those surviving his demise. A person who dies is survived by only those members of his family who did not die.

Understood according to our ordinary uses, then—the way we understand (3)—question (2) is as silly as

(4) Could a right triangle have four sides?

For, as we speak and think in everyday contexts, 'dead' and 'surviving' exclude each other every bit as much as 'triangular' and 'four-sided' do. If we interpret (2) according to our customary ways of speaking, as a straightforward question, then, the answer to it must be a plain and unequivocal "No." Interpreted in this way, indeed, (2) is just a silly question.

But someone who seriously raises the question (2) surely does not intend to be asking something absurd. She wants to be asking a sensible question and, what is more, an important one—a question to which the answer might be "Yes" and to which a "Yes" answer would be a matter of considerable interest. And so she must be asking—or trying to ask—something quite different from what she appears to be asking. But—and this is the crucial point—it is not at all obvious any longer what she wants to ask.

Despite appearances, (2) must actually be a question very different from (3). But while it may now be clear that (2) does not ask what it seems to, it is no longer clear just what (2) does ask. That is why I call it a very peculiar question. And that suggests what we need to do next. Our next job must be to figure out what, if anything, a person who poses question (2) is trying to find out. Is there any way of formulating the intended question here which does not take the form of a straightforward absurdity, which is not a silly question? Answering this question—a question, notice, not about death but about another question—will be our next order of business.

1.2: SOME OTHER SILLY QUESTIONS

By this time, the reader may well be getting a bit annoyed with me. Put into words, his annoyance might sound like this:

> "You are doing a fine job of demonstrating just what's wrong with contemporary philosophy. Your petty, nit-picking linguistic literalism is as bad as mediaeval debates about how many angels can dance on the head of a pin. Such logical hairsplitting is simply perverse. You know perfectly well what the question is. What people want to know is
>
> (5) Is there life after death?
>
> This is a clear, straightforward question with a yes-or-no answer. If you have something to say that is relevant to the matter, then say it. Otherwise stop wasting our time. Playing word-games with 'dead' and 'surviving' is pointless and sterile."

Now I can sympathize with this reaction. My "analytic philosophy" certainly doesn't seem to be getting us anywhere. But I want nevertheless to insist that this is no fault of analytic philosophy. For once again, I claim, it is not yet clear that there is anywhere we are being urged to go.

Consider question (5). It is a very popular question. Our objector claims that it is a clear, straightforward question with a yes-or-no answer. Well, there is a clear, straightforward question which one can ask by asking (5), and it does have a yes-or-no answer. Its answer, however, is also a plain, unequivocal "No." For death, after all, is the end of life. Asking straightforwardly whether there is life after death, then, is asking

(6) Is there life after the end of life?

Like

(7) Does the road go on after the road comes to an end?

this is again a silly question. But it does have a yes-or-no answer. Its answer is "No."

Where did I get "Death is the end of life," by the way? Well, I got it out of a dictionary.[1] Now dictionaries are books of limited usefulness. People who compile them typically believe that all adjectives stand for properties and that every noun is the name of a person, place, or thing. But dictionaries are repositories of customary usages and common understandings. When I am told to interpret (5) as a clear, straightforward question, then, a dictionary becomes a pertinent place to look, for it records just those everyday uses which constitute most people's ordinary "clear, straightforward" understandings.

Some dictionary entries are less direct, of course. Under 'death,' for instance, I also find

(a) the act of dying

and

(b) the total and permanent cessation of all the vital functions of an animal or plant.

Entry (a) directs me to 'dying' under which I find, of course, "ceasing to live." Question (5), then, can evidently also be paraphrased by

(8) Does a person continue to live after he ceases to live?

Alas, it is still a silly question, and its answer is still "No."

To come to terms with entry (b), I need to find out which functions of a plant or animal are its vital functions. Not surprisingly, they turn out to be the ones necessary to life. This gives us another paraphrase of question (5), namely

(9) Does life continue after the total and permanent cessation of all the functions necessary to life?

Well, the answer is still "No," isn't it? Functions necessary to life are just those functions in the absence of which life cannot continue.

So far, then, we are no better off with the question "Is there life after death?" than we were with the question "Can a person survive his death?" The person who poses either of these questions surely cannot be asking what he appears to be asking—for he appears to be asking a silly question. But it is no longer obvious what he does want to find out. Dictionaries, it turns out, are no help at all. They are fine as far as they go, but where they go is in tight little circles. Being told that death is the end of life, and then that life is "the condition that distinguishes animals and plants from inorganic objects and dead organisms" (and surely that should be "living animals and plants"!) does not tell us what we need to know in order to understand questions (1) and (5). So we need to take another tack. One way to proceed is by continuing to take our dictionaries to task. For they do not only move in circles; sometimes they are just wrong.

1.3: THE END OF LIFE— AN EDIFYING TALE

To say that death is the end of life suggests that all living things die. That's just wrong. There are other ways for a life to come to an end besides death.

Consider amoebae, for example. Some amoebae, to be sure, do die. Sometimes an amoeba cannot get sufficient food or oxygen or moisture to sustain its life, and that kills it. But some amoebae do not get an opportunity to die. Something else happens to them first. They divide.

As an example, let us take a well-fed, healthy amoeba alone in a drop of well-oxygenated pond water. I shall call it "Alvin." Alvin, let us suppose, lives happily through Tuesday and, precisely at the stroke of midnight, divides, producing two offspring whom I shall call "Amos" and "Ambrose."

On Wednesday, then, we find two amoebae—Amos and Ambrose—swimming happily about in our drop of pond water. But what has become of Alvin?

One thing is quite clear: Alvin is not an inhabitant of our drop of pond water on Wednesday. Alvin is one amoeba; our drop of water contains two amoebae; and one amoeba cannot be identical to two amoebae. Nor can we coherently hold that Alvin is identical to only one of the two amoebae we find on Wednesday. For the relationship between Amos and Alvin is exactly the same as the relationship between Ambrose and Alvin. If we held that this relationship implied that, say, Amos was identical to Alvin, we would also need to hold, for the same reasons, that Ambrose was identical to Alvin. It would then follow, however, that Amos was identical to Ambrose—which is impossible. Amos and Ambrose may be ever so similar, but they are two distinct amoebae, not one and the same amoeba.

So Alvin is no longer with us on Wednesday. He is no longer "among the living." His life, therefore, must have come to an end. But it is equally clear that Alvin did not die. At no time on Tuesday or Wednesday did any organism undergo "the total and permanent cessation of all its vital functions." We will search in vain for Alvin's remains. Alvin's life came to an end, but Alvin did not lose his life. Alvin's life came to an end in a different way. It ended, precisely at the stroke of midnight, not with his death but with his division. Alvin became (was transformed into) two new amoebae—Amos and Ambrose.

Death may be an end to life, then, but it is not—in spite of our dictionaries—the only end to life. Not all living things die.

1.4: A HELPFUL DISTINCTION— AND A SENSIBLE QUESTION

We need a distinction. I want, in particular, to distinguish between life and a life. In accord with the customary understandings recorded in our dictionaries, I have been using 'life' to speak of a condition of organisms. Now conditions, like smiles, are merely nominal objects. An organism which has or is in the condition of life is just an organism which is alive. It is a living organism. Just as we do not have people and smiles in the world, but only smiling people, so, too, we do not have organisms and life in the world, but only living organisms. Still, no harm is done by continuing to speak of life as a condition of organisms once this has been noted—just as no harm is done by continuing to speak of Mary's warm, welcoming smile, once we understand what such talk amounts to—so I shall continue to employ the word 'life' in this sense.

A life, however, is something different. A life is someone's or something's life—Alvin's life, for example. It consists of happenings, of events and occurrences. Take the life of Aristotle as an example. The life of Aristotle is what one might recount in a biography of Aristotle (or what he could have recounted in his autobiography, had he written one). What one recounts in such a biography are the happenings of which Aristotle was a part—the things that he did and the things that happened to him. One recounts, that is, Aristotle's history.

A life is a life-history. The history of Aristotle's life is just the history of Aristotle. Histories, of course, are nominal objects, too. We do not have persons and their histories, but only persons who do things and to whom things happen—acting persons and experiencing persons. Here, too, however, I shall stick to the customary manner of speaking.

What came to an end at the stroke of midnight was Alvin's life, that is, Alvin's history. It came to an end when Alvin came to an end, when Alvin ceased to exist. On Wednesday, as we have seen, Alvin existed no longer. But Alvin's history came to an end without any loss of life, that is, with no cessation of the condition of life. Alvin's history came to an end with the event of his division (the same event with which the histories of both Amos and Ambrose began), but dividing is something that only a living amoeba can do.

And now I think that we have the conceptual apparatus which we need in order to formulate the question which someone who asks (1) or (5) wants to ask. It is, surprisingly enough, the question of whether our dictionaries are right. Is death even an end to life? The question, we now see, is ambiguous. Death is certainly an end to the condition of life. To die is to cease to live, to cease to be in the condition of life, to lose one's life. But is it to cease to be, to cease to exist? Death is an end to the condition of life, but is it an end to a life? That, I submit, is the question that someone who asks (1) or (5) intends to be asking. In terms of our distinctions, we can frame it this way:

(10) Does a person's history necessarily come to an end with that person's death?

This, at least—at last!—is not obviously a silly question. But it could easily become one. What is now crucial is what a person is. For suppose that persons were necessarily living organisms. A person's history would then be the history of a living organism, and such a history would necessarily come to an end with the death of that organism, that is, with its ceasing to be living. Question (10), in short, immediately brings a further question along with it:

(11) Are persons necessarily living organisms?

And now we have our work cut out for us. To find out how to think clearly about death, we need to find out how to think clearly about persons. We need to find out what a person is—or might be. And that project will lead us down some curious paths. Before setting out on this trip, however, there are still a few matters about our questions which need to be tidied up. Perhaps now that we have located at least one sensible question to be asking, the reader will bear with me a moment while I do this tidying up.

1.5: OF LIFE AND DEATH . . .
AND OTHER "OPPOSITES"

After some considerable fussing,we have arrived at a useable version of our main question:

(10) Does a person's history necessarily come to an end with that person's death?

Framed differently, this is the question:

(12) Is a person's death an event in that person's history?

Now death is the loss of life. A person who dies ceases to be alive. He is, at least, no longer a living person. If death is an event in a person's history, then, it will presumably be an event of a certain kind. It will be a change of condition. For 'life,' we have noted, picks out a condition of persons. If the history of a person continues beyond the death of that person, then, the subsequent portion of that history will not be the history of a living person but presumably of a person in some other condition. So our question (10) is also equivalent to

(13) Is a person's death a passage between two conditions?

Now it might seem that question (13) admits of an easy answer. It runs something like this:

"Of course death is a passage between two conditions. A person who dies passes from the condition of life (being alive) to the condition of death (being dead). A living person becomes a dead person. And that's enough to show that a person's history does not come to an end with his death. For lots of things can happen to dead persons. They can be buried or cremated, for example. They may also be honored in various ways—canonized, for instance, or awarded various prizes posthumously. The answer to question (13), in other words, is obviously "Yes." And if question (13) comes to the same thing as question (10), then the answer to (10) will be "No.""

This "easy answer" has a long and distinguished history. Plato, in fact, endorsed something rather like it in his *Phaedo*.[2] I want to argue, however, that the answer simply will not do. It trades on ambiguities and confusions—which, parenthetically, it is worth taking the time to sort out independently.

'Life' and 'death', 'alive' and 'dead' are opposites. They are, more precisely, contraries. They exclude one another. What our "easy answer" presupposes, however, is that they are contrary conditions. Yet this is not at all obviously correct. For opposites are not all of a piece. There are many sorts of contraries, only some of which pick out contrary conditions. Let me illustrate the point by reminding you of some things which you already know.

'Tall' and 'short', for example, are opposites. We are inclined, at first glance, to treat them as simple contraries as well. Nothing, we may say, can be both tall and short. Well, the fact of the matter is that nothing can be either tall or short period. Nothing is merely tall or short, but only a tall this or a short that. Whether or not something is tall or short, in other words, depends not only upon its height but also upon its kind. Even a very tall person is still shorter than a short giraffe; a short building is still taller than a tall sunflower. It follows that one and the same thing can be both tall and short—for one and the same thing can belong simultaneously to various kinds. A short sequoia is nevertheless a tall tree; a tall dwarf is at the same time a short person.

The reason for this is that, in the tall-short family, it is the comparative forms, 'taller' and 'shorter', which wear the logical trousers. 'Tall' and 'short' are explained in terms of 'taller' and 'shorter.' Whether something is a tall or short thing of some kind depends upon the average height for things of that kind. A tall person is one who is significantly taller than a person of average height. A short giraffe is one which is significantly shorter than average for giraffes. That is what I meant when I said that 'tall' and 'short' are explained in terms of the comparative forms. And what is more, the notion of "average height" is also explained in terms of the comparative forms. A woman of average height, for example, is one such that there are about as many women who are taller than she is as there are women who are shorter than she is. So here it is 'taller' and 'shorter' which wear the logical trousers. They come first in the order of understanding.

'Tall' and 'short' are paradigms for one sort of opposites. It is a large family. It includes, for instance, hot-cold, large-small, fat-thin, heavy-light, fast-slow, and myriad others. But not all others. There are other sorts of opposites. Our dictionaries and our grammar books tell the same kinds of stories about 'wet' and 'dry', for instance, as they do about 'tall' and 'short'. The linguistic appearances are quite similar. But the linguistic realities are very different.

The quickest way to see this is to notice that a dry road, for example, is not one which is significantly drier than average for roads. A dry road is simply one which is not (at all) wet. In the wet-dry family, in fact, it is 'dry' which occupies a logically central position. Its special status is signaled by the availability of some special adverbial modifiers: Something can be totally, completely, absolutely, or perfectly dry. It makes no sense, in contrast, to speak of something's being absolutely wet—or perfectly tall, completely short, totally fast, and so on. Earlier we explained 'tall' and 'short' in terms of 'taller' and 'shorter'. Here, however, we analogously explain 'drier', 'wetter', and 'wet' in terms of (absolutely) 'dry'. One thing is drier than another, for instance, if it is more nearly (perfectly) dry than the other. And something is (more-or-less, to some degree) wet just in case it is not (absolutely) dry.

Opposites in this wet-dry family behave as if one were dealing with various quantities of some sort of "stuff." In the case of 'wet' and 'dry', the "stuff" is moisture. For something to be totally dry is for it to have a total absence of moisture. The more moisture there is in or on something, the wetter that thing is. We must be careful not to take this notion of a "stuff" too literally, however. Absolute darkness is the total absence of light—and light, perhaps, can still qualify as a "stuff." But absolute ignorance is the total absence of knowledge—and, although we do speak of "bits" or "pieces" of knowledge, knowledge is only metaphorically a sort of "stuff." Again, absolute straightness is the total absence of curvature—but now curvature is not even metaphorically a "stuff." Light-dark, knowledgable-ignorant, straight-curved, flat-bumpy, rough-smooth, and myriad others belong to this second group of opposites—the wet-dry group.[3]

But 'living' and 'dead' belong to neither of these groups. Members of both the tall-short group and the wet-dry group of opposites have active comparative forms. Height, speed, size, wetness, knowledgeability, curvature, and so on are all matters of more-or-less. As the tradition puts it, they "admit of degree." Life and death, however, do not. There are no shades of grey here, only black and white. In this respect, at least, 'alive' and 'dead' do resemble the classic paradigm of a pair of contrary conditions—'awake' and 'asleep'.

'Awake' and 'asleep' exhibit the pattern which our "easy answer" takes for granted applies to 'alive' and 'dead'. Persons who are awake and persons who are asleep are two kinds of persons. Being awake and being asleep are both conditions of persons. The events of waking up and falling asleep are both changes of condition, and both are events in a person's history. Finally, neither condition admits of degree. One person can be drowsier or sleepier than another, but not more asleep than another. ("More deeply asleep" is all right, of course. But if Herbert is more deeply asleep than Harold, it does not follow that Herbert is more asleep than Harold. Both are equally (in the condition of being) asleep, that is, both are equally sleeping persons.) Similarly, one person can be more animated or alert or responsive than another (and so, metaphorically, "more awake"), but one person cannot be literally more awake than another.

Not every pair of opposites which do not admit of degree belongs to the awake-asleep family, however. As we saw earlier, 'genuine' and 'counterfeit' do not. One passport cannot be more or less genuine (or counterfeit) than another. But genuine passports and counterfeit passports are not two kinds of passports. Counterfeit passports are not passports at all. Thus 'genuine' and 'counterfeit' do not pick out two contrary conditions of a document, and there is consequently no possibility of a document's passing from one of these "conditions" to the other.

Our "easy answer" takes it for granted that living persons and dead persons are both kinds of persons, that 'alive' and 'dead' pick out contrary conditions of a person, and that it is possible for a person to pass from being in one of these conditions to being in the other while continuing to exist. But it is not obvious that a dead person is a kind of person. A counterfeit passport is not a kind of passport, and a Welsh rabbit is not a kind of rabbit. Not all adjectives stand for properties, after all.

1.6: WHAT DIES AND WHAT WE BURY— A DECEPTIVE IDIOM

Now it is, once again, easy to be misled by linguistic appearances here. We say such things, for example, as

(14) My Aunt Ethel died last week, and we're burying her tomorrow.

Sentences like (14) typically do not raise any eyebrows. Idiomatically, (14) is perfectly in order. Logically, however, (14) is a mess. Taken at face value, (14) appears to refer to my Aunt Ethel twice. It says, in essence, that there is one thing—presumably one person—Ethel, of which two things are true:

that it (she) died last week

and

that we are burying it (her) tomorrow.

But this double reference is only a linguistic appearance. There is no one thing which both died last week and will be buried tomorrow. What died last week was Aunt Ethel. What will be buried tomorrow, however, is not Aunt Ethel but rather Aunt Ethel's remains. What will be buried tomorrow is a corpse, Aunt Ethel's corpse. But a corpse is not a person. Aunt Ethel's corpse is not Aunt Ethel. Now sometimes we might use the expression 'dead person' to refer to what we bury, to refer to a corpse. ("The battlefield was littered with dead people.") But a corpse is not a kind of person, and so a dead person, in that sense, is not a kind of person either.

Of course, if (14) is true, there is another sense of 'dead person' in which Aunt Ethel herself is a dead person. For if (14) is true, Aunt Ethel is a person who has died. But having died is not a condition of persons. A person who has died is not a person who is now in some special condition but a person to whom something previously happened.

Here we have a particularly subtle sort of linguistic appearance, for what is merely apparent is the present tense of, for example,

(15) Aunt Ethel is dead.

Being dead, we might say, is only a "nominal condition" in the same way that smiles are merely nominal objects. Just as we could paraphrase apparent reference to smiles as actual reference to smiling people, so too we can paraphrase apparent reference to people who are dead as actual reference to people who have died. (15), for example, says just what

(16) Aunt Ethel has died

says.

Genuine conditions do not allow this sort of "elimination through paraphrase." There is no past tense equivalent to

(17) Uncle Harry is alive.

That is, nothing stands to (17) in the same relationship that (16) bears to (15). (If we go to the past tense, we must make it a negative, and change the verb from 'to live' to 'to die': Uncle Harry has not yet died.)

Being dead, in this sense, resembles being the winner (of a race). Someone is the winner of a race just in case he (has) won it. Being the winner, like being dead, is only a nominal condition of persons. Once again, then, a dead person is not a kind of person. That is, being dead is not a condition of persons coordinate with being alive. A living person is a person who is alive; a dead person, however, is a person who has died.[4]

It remains an open question, then, whether persons who have died still exist, that is, whether their histories continue beyond the point of their deaths. The fact that we canonize or award posthumous prizes to people who have died does not by itself show that the answer to this question must be "Yes." For it is not clear that its subject's existing now is a requirement for our engaging in either activity. It may well be sufficient that the to-be-canonized individual or intended recipient of the posthumous prize previously existed.

Our "easy answer" trades on the fact that we sometimes speak of dead persons. It takes it for granted that this way of speaking is completely analogous to our speaking of living persons, that is, that being dead is a condition of persons in the same way that being alive is a condition of persons. But this is to mistake linguistic appearances for linguistic reality. For, as we have seen, in our customary speech, the expression 'dead person' picks out either a corpse—which is not a person at all—or a person who has died. People who have died might, for all that, still exist in some condition alternative to the condition of life. Whether they could, indeed, is our leading question. But 'being dead', when understood according to our ordinary, everyday manner of speaking, does not pick out such an alternative condition of persons. 'Being dead', as we customarily speak, picks out only the "nominal condition" of having died—and nominal conditions are no more conditions than nominal objects are objects. A negative answer to (10), in other words, is not built into our language. We cannot get it that cheaply, if we can get it at all. That is another, perhaps regrettable, moral of analytic philosophizing: There is no substitute for hard work.

1.7: MARKING TIME—
PROCESS, EVENT, AND INSTANT

The traditional analogizing of the living-dead pair with the waking-sleeping pair supplies a useful vehicle for gaining a clear view of some of the subtler points concerning the temporal structure of our talk about death.

Consider, for example, the events of my waking day. Being awake is a condition of persons. While I am in this condition—while I am awake—I do certain things and certain things happen to me, and these doings and happenings constitute the events of my waking day. My waking day is bounded at both ends by two particular events: It begins with my awakening, and it ends with my falling asleep. The important point which needs to be made here is that both 'awakening' and 'falling asleep' are ambiguous. They can be used to pick out occurrences of quite different temporal structures. Let me explain.

The most fundamental temporal contrast of interest to us here is that between a process and an event. Intuitively put, the contrast is this: A process occurs during a time; an event, at a time. Processes last for a time; they take time; they are clockable. Events, in contrast, are dateable. For a process, the leading question is "How long did it take?"; for an event, "When did it happen?" The most significant fact about the contrast between process and event, however, is that it is, to begin with, context-dependent. Whether some occurrence is a process or an event depends upon the sort of discourse about it in which we are engaging.

To begin with, indeed, events are the boundaries of processes. The voyage of the Titanic, for example, is a process. The sinking of the Titanic is the event which bounds one end of that process. The Senate's deliberations over the budget may count as a process; the final vote on the budget as the event which brings that process to an end.

But if we shift the focus of our attention and concern, what was in these contexts an event may count, in our next context, as a process. The sinking of the Titanic, for example, may be considered as a process in its own right, beginning when the ship collided with an iceberg and ending when the stern vanished below the waves. The final Senate vote on the budget can be viewed, not only as the event which ends the Senate's deliberations, but as a process beginning when the first senator casts his vote and ending when the hundredth casts his.

We can, in other words, apply in our thought a sort of "temporal magnifying glass," shifting from a context in which an occurrence is thought of as occupying one point in a temporal continuum—say, the beginning point or ending point of a stretch of time in which we have an interest—to a context in which the same occurrence is itself thought of as a temporal continuum—a stretch of time in which we now take an interest—having its own beginning and ending points, and itself subdividable into smaller stretches of time. (E.g., the first lifeboat's being lowered, the band's playing "Nearer My God To Thee," water flooding the dining salon, etc.)

Once the possibility has been noted, however, we see that we can think of this process of attending to ever-shorter stretches of time in the limit. That is, we can form the idea (the concept) of a stretch of time of zero duration, of a temporal point or instant—and with it, of course, the idea of an event which occurs at such a durationless point, of an instantaneous event. Unlike our context-dependent processes and events, however, there is nothing in experience which matches up with this idea of an instantaneous event—as something in experience does match up with, for instance, the Titanic striking an iceberg or some senator casting a vote. Instantaneous events do not belong to our experience but to our manner of thinking about what we can experience—to our idea, for example, that we might take ever-more-speeded-up movies of, say, a bullet striking an egg or a drop of water falling into a pond and then, playing them back in slow motion, distinguish ever-smaller subprocesses of these processes, occupying ever-shorter intervals of time.

The notion of an instantaneous event, in other words, does not correspond to some special, privileged context, but rather to the idea that, however finely we divide our temporal intervals, we remain free to divide them more finely still. The notion of an instantaneous event corresponds, that is, to our ability to change contexts in the direction of attending to ever-shorter stretches of time—but that ability is not itself another, special, temporal context. Instantaneous events, in brief, are merely "nominal events," in much the same way that smiles were "nominal objects." They are products of one way in which we talk and think about genuine, that is, context-dependent, events and processes, just as smiles turned out to be products of one way in which we talk and think about smiling persons.[5]

With these distinctions in hand, then, we can say—and see—in what way 'falling asleep', for example, is an ambiguous expression. It may be intended to pick out an event, or a process, or an instantaneous event. Thus:

I brush my teeth; I climb into bed; I turn out the light; and I fall asleep.

Here falling asleep is an event. It is the last event of my waking day, when that day is considered as a process. It is the event which bounds that process at one end. But, of course, falling asleep may itself take some time. One can fall asleep swiftly or slowly, easily or only with difficulty. Here we have shifted context. Now falling asleep is a process, containing such subprocesses as yawning, punching the pillow, tossing and turning, counting sheep, and so on. This process of falling asleep is only vaguely bounded at its beginning. There is no customary procedure for deciding when, after tossing and turning for several minutes, I finally begin to fall asleep. But once begun, this process of falling asleep (sometimes we call it "dropping off to sleep") must presumably come to an end. But how does it end?

It ends when I, finally, fall asleep. Now this falling asleep is an instantaneous event. It is, we might say, the "ideal limit" of the process of dropping off to sleep. It is, to put it another way, a sort of "boundary marker" which we erect in our thinking and speaking between two conditions: the condition of being awake and the condition of being asleep. But the instantaneous event of falling asleep is merely a nominal event, that is, a product of one particular way we have of speaking and thinking about a change from one condition to the other. There are waking people and sleeping people, and a person may pass from being awake to being asleep. The process which culminates in this change of condition is "dropping off to sleep." The idea of an instantaneous event of falling asleep derives from our manner of thinking

about such a change of condition—from our idea, for instance, that we could "bracket" ever-shorter intervals which contained both stretches of time during which the person was (still) awake and stretches of time during which he was (just barely) asleep, and so in the limit arrive at a durationless point or instant at which he "crossed over" from wakefulness into sleep. But nothing in our experience answers to this "arriving at the limit." It is simply a way in which we (sometimes) choose to speak and think about what we do experience—wakeful people and sleeping people and transitions from one condition to the other.

1.8: THE "WHEN" OF DEATH

'Death', as the name of an occurrence, is ambiguous in much the same way. A person's death is the last event of that person's life (life-history), when that history is considered as a process.

> He went on a hunting trip; he caught pneumonia; his condition gradually worsened; and he died.

Here 'his death' would pick out a terminal event in the process of a life-history, an event correlative to other events in that history (the hunting trip, the gradual worsening of the illness, and so on). But, of course, a person's death may itself take some time. One can die quickly or slowly. One's death can be swift and painless or agonizing and protracted. Here, once again, we have shifted temporal contexts. 'A person's death' here picks out a process—the process we call 'dying'. Like the process of dropping off to sleep, the process of dying is only vaguely bounded at its beginning. It is only very rarely, for example, that we can confidently isolate some event which counts as a person's entering into an "irreversible decline." But once begun, the process of dying must presumably come to an end. How does it end?

It ends when the person, finally, dies. It ends with that person's death. Here 'that person's death' is intended to pick out an instantaneous event. As before, it is an "ideal limit" of a process, a boundary marker which we erect in our thinking and speaking. But—and this is a crucial disanalogy—it is not a boundary marker erected between two conditions of a person. For no condition of a person answers in our experience to the "far side" of this boundary. What answers in our experience to the far side of this boundary is a lifeless corpse—and a corpse is not a person, but merely a person's remains.

The notion of an instantaneous event of death is once again essentially a product of a certain manner of speaking and thinking about our experiences. Once again, it answers only to our presumed unlimited ability, at least in imagination, freely to change temporal contexts, to focus our attention on ever-shorter stretches of time. But where the time-intervals which were hypothetically "bracketed" in this way in the case of falling asleep contained a person throughout, wakeful during the first part of each interval and sleeping during the second, the time-intervals which we hypothetically "bracket" in the case of death do not. They are time-intervals at the beginnings of which we find a person, still (only barely) alive, and at the ends of which we find a corpse. A corpse, however, is not a person. It is a person's remains.

One consequence of this observation is that the so-called "moment of death" is itself, once again, a merely nominal object (or, more precisely perhaps, a merely nominal instant). It is not something discoverable, something about which one could be right or wrong, but rather a kind of fiction, created by our manner of speaking and thinking about death. There is no fact of the matter about the "moment of death." It is not difficult to find, say, a one-hour period at the beginning of which we confront a still-living person and at the end of which we confront a corpse. With the help of, for instance, stethoscopes and mirrors to test for fogging by the breath, we might narrow down this "bracketing" time-interval to a few minutes—living person at the beginning, corpse at the end. Technical refinements, electrocardiographs, and electroencephalographs might let us bring the interval down to a few seconds. But there is no guarantee that we will in practice—as opposed to in our imaginations—be able to bring that interval down to an arbitrarily short stretch of time—a millionth or a billionth of a second. And there is simply no sense to be made of the suggestion that we might narrow it down to no time at all. The idea of such an instantaneous event, of the "moment of death" answers to nothing in our experience beyond those "bracketings" which we are able, in practice, to effect—and our imaginative consideration of the ideal limit of such ever-narrower bracketings, indefinitely repeated. The "moment of death" is a merely nominal instant, a linguistic appearance created by one of the ways in which we, from time to time, talk and think about the deaths of persons.[6]

1.9: CHANGING THE SUBJECT—
WHY DEATH ISN'T SLEEP

Our examination of the temporal structure of talk about death reveals, however, also a second moral—one which will be important for structuring the remainder of our investigations. It grows out of the crucial disanalogy which we have discovered between an event such as falling asleep and the event of a person's death.

One way of putting the point is as follows: Whereas the nominal instantaneous event of falling asleep is automatically, by reason of the particular idealization of experience which talk of such an instantaneous event actually encodes, nominally an event in the history of a person, the nominal instantaneous event of that person's death is not.

Talk which appears to be about a special sort of event in the case of falling asleep derives from our manner of thinking and speaking about our experiences of persons in two conditions—awake and asleep—and of the passage between them. The change which answers in our experience to our talk about the instantaneous event of falling asleep is an experienced change of condition. We confront first a wakeful person and then that very person sleeping. But our analogous talk in the case of death derives from our manner of thinking and speaking about our experiences of confronting first a living person and then a corpse, which is not a person. The change which answers in our experience to our talk about the instantaneous event of death is, consequently, not an experienced change of condition. It is an experienced change of subject. The subject of our predeath experiences, the person (e.g., Aunt Ethel), is not the subject of our postdeath experiences, the corpse (e.g., Aunt Ethel's remains).

This observation, however, gives us two questions. One of them is what we have been taking as our main question all along: What becomes of the person? That is, does the person cease to exist at the point of his death, or does the history of the person continue beyond that person's death? But there is a second question which needs to be asked at this point as well, for there are two subjects of experience and discourse which need accounting for. We must not only inquire about the person. We must also inquire about the corpse. For, after all, following the death of some person, we do have a corpse on our hands. This corpse is not a person. It also did not exist prior to the person's death. So it must have come into existence at the point of that person's death. And this gives us our second question: Where does the corpse come from?

One answer, I think, we can dismiss as silly. We do not want to be forced to say that the corpse was created *ex nihilo,* that it sprang into existence "from nothingness" when the person died. But this leaves only one alternative: Something else became that corpse. If the corpse did not spring into existence "from nothingness," then there must have already existed something else, prior to the person's death, which changed into a corpse when the person died. Now, what might this "something else" be?

The most straightforward answer, surely, is that what changed into a corpse was the person himself. According to this answer, a person's death is simply the event of that person's becoming a corpse. On this account, death is not a change of condition but rather a change of kind. One kind of thing, a person, changes into another kind of thing, a corpse. This might sound mysterious, but it is really quite commonplace.

We have already encountered a similar case. Recall the case of our amoebae—Alvin, Amos, and Ambrose. One amoeba, Alvin, became (changed into) two amoebae, Amos and Ambrose. Now this is not a change of kind, but neither is it a change of condition. Being two amoebae is not a condition of one amoeba. Amoebic fission, in fact, is a change of number. What changed was how many amoebae existed in our water-drop.

There are numerous familiar examples of changes of kind as well, however. Probably the most familiar is metamorphosis: A caterpillar changes into (becomes) a butterfly. The phenomenon is not limited to the organic world though. Radioactive decay is also a change of kind. An atom of one kind, say Uranium 238, emits an alpha particle and becomes (changes into) an atom of a different kind, Protactinium 235.

If we adopt this answer to our question about the corpse, however, we immediately obtain an answer to our question about the person. For, just as changing into a butterfly is one way in which a caterpillar may cease to exist, and changing into an atom of Protactinium 235 is one way that an atom of Uranium 238 may cease to exist, so, too, changing into a corpse will be one way in which a person ceases to exist. On this account, in other words, there remains no logical room for the possibility that a person's history continues beyond that person's death.

If what becomes a corpse is the person himself, then, that person's history will come to an end with his death. The history of a corpse, to be sure, will begin with the same event—but just as a corpse is not a person, so too the history of a corpse is not the history of a person. On this account, in short, we have one answer to both the question of what becomes of the person and the question of where the corpse comes from: the person becomes (changes into) the corpse. 'Death' will be a name for an event of this sort, for a change of kind. It follows, however, that death, so understood, cannot be an event in a person's history, for it is the event with which that history comes to an end.

1.10: THE DUALISTIC PULL

If we are going to find logical room for the possibility that a person's history continues beyond that person's death, therefore, we must locate a different answer to our question about the corpse. We must, that is, be able to identify something other than the person himself which changes into a corpse when the person dies. What might this other something be?

Well, whatever it is, let us notice that we will be committed to holding that it existed as well before the person died. On this alternative, in fact, what we call "the person's death" will turn out to consist of two events. One of them will be something that happens to the person:

> The person undergoes a change of condition, from being a living person to being a person in some other (postdeath) condition.

The other event, however, will be something's happening to something other than the person:

> Something which is not a person undergoes a change of kind; from being whatever it is, it becomes a corpse.

To make room for the mere possibility of a person's history continuing beyond that person's death, in short, we must be able to construct a coherent account of what we call "a person's death" in which we find two events, two subjects of change (a person and something other than a person), and two sorts of change (a change of condition and a change of kind). The very possibility of a person's history continuing beyond that person's death, it turns out, logically demands some sort of dualistic world-picture. We need a world which not only contains persons, who die, but also things other than persons, which become the corpses we are left with when people die.

Now there is, of course, a classical dualistic world-picture already prepared and waiting for us. According to this ancient account, a living person itself precisely is a union of two distinct sorts of beings. A living person consists of a soul (or mind) and a body. What we call "the person's death" is the separation of the soul from the body. And what we call "a corpse" is nothing but an unsouled body. It is the person's body, then, which becomes a corpse when the person dies. But the history of the person also continues beyond that person's death, for the person continues to exist as a disembodied soul.

Our next job, then, is to examine this classical, dualistic, account. I will want, in fact, to ask two questions about it. We need to know, of course, whether the account as it stands makes any sense. We know how it goes, to be sure, but we also know how Jabberwocky goes—it's the toves that were slithy and the borogoves that were mimsy, and not the other way around—and, for all that, Jabberwocky remains a piece of (inspired) nonsense.

At the same time, however, I will want to be asking another question: Even assuming that the classical dualistic account makes sense more or less as it stands, does it do the job for which a dualistic world-picture is needed in the first place? Does this form of soul-body or mind-body dualism, in other words, supply satisfactory answers to our earlier questions about the person and about the corpse? The surprising fact of the matter, I think, is that it does not—and could not. Understanding why not will take us a step further along the road toward our goal of thinking clearly about death.

CHAPTER 2

Bodies and Souls, I: The Limits of Theorizing

2.1: A FIRST TRY—
THE 'HAVING' THEORY

We now have a picture before us which appears to contain three entities—a soul, a body, and a person. These entities, of course, are not presumed to be independent of one another, and that leads us immediately to our next specific question: How are soul, body, and person supposed to be related to one another? It turns out, in fact, that there are three quite different theories apparently implicit in our customary ways of speaking about these matters—three theories which, it also turns out, are all too easily confused with one another.

The first of these theories derives from the most straightforward bit of what one might call "ordinary body-and-soul talk." We sometimes say such things, for example, as these:

    i.   He has a muscular body.

    ii. She has a generous soul.

This manner of speaking identifies a body and a soul as things which a person has. Accordingly, I shall call our first theory, Theory 1, the 'Having' Theory:

    T.1 A person has a soul and a body.

According to T.1, in other words, the relationship between a person, on the one hand, and a soul or a body, on the other, is some form of possession or ownership, signaled by the word *has*. Can Theory 1 supply coherent answers to our questions concerning a person who dies: "What becomes of the person?" and "Where does the corpse come from?" I want next to argue that it cannot.

The reason, quite simply, is that no account of the history of a person's possessions following his death has any consequences regarding the history of the person himself following his death. Theory 1, accordingly, supplies at best an answer only to the second of our two questions concerning death. It does, apparently, provide us with something other than the person himself to become (change into) the corpse with which we are left upon the death of the person—namely, the body which, according to T.1, the person has. On the question of what becomes of the person himself, however, Theory 1 is completely silent. For, according to Theory 1, a soul is also something which the person has, and knowing what becomes of it is not yet knowing what becomes of him.

An analogy might be helpful. A pancreas is also something which a person has. Suppose, then, I were assured that, upon my death, my pancreas would be surgically removed and henceforth and forever kept healthy and functioning in a chemical nutrient solution. The history of my pancreas, in other words, would continue after my death. Would it follow that my history would continue after my death? That I would not cease to exist at the point of my death? Clearly, it would not. The fate of my pancreas might be a matter of interest to me, after the fashion of a curiosity, but it would not be my fate. While I might find the fact that my pancreas will not perish upon my death an interesting one, then, it would be out of place for me to find it especially important.

On Theory 1, however, the relationship between a person and his soul is no different in essence from the relationship between a person and his pancreas. Each is something which the person has. The information that my soul would not perish upon my death, then, while it might—as a curiosity—be of equal interest to me as the analogous information concerning my pancreas, would not be of any more importance to me than the analogous information concerning my pancreas. It would not follow from the fact that my soul would continue to exist following my death that I would continue to exist following my death. The fact that the history of my soul continues after my death does not, on Theory 1, imply that my history continues after my death, any more than would the analogous fact about my pancreas. Theory 1 leaves my fate so far completely undetermined. It cannot, therefore, supply a coherent answer to both of our questions concerning death—the question concerning the corpse and the question concerning the person.[1]

2.2: HAVING A SOUL—
IN A MANNER OF SPEAKING

Now you have probably been struck by the peculiarity of the discussion which I have just concluded. Surely, you may be inclined to protest, a person's having a soul is a very different sort of thing from a person's having a pancreas. My analogy, consequently, must be ill-chosen, and the conclusions which I drew from it somehow mistaken.

I think that your intuitions here are, indeed, quite correct, but we must be rather careful as to how we spell them out. A person's having a soul is, indeed, a very different sort of thing from a person's having a pancreas. But this is not for the reason that a person's having a soul is a very special form of possession or ownership. Rather, it is because a person's having a soul is not a form of possession or ownership at all. The fact of the matter is that the souls which people have—and the bodies which they have, as well—are not things or entities at all. They are merely nominal objects, that is, illusions of linguistic appearance. Let me explain.

We derived Theory 1 from a common manner of speaking in which we say such things as:

> i.   He has a muscular body.

and

> ii.   She has a generous soul.

Taking linguistic appearances at face value here, each of i. and ii. appears to state a relationship—of having, possession, or ownership—between two things, a person and a body or a person and a soul. Thus the surface grammar of i. and ii. is fully analogous to the surface grammar of sentences which do state such a relationship, for example:

> iii.   He has an enlarged liver.

and

> iv.   She has a red Pontiac.

To dispel the illusion generated by these superficial grammatical analogies, however, consider a few more examples of the same surface forms:

> v.   He has a short temper.
> vi.   She has an even disposition.

Here there is no temptation, I think, to suppose that there are things or entities—a temper and a disposition—which have histories of their own, independent from the histories of the persons who have them, and which are owned or possessed by those persons. Rather, we recognize v. and vi. as idioms, mere manners of speaking, and we know well enough how to paraphrase them to remove the misleading impressions:

> v*.   He is irascible, testy, easily provoked to anger.
> vi*.   She is calm, unflappable, not easily disturbed.

Rather than stating a relationship between two things—a person and something else—sentences v*. and vi*. simply attribute properties to one thing—a person. Each of v*. and vi*. says what a person is like, not what a person possesses. But v*. and vi*. are paraphrases of v. and vi. That is, the two sets of sentences say the same thing, state the same facts. It follows that v. and vi. also do not, despite appearances, say what a person possesses, but only what a person is like. Despite appearances, sentences v. and vi. are also each only about one thing—and the temper and the disposition seemingly referred to in those sentences are not things or entities in their own right but merely nominal objects. Like smiles, they are products of a manner of speaking.

The souls and bodies which people (are said to) have are not, like the livers and Pontiacs which persons may possess or own, things in their own right. Rather, they, too, are merely nominal objects, cousins of smiles and tempers and dispositions. The therapy of paraphrase which we applied to v. and vi., we can apply to i. and ii. as well. For to say that

    i.   He has a muscular body.

is simply to say that

    i*.   He is muscular.

And to say that

    ii.   She has a generous soul.

is simply to say that

    ii*.   She is generous.

Nothing of this sort, however, can be done to sentences iii. and iv.—for an enlarged liver and a red Pontiac are things in their own right, with histories of their own, which, for better or for worse, a person can own or possess. Each of sentences i. and ii., in contrast, only appears to state a relationship between independent entities. What i. says is the same as what i*. says, and what ii. says is the same as what ii*. says—but neither i*. nor ii*. says anything about what a person possesses. Each of i*. and ii*., rather, says something about what a person is like—and so, consequently, do both i. and ii. The souls and bodies which, according to these customary modes of speech, people are said to have are merely nominal objects.

Theory 1, however, treats the souls and bodies seemingly referred to in these idioms precisely as if they were things in their own right, entities with histories of their own which stand in special relationships to persons. T.1, consequently, is even worse off than it seemed to be a moment ago. Earlier, I concluded that Theory 1 could, at best, supply an answer only to our question concerning the origins of a corpse, but no answer to our question concerning the fate of a person. We see now, however, that the theory cannot even do this much for us—for it rests from the very beginning upon a misunderstanding. It mistakes linguistic appearance for linguistic reality. Theory 1, it turns out, is just a muddle. If we are going to find a dualistic picture with which to answer our questions about death, we shall need to look elsewhere than at these customary modes of speech.

Parenthetically, it would be of no help at all to substitute the word 'mind' for the word 'soul' here, for the minds which people are also often said to have are equally merely nominal objects. To say that

> vii.   She has a logical mind.

is, once again, not to state a relationship of possession or ownership between a person and something else which is a thing in its own right, but rather, again, to say something about what a person is like. For to assert vii., it should by now be clear, is only to say that

> vii*.   She is logical (i.e., reasons well, draws sensible conclusions from the evidence, etc.).

Talk of the minds which people have, then, gives no more aid and comfort to the notion that a person's history might continue beyond his death than does talk of the souls or bodies which people have.[2] It is time, in short, to leave the 'Having' Theory, and the manners of speaking which give rise to it, entirely behind us. Our next question therefore must be: Is there then an alternative?

2.3: A SECOND TRY— THE 'TEAM' THEORY

Theory 1—the hypothesis that the relationship among persons, souls, and bodies is some form of having—we have seen, is doubly a failure. It misconstrues the linguistic appearances which give rise to it, and so, in fact, does not even place before us three independent entities which might stand in relationships at all. But, even if we pretend for a moment that the souls and bodies which people are said to have are genuine entities and not merely nominal objects, the theory still offers no answer at all to the question concerning the history of a person who dies.

When I originally presented the dualistic, soul-and-body picture, however, I did not present it in the idiom of ownership or possession. When I originally sketched this picture, I sketched it in the idiom of constitution or composition. A person, I said, is thought of as the union of a soul and a body—not as some third, independent thing which has both a soul and a body but as a derivative, built-up thing which consists of (is composed of) a soul and a body. This way of speaking gives rise to our second theory concerning the relationships of person, soul, and body:

> T.2   A person is (consists of) a soul and (united with) a body.

I shall call Theory 2 the 'Team' Theory, for it holds that what we ordinarily call a person is something that results when a soul and a body "team up" together to form a composite thing. Now, is the 'Team' Theory any better than Theory 1 with regard to our two questions?

Well, it turns out that it is. Theory 2 can supply answers to both the question concerning the origins of corpses and the question concerning the histories of persons following death. The catch, however, is that, from the point of view which motivates it in the first place, Theory 2 supplies the wrong answer about persons. For it follows from Theory 2 that the history of a person cannot continue beyond the point of that person's death.

According to Theory 2, a person is a particular sort of team. Consider, by analogy, the battery of a baseball club. According to the handiest dictionary, a *battery* (in baseball) is "a team's pitcher and catcher for a game considered as a unit." (Similarly, we might formulate Theory 2 by saying that a person is "a soul and a body together considered as a unit.") At the start of any given game, then, each club fields a (starting) battery. In parallel with T.2, we can say that

T.B   A battery is (consists of) a pitcher and (working together with) a catcher.

Now what death is, on the picture supplied by Theory 2, is the separation of soul and body, the dissolution of their union. Each goes its separate way. Let us, then, say analogously that when either the pitcher or the catcher in a given game is replaced (or when both are) the battery composed of that pitcher and that catcher is retired. We can now formulate questions analogous to our questions concerning death. We can ask, for example, what becomes of the starting pitcher when the starting battery is retired. There are two possible answers: Either the pitcher continues to pitch (for the starting battery can be retired by replacing the catcher) or the pitcher is sent to the showers. In either case, the starting pitcher will have a history which continues beyond the retirement of the starting battery. The same holds true, of course, for the starting catcher. But what about the starting battery itself? Does its history continue beyond the point at which it is retired?

The answer, clearly, is that it does not. Of course, if the game is not finished, the club will still be fielding some battery or other—but it will no longer be fielding that battery. For that battery (the starting battery) consists of that pitcher (the starting pitcher) and that catcher (the starting catcher) working together. When a battery is retired, however, its pitcher and its catcher precisely cease to work together. When either the pitcher or the catcher of the starting battery is replaced, then, there no longer exists anything of which it is true to say that it consists of that pitcher (the starting pitcher) and that catcher (the starting catcher) working together. But that is what the starting battery consisted of. It follows that, upon being retired, the starting battery itself ceases to exist. It is replaced in the game by a different battery, and its history comes to an end.

Theory 2 supplies answers both to the question concerning the origins of corpses and to the question concerning the histories of persons following death. It is, of course, the body which becomes (changes into) the corpse which we are left with upon a person's death—just as it may be, for instance, the starting pitcher who becomes the dejected player we find in the showers upon the retirement of the starting battery. And just as the pitcher and the catcher of some starting battery both have histories which continue beyond the retirement of the battery composed of them, so, too, Theory 2 proposes that the soul and the body have histories which continue beyond the death of the person composed of them, that is, beyond the dissolution of their union.

But the person himself is precisely in the same circumstances as the battery itself. The person himself no more has a history which continues beyond his death than the battery itself has a history which continues beyond its retirement. For, according to Theory 2, a person consists of a united soul and body, and a united soul and body necessarily ceases to exist when the soul and the body becomes disunited in exactly the way in which the starting battery necessarily ceases to exist when one of its members is sent to the showers.

If a person is a composite entity of the sort which the 'Team' Theory takes a person to be, then, there will be no logical room for even the possibility that the history of a person continues beyond that person's death. A person will no more be able to have a history continuing beyond the point of his death than a federation can have a history beyond the point at which all of its members secede or a team can have a history beyond the point at which it breaks up or disbands. The soul and the body, to be sure, might each have such a continuing history, just as individual players or federated states will (or can) have histories continuing beyond the disbanding of a team or the dissolving of a federation. But just as no single player is a team and no single state is a federation, so too, on the account offered by Theory 2, neither the body nor the soul is the person. Their continuing histories, consequently, will not be his continuing history. But there is nothing else specified by the 'Team' Theory, the history of which could be the history of that person following his death—and it follows that, on Theory 2, the person simply does not have a history following his death. His history comes to an end with his death. The person, the union of soul and body, ceases to exist. Far from opening the possibility of an "afterlife" for persons, then, Theory 2 is logically incompatible with that possibility.

2.4: . . . AND TRY AGAIN

Our discussion in this chapter is motivated by the observation that the very possibility of a person's history continuing beyond that person's death requires some sort of dualistic view of persons. The traditional dualistic view which lay most readily to hand was soul-body (or, equivalently for our purposes, mind-body) dualism. Our most recent efforts have been dedicated to finding a version of that view which was both internally coherent and did leave open the possibility that a person's history continues beyond his death. Theory 1, the 'Having' Theory, failed on the first of these counts. It was based upon a linguistic illusion and so, it turned out, no authentic dualism at all. Theory 2, the 'Team' Theory, in contrast, failed on the second count. If a person is (consists of) the union of a soul and a body, there is no logical room left for the possibility that a person's history continues beyond the disuniting of that soul from that body.

We are thus led to attempt a third interpretation of soul-body dualism. It is not that a soul and a body are both things which a person has, nor that a soul united with a body is what a person is. Those theories we have tried and found wanting. To leave open the possibility that a person's history continues beyond that person's death, what we would need to hold is that a person is a soul, period. A living person would not then be a soul and a body. A living person would be a soul in a body. I shall call this version of dualism, Theory 3, the 'Soul' Theory:

T.3   A person is a soul.

Theory 3, at last, not only provides the resources for answers to both of our questions concerning death, but in fact provides resources which leave open the possibility that the history of a person does continue beyond his death. On this view, the history of a person is the history of a soul. Death is an event within the history of the body. It is, to be more precise, the event of that body's becoming desouled. A corpse, according to Theory 3, is just a desouled body. The event of a body's becoming desouled is also, of course, an occasion of a soul's becoming disembodied. It does not follow, however, that death is an event within the history of a soul. For it might, alternatively, be the case that the disembodiment of a soul is the event with which the history of that soul comes to an end, just as the division of an amoeba is an event with which the history of that amoeba comes to an end.[3] It remains, then, an open question whether the history of the soul continues beyond the point of its disembodiment and, consequently, also an open question whether the history of the person who is that soul continues beyond the person's death which is that disembodiment.

But the 'Soul' Theory at least leaves open the possibility that a person's history might continue beyond that person's death, for, unlike Theory 2, Theory 3 does not identify a person as something whose nonexistence would be a logical consequence of the separation of soul and body. If we can make sense of the notion of a soul as something which (i) a person is (rather than has) and (ii) is capable of existing in two conditions (embodied and disembodied), then, we can at least make sense of the possibility that the history of a person continues beyond that person's death, and of the idea that the death itself is a change of condition rather than a change of subject—a change from a living (= embodied) person (= soul) to a disembodied person (= soul). If Theory 3 is internally coherent, in other words, it will be a view of persons which allows, but in no way guarantees, an "afterlife" for persons. It would then become a further question whether there are any reasons to suppose that a soul does continue to exist once it has been disembodied, that is, whether the history of a soul continues beyond the disembodiment of that soul, or whether disembodiment is to souls what division is to amoebae or metamorphosis to caterpillars, an event which puts an end to their histories.

The first question, however, must be whether the 'Soul' Theory is internally coherent to begin with. Our discussion of Theory 1 emerged with the result that the souls which people are often said to have are merely nominal objects. They turned out to be products of linguistic appearances, not things in their own right. Now Theory 3 speaks of souls as well, not souls which people are said to have but souls which people are said to be. So far, however, all that we have to work with is this new manner of speaking. We do not yet know how this manner of speaking is to be interpreted and how—or even whether—it can be understood. Exploring the 'Soul' Theory—as opposed to merely formulating it—must therefore be our next order of business. For all that we have so far said, it could still turn out that the souls which people are said by Theory 3 to be are also not things in their own right, but rather objects every bit as nominal as the souls which, according to T.1, people may be said to have.

2.5: THE BANAL
AND THE SPECIAL

In formulating Theory 1, I traced the notions of a soul and a body which people may be said to have to certain common idioms. In formulating Theories 2 and 3, however, I have simply availed myself of the words 'soul' and 'body' without raising the question of whether the words as thus used also figure in our customary, nontheoretical talk about persons. It now becomes important to recognize that, at least in the case of Theory 3, they do not. It is important, that is, to recognize that what I am calling the 'Soul' Theory, while it borrows some old words, in fact introduces a new manner of speaking about persons. It proposes a certain contrived way of talking and thinking about persons, one tailored precisely to allow, as our customary modes of speaking evidently do not, for the coherent formulation of the very possibility that a person's history continues beyond that person's death.

Theory 1, as we saw, derived a certain spurious plausibility from the common idioms which give rise to it. Even for Theory 2, as I shall argue in a moment, we could have found some motivation in our customary ways of thinking about persons—although the plausibility thus conveyed to the 'Team' Theory would have once again been only spurious, as we shall also shortly see. But Theory 3 will receive aid and comfort neither from those idioms inspiring T.1 nor from those considerations which might have tempted us to espouse T.2 If the 'Soul' Theory is to advance in our discussions from the status of a mere verbal formula to that of an intelligible hypothesis—something for which there could be reasons and which could serve as a point of departure for further inquiry—then it will need, so to speak, to "go it alone." We will not, in other words, be able to discover an interpretation of T.3 already implicit in our linguistic practices, but rather shall need to ask whether a coherent understanding of the theory can be constructed. And if it cannot, then "Persons are souls" will suffer the same fate as "There is an undetectable gremlin in my refrigerator." It will be revealed as an empty sentence which, far from opening a real possibility of an "afterlife," will prove incapable of being used to state a fact or make a claim about the world at all.

But let us pursue our investigations in an orderly fashion. What we need to do first is to explore those features of our everyday ways of talking and thinking about people—over and above such nominal idioms as "has a soul" and "has a body"—which motivate talk of souls versus bodies in the first place, and which, in particular, might motivate the idea that what we naturally identify as a person is actually, in some sense, composite, the union of two distinct sorts of beings.

To focus our discussion, let us equip ourselves with an exemplary person, named, let us suppose, Pierre. And let us construct a list of some of the indefinitely many things which might be true of Pierre, some of the indefinitely many things which we might truly say about him. For example, it could be true that

(sp1)   Pierre thinks (believes, knows, sees) that it is raining outside.

(sp2)   Pierre intends (wants, expects) to go dancing tonight.

(sp3)   Pierre remembers (recalls, recollects) having eaten eggs for breakfast.

(sp4)   Pierre is fond of (dislikes, is intimidated by) his employer's wife.

And it could also be true that

(bp1)   Pierre weighs 87 kilograms.

(bp2)   Pierre is 185 centimeters tall.

(bp3)   Pierre is currently in Detroit.

(bp4)   Pierre is composed of chemicals worth $4.95.

Now, confronted with a list of this kind, we might be struck by the fact that we can apparently say quite different sorts of things about Pierre. In particular, we might well be inclined to claim that the sentences in the (sp) group all say one sort of thing about Pierre, while the sentences in the (bp) group all say another sort of thing about him. The sentences in the (sp) group are, roughly, sentences which attribute to Pierre thoughts, beliefs, perceptions, intentions, desires, memories, or feelings. The sentences in the (bp) group attribute to Pierre mass, size, shape, location, or material composition.[4]

But while it might seem obvious that there is a difference between the sorts of things attributed to Pierre by (sp) sentences and the sorts of things attributed to him by (bp) sentences, it is not quite so obvious exactly what that difference amounts to. In order to make the difference precise, we need to articulate a principle for sorting still other sentences about Pierre into the (sp) group or the (bp) group. The original classification is rather rough-and-ready, and so does not lend itself especially well to the formulation of a sharp principle of classification. After a bit of groping, however, we seem to come out with something like this:

> What (sp) sentences say about Pierre could sensibly be said only about living organisms,

but

> What (bp) sentences say about Pierre could also sensibly be said about, for example, a rock (or, for that matter, about Pierre's corpse).

Let us call those of Pierre's features or characteristics which could also be features or characteristics of a rock or a corpse "banal" properties or, for short, "b-properties," and let us call those of his characteristics which could be characteristics only of living organisms "special" properties, or "s-properties" for short. Pierre, our typical person, then, is one thing which has two sorts of properties, banal b-properties and special s-properties. Pierre's corpse, the remains of our typical person, in contrast, would be a thing which would have only one sort of properties, banal b-properties.

So far there is nothing the least bit problematic about these observations. We are now equipped with the linguistic machinery we would need to say such things as "A corpse cannot have s-properties," but we must be clear that there is nothing exciting about such claims. They are true, so to speak, "by definition." They do not express a discovery about persons or corpses, but a decision to divide the features or characteristics of persons into two groups, depending upon whether or not they could also be features or characteristics of corpses. So far, in other words, nothing we have done requires that we have any kind of dualistic theory of persons at all.

But while our machinations to this point do not entail a dualistic view of persons, they may nevertheless inspire one. In particular, the distinctions which we have been making may lead us to formulate something like Theory 2, the 'Team' Theory. All that is necessary is that we allow ourselves to become puzzled about how one thing, Pierre, could have both s-properties and b-properties. If we develop such a puzzlement, and suitably nurture and encourage it, we may be led to formulate the view that while, speaking according to our customary fashions, Pierre is correctly said to be one thing, for all that, Pierre is not ultimately one thing. Rather, Pierre is one thing only in the way in which a baseball club's starting battery is one thing. Pierre is one composite thing. He consists of the union of two other things—one of which, like his corpse, has only b-properties but no s-properties, and the other of which has only s-properties but not b-properties. And while we do not have any ready-made names for these two theoretical constituents of Pierre, we can borrow some from an idiom with which we are already familiar. We can call the constituent of Pierre which has only banal b-properties a body, and we can call the constituent of Pierre which has only special s-properties a soul. In this way, we might well arrive at Theory 2:

> Pierre is (consists of) the union of a body and a soul.

To say that Pierre has both b-properties and s-properties, on this theory, then, will be rather like saying that some battery has both a batting average and an earned run average (in a league which makes use of designated hitters). The battery has both a batting average and an earned run average precisely in the sense that the catcher has a batting average and the pitcher an earned run average, where the battery consists of that catcher and that pitcher. Analogously, Pierre will have both b-properties and s-properties only in the sense that some body has b-properties and some soul s-properties, where Pierre consists of that body united with that soul.

2.6: FIVE WAYS TO TALK ABOUT BODIES

I claimed earlier that Theory 3, the 'Soul' Theory, introduces a contrived use of the words 'body' and 'soul'. If what I have just finished saying is correct, however, it turns out that the same thing was already true of Theory 2 as well. For the 'Team' Theory, I have claimed, borrows the terms 'soul' and 'body' from the idiom in which we speak of persons having souls and having bodies—uses of the terms in which they do not designate things in their own right—and gives them a new use—as supposedly picking out two distinct entities of which the person, Pierre, is theoretically composed. I want now to argue in some detail that this is indeed the case. That is, I want to argue that the only customary use of the term 'body' in which it is opposed to the term 'soul' (or to the term 'mind') is that idiomatic use in which persons are spoken of as having souls (or minds) and bodies.

The term 'body' is a remarkably versatile one. We can distinguish at least five common contexts in which the word is correctly used.[5] There is, for example, the sort of context in which, say, a physicist might speak of "moving bodies" or "falling bodies." In this use of the term 'body'—let us call it 'body-1'—a body is, roughly, a mass, that is, a chunk of material which occupies space and obeys the laws of motion. Both a rock and a person pitched from a third-story window immediately become falling bodies-1. But the notion of a body-1, it should be clear, is not the notion of something having only b-properties. A person who has had the misfortune to become a falling body-1 is no less the subject of s-properties than one seated comfortably at his dining room table. He continues to perceive, think, remember, feel, and desire—even though his dramatic circumstances surely alter what he is, for example, thinking about.

Secondly, there is the use of the term 'body' in which a marksmanship instructor might tell his students to "aim for the body." Here the term 'body'—let us call it 'body-2'—is opposed, not to 'mind' or 'soul', but to 'head', 'arms', and 'legs'. A body-2 is, roughly, a torso. While a person may, indeed, be said to consist of a body-2 and something else, the "something else" here is not a soul but rather a head, neck, arms, and legs. The term 'body' which appears in Theories 2 and 3, in other words, is not 'body-2' any more than it was 'body-1'.

Exactly the same sort of thing is true of that use of the term 'body' in which it is opposed to 'brain', 'heart', 'lungs', and 'liver'. Here we might say, for instance, that a surgeon has transplanted Smith's heart into Jones's body. This use of the term 'body'—call it 'body-3'—is analogous to that in which we speak of the body of an automobile, as opposed, for example, to its engine or drive train. "The engine needs a valve job and the gears in the transmission are stripped, but there isn't a speck of rust on the body." A body-3 is, roughly, a chassis, and, especially in medical contexts, we may speak of the body-3 of a person when we wish to contrast a sort of stable "shell" or "container" to some "inner mechanisms" or "works" that a surgeon is fooling around with. But the term 'body' which appears in Theories 2 and 3 is also, obviously, not 'body-3'.

We have already met that use of the term 'body'—call it 'body-4'—in which we speak of a person's corpse as a "dead body." A body-4 just is a corpse, a cadaver—and, for that reason, cannot be the body supposedly referred to in Theories 2 and 3. True, a body-4 (that is, a corpse), like the body supposedly referred to in the 'Team' Theory, has—by definition, as it were—only banal b-properties, for the notion of b-properties was introduced precisely as the notion of those properties of persons which could also be properties of corpses. But that is not enough to allow the term 'body' in Theory 2 to be interpreted as 'body-4'. For the body in T.2 is supposed to be something which (i) is a constituent of a living person and (ii) becomes a corpse when the person dies. If we were to interpret the term 'body' appearing in T.2 as 'body-4', then, in stating the theory, we would be uttering such absurdities as (i) a living person consists of a soul and a corpse, and (ii) a corpse becomes a corpse when the person dies. Since, we may presume, an advocate of the 'Team' Theory does not intend to be offering us such absurdities as these, we are barred from interpreting his use of the term 'body' as a use of 'body-4'. The proper opposite to 'body-4', in other words, is not 'soul' but rather 'living organism', for it is to living organisms that we contrast "dead bodies," that is, corpses.

Finally, there is our old friend, the use of the term 'body'—call it 'body-5'—in the idiom of possession or ownership, in which we speak, for instance, of Pierre's body, the body which Pierre has. 'Body-5', as we have seen, does properly contrast with 'soul' (or 'mind'). But, as we have also already seen, bodies-5 are not things in their own right which could be constituents of persons but merely nominal objects, illusory products of a certain manner of speaking. This manner of speaking is always available to us when we are attributing b-properties to a person. Instead of saying that Pierre weighs 87 kilograms, is 185 centimeters tall, is currently located in Detroit, and is composed of chemicals worth $4.95, we have the option of saying these things about Pierre's body. But this no more shows that a body-5 is a thing in its own right than does the fact that we could express the claim that

    (a)   Pierre is compact, muscular, and well-developed

by saying

    (b)   Pierre has a compact, muscular, and well-developed body.

For we could also express the claim (a) by saying

    (c)   Pierre has a compact, muscular, and well-developed physique.

But that would give us no grounds for holding that physiques are things in their own right—nor, I suspect, would it tempt us for even a moment to suppose that Pierre is a composite entity, one constituent of which is a physique. Like tempers and dispositions, physiques are pretty obviously merely nominal objects, not things in their own right which might be constitutents of composite beings.

In many of our uses of 'body-5', a body-5 just is a physique. But even in those cases in which we could not comfortably replace the term 'body' (i.e., 'body-5') by the term 'physique', we should not conclude that the body-5 which a person is said to have (or which is said to be his) is a thing in its own right. We reserve the term 'physique' for those attributions of b-properties to persons in which what interests us are matters of musculature, posture, and carriage, rather than mass, size, and chemical composition. (Thus we are happy speaking about the physique of a realistic Greek statue, but not about the physique of the piece of marble from which it was carved—although talk about mass, size, and chemical composition is appropriate in both cases.) But even where talk of physique is out of place and we nevertheless employ a manner of speaking of the form

> Pierre's body has properties X, Y, and Z,

there is no reason to interpret this idiom as meaning that

> There is something which (i) can have only b-properties and (ii) has the properties X, Y, and Z, that Pierre has (owns, possesses) or that is a constitutent (component, part) of Pierre.

For what we are saying can be understood much more straightforwardly as it is ordinarily understood—apart from special philosophical (or theological) theories about persons—as meaning that

> Pierre (the person) has properties X, Y, and Z,

and as indicating, by availing ourselves of the body-5 idiom, that

> Properties X, Y, and Z are banal b-properties (i.e., properties that a rock or a corpse might also have).

To put the point in a nutshell, talk of bodies-5 in the idiom of ownership or possession does not ordinarily serve the function of indicating a special subject, a nonperson, to which certain properties are to be ascribed, but rather serves the function of making a comment about certain properties which are ascribed to a person, namely that they are not exclusively properties of persons (or of living organisms in general). And talk of souls in the idiom of ownership or possession does not ordinarily serve the function of indicating a different special subject, also a nonperson, to which certain different properties are to be ascribed, but rather serves the function of making a different comment about these other properties, namely that they are exclusively properties of living organisms, that they could not also be sensibly attributed to corpses or to rocks. To take a comment about the properties of persons to be reference to special subjects which are not persons but rather constituents of persons or things possessed by persons is, once again, to mistake linguistic appearance for linguistic reality. It is to be taken in by an illusion of surface grammar, which, consistently pursued, would populate our world, not just with souls and bodies, but with tempers, dispositions, physiques, and ghostly smiles as well. The term 'body' which occurs in Theory 2, then, is also not our ordinary term 'body-5', for the bodies spoken of in the 'Team' Theory are intended to be things in their own right, constituents of persons, and bodies-5, we have seen, are not. Bodies-5 are merely nominal objects, the illusory products of a common manner of speech.

But how, then, are we to interpret the term 'body' which occurs in Theory 2—if not as 'body-1' or 'body-2' or 'body-3' or 'body-4' or 'body-5'? If our customary manners of speaking and thinking do not include the conceptual resources for understanding the term 'body' as it appears in T.2, where shall we turn for such an understanding? Clearly, there is no place to turn except to the theory itself. The notion of a body as a constituent of a person was introduced into Theory 2 to explain something, to solve some problem. To understand this notion of a body, then, what we need to understand is that problem and that explanation. Let us return, therefore, to the considerations which motivated the 'Team' Theory in the first place, and see what, if anything, the problem is; what, if anything, needs to be explained.

2.7: WHAT'S STRIKING ABOUT DEATH

The line of thought which leads up to the formulation of the 'Team' Theory—or, for that matter, to the formulation even of the 'Having' Theory—is an intricately tangled interplay of confusions. I am not sure that I can successfully unravel all of its strands. But I shall try to say enough to indicate why I am convinced that the supposed problem which such theories are invoked to "solve" is misconceived from the outset. And I shall also try to show how, once we have convinced ourselves that there is a problem here, the superficial appearances of our language can seduce us into supposing—falsely—that we already have coherent concepts of a "soul" and a "body" which can be invoked to "solve" it. Let me begin, then, by asking: What is the fundamental observation about persons which provokes people to talk about "souls" as opposed to "bodies" in the first place?

The answer, surely, is that people are very different from, say, rocks. A person can move and grow, see and hear, feel and need. A rock can do none of these things. This much, of course, is not exclusively true of persons. Fish and dogs and apes, for instance, also move, grow, see, hear, feel, and need. But people are still, for all that, very different from fish and dogs and apes. A person not only sees and hears but also reasons about what he sees and hears. A person not only feels and needs but also deliberates about what he feels and needs. A person, in other words, is a rational being—a being capable of both theoretical rationality (which issues in hypotheses, theories, descriptions, and explanations comprising an understanding of the world) and practical rationality (which issues in goals, aims, plans, intentions, and actions for coping with the world of which theoretical reason delivers an understanding).

This picture of the uniqueness of persons can, to be sure, be indefinitely elaborated upon. Persons, it can be stressed, are not merely social beings—as are bees and ants, for instance—but political beings, whose collectivities are structured and mediated by exercises of their rational capacities. Again, it may be emphasized that persons do not merely communicate—as do crows and beavers, for example—but genuinely converse. Human languages are not closed collections of mere signals but full-fledged systems of symbols, embodying a conception of the world which is capable of indefinite creative modification, expansion, and enrichment. But however formulated and however elaborated, this picture of the specialness of persons is a very powerful one. And this is the picture which, in the last analysis, lies at the motivational root of talk of "souls" or "minds" as opposed to "bodies" and, indeed, lies at the root of vast quantities of traditional theology and classical philosophy in general.

Here, parenthetically, is a point at which I can say something useful about the distinction between "souls" and "minds." The collection of differences between persons and things other than persons to which I have just been calling attention is a fairly mixed bag, and it is consequently possible to cut it up in different ways. If one is primarily impressed by the differences between living organisms in general and, say, rocks, one will probably emerge from such ruminations on specialness speaking of such things as a "vital principle" or an "entelechy." This is the classical notion of a "soul"—the one which figures in the philosophies of Plato and Aristotle, for example.[6] If, on the other hand, one is most impressed by the differences between, say, dogs or fish and people, then one is likely to emerge speaking of such things as a "mind" or an "understanding." This tendency reached its full flowering only in the modern era—in the philosophies, for instance, of Descartes and Locke.[7] The primary notion of a "soul," in other words, is the idea of something that explains life (growth, reproduction), whereas the primary notion of a "mind" is that of something which explains reason (intelligence, rationality).

Historically, these two notions have become thoroughly muddled together. I have respected this historical tradition by muddling them together in my own discussion as well. The collection of properties which I called s-properties, for example, while it tracks more-or-less with the living/nonliving distinction, is really itself in the last analysis rather a mixed bag, and I have deliberately made no attempt to unmix it. For what we are investigating in this study, the muddling together of "minds" and "souls" turns out to be unimportant. I shall therefore continue to talk, for the most part, of "souls," but the reader remains free to substitute 'mind' for 'soul'. The points I shall be making will all remain valid and in force.

What is important to our investigations is what happens when the general picture of the specialness of persons is brought up against the phenomenon of death. For there, imbued with this picture, we encounter in a moment a dramatic transition: from a living person in all his specialness to a corpse—something which looks ever so much like the person who has just died; something, indeed, which is intimately related to the person who has just died; but something which is not special at all. We confront a transition from a person to a mere object, a thing among things, no different in any significant respect from the commonest stone or clay. (That is why, in my division of special s-properties from banal b-properties, it is the notion of b-properties which logically comes first. B-properties are those properties of persons which are also properties of mere objects. S-properties are all the rest of them—the properties that make persons special.)

In the phenomenon of death, in other words, something striking happens. Specialness disappears from the world. To one imbued with the picture of the specialness of persons—even to one not so caught up with that picture—the phenomenon cries out for an explanation. The phenomenon of death dramatically brings the specialness of persons into sharp and vivid focus. It creates a demand for an account of the specialness of persons which will allow us to explain the manifest vanishing of that specialness in death. What talk of "souls" as opposed to "bodies" is, and always has been, is an attempt to meet that demand—to supply that account and that explanation. But it is, I shall argue, a radically failed attempt. Radically failed, for not only does it mislocate and misconceive the question which motivates it, but the story which it offers in response to that question is incoherent in ways which logically preclude the very possibility of its counting as an intelligible answer to that question.

2.8: A VERY BAD ARGUMENT

It is easy enough to see how the multiple ambiguities of the term 'body' can interact with demands for understanding generated by the felt specialness of persons and the striking phenomenon of death to give rise to such theories as the 'Having' Theory and the 'Team' Theory, and to the notion of a soul which is a thing in its own right. All that is needed is that one suppress those ambiguities in one's thinking and speaking about the matter. Implicitly or explicitly, then, something like the following line of reasoning becomes open to one:

(1) A corpse is a body.

(2) A corpse can have only b-properties.

(3) Therefore, a body can have only b-properties.

(4) But a person can have both b-properties and s-properties.

(5) Therefore, a body is not what a person is.

(6) But a person has a body.

(7) That is, there is something, namely a body, which a person has that can have only b-properties.

Which means either

> (7a)   A body is something which a person owns or possesses that can have only b-properties. (Theory 1)

or

> (7b)   A body is something which is a part or constituent of a person and which can have only b-properties. (Theory 2)

> (8)   Since, (4), a person can have both b-properties and s-properties, but, (3), a body can have only b-properties, there must be something else which a person has which can have s-properties, but which is not a body.

> (9)   What a person has besides a body is a soul (or: a mind).

> (10)   That is, a soul is something which a person has that can have s-properties and which is not a body.

Which means either

> (10a)   A soul is something which a person owns or possesses that can have s-properties and which is not a body.

or

> (10b)   A soul is something which is a part or a constituent of a person, that can have s-properties, and which is not a body.

Thus one is led, step by step, to the view that souls and bodies are things in their own right, and either—following (7a) and (10a)—to

> T.1:   A person has a soul and a body.

or—following (7b) and (10b)—to

> T.2:   A person is (consists of) a soul united with a body.

In terms of the distinctions which we have already had occasion to make, of course, it is easy enough to see what has gone wrong here. In fact, quite a few things have gone wrong, which is why I earlier called the emergence of Theories 1 and 2 a "tangled interplay of confusions." The quickest way to lay our hands on a bunch of these confusions is to attempt to tag the various occurrences of the term 'body' with appropriate numerical identifiers—that is, to disambiguate the various uses of the term—in a manner which makes as much of the argument as possible come out true.

Steps (1) through (5), for example, are perfectly in order, provided that we understand the term 'body' which occurs in them as 'body-4', that is, as simply synonymous with 'corpse'. Step (3) is the only one which might then give us a moment's pause, but all that we need do to allay any doubts about it is remember that the notion of a banal b-property was introduced precisely as the notion of a property of a person which could also be a property of a corpse. Step (3), in other words, is "true by definition," when we interpret 'body' as 'body-4'.

Unfortunately, step (6) requires us to interpret its use of the term 'body' as 'body-5'—the idiomatic use of the term 'body' which does not pick out an object in its own right—for it is simply not true that a person has a body-4, that is, that a person has a corpse. And once we have shifted from 'body-4' to 'body-5', there is no way of saving step (7). (7a) is simply hopeless, for it requires us to treat the nominal object apparently referred to in the idiomatic step (6) as a thing in its own right, that is, to mistake linguistic appearance for linguistic reality. Interestingly enough, there is an interpretation of (7b) which makes it come out true—two interpretations, in fact. All that we need to do is interpret 'body' as 'body-2' (that is, torso) or as 'body-3' (that is, roughly, chassis). Both a torso and a "shell" are (different) parts or constituents of a person, parts which might consistently be held to have only banal b-properties, i.e., only such properties as a corpse (body-4) or a rock might also have. But reading (7) as (7b) and interpreting (7b) in terms of 'body-2' or 'body-3' makes a disaster of step (9), for what will then be opposed to 'body' will not be 'soul' (or 'mind') but rather such things as a head, neck, arms, and legs, in the one case, or a brain, heart, lungs, and kidneys, in the other.

The upshot, clearly, is that there is no single ordinary way of understanding the various occurrences of the term 'body' in this line of reasoning by which it comes out a piece of good reasoning. And that is just to say that we do not already have coherent concepts of a "soul" and a "body" which can be invoked to solve the problem—that is, to meet the demand for an account of specialness and an explanation of the manifest vanishing of specialness in death—which motivates the reasoning in the first place.

2.9: BEYOND "COMMON SENSE"

Here, however, it may be protested that I am losing sight of the urgency of the question. If our ordinary understandings of a term such as 'body' do not supply adequate resources for constructing an answer to the question which exercises us here, it may well be said, then so much the worse for our ordinary understandings. Instead of trying to interpret the line of reasoning leading up to such theories as T.1 and T.2 in terms of our customary usages, let us instead allow the reasoning itself to teach us a new way of speaking and thinking about persons. Let us, in other words, view the argument which I have sketched as making use of a new term 'body'—call it 'body-6' or, perhaps better, 'boddy'—which we are to understand precisely by stipulating that all of the things which steps (1) through (10) say are true of bodies are true of boddies (bodies-6). This, after all, is nothing but good science. If we are allowed to postulate, say, forces of gravity to make sense of falling apples and orbiting planets, or molecules to make sense of chemical reactions and the behavior of gases, then why should we not simply postulate souls (or, better, "soulls") and boddies to make sense of the specialness of persons and the vanishing of that specialness with the coming into existence of a corpse in death?

Well, the first thing to notice about this strategy is that it represents a radical shift of ground. It no longer offers its talk of bodies and souls as "just common sense" or "what we all believe anyway," but explicitly acknowledges these various dualistic theories of persons as theories. That is, it makes of soulls and boddies theoretical entities. They are no longer to be understood as things with which we are acquainted, but rather as things which we must hypothesize in order to make explanatory sense out of what we encounter. And the most important consequence of this shift of ground is that it immediately brings into play a certain set of criteria of assessment—for, if body-and-soul (boddy-and-soull) talk is to be understood as an explanatory theory, it immediately becomes appropriate to ask how good an explanation it offers of what it purports to explain. And this, in turn, leads us to refocus our critical attentions from the notion of a body to the notion of a soul. It leads us, in fact, to take a careful look at a piece of the implicit reasoning which has so far escaped scrutiny—at step (8).

Step (8), we recall, looked like this:

(8)   Since, (4), a person can have both b-properties and s-properties, but, (3), a body can have only b-properties, there must be something else which a person has that can have s-properties, but which is not a body.

Step (8), in other words, is the move in the reasoning which introduces the notion of a soul (soull) as a postulated or hypothesized something— possession or constituent of a person—precisely to explain how a person can have s-properties as well as b-properties, that is, to explain how it comes about that a person is special. And the ostensible explanation is that a person is special because a person owns or contains something which is not a person, a soull, which is special. Unfortunately, this is about as clear a case of a nonexplanation as one could ever expect to find.

Perhaps the tidiest parallel would be Moliere's physician, who, when asked to explain how it comes about that the administration of opium puts people to sleep, replied that opium contains a *virtus dormativa*, a "dormative virtue." Since a "dormative virtue" just is the power to put people to sleep, what the doctor's reply amounted to was the assertion that opium does put people to sleep because opium can put people to sleep. Well, it is, of course, true that opium both can and does put people to sleep. That is not the problem here. The problem is with the 'because'. For the fact that opium can put people to sleep does not explain the fact that it does.

The attempt to explain the specialness of people by invoking the specialness of soulls is like that. What puzzles us about persons, we are supposing, is how it can be that a person is special—how it can be that a person can think, perceive, plan, decide, feel, and remember. But we are not helped out of our puzzlement by being told that, really, it isn't people who think, perceive, plan, decide, feel, and remember, but only possessions or parts of people who do. For what puzzles us, surely, is how anything at all can be special in these ways. Far from explaining the specialness of persons, this appeal to soulls not only retains and relocates the original puzzle of specialness but, worse, equips us with a new puzzle—the puzzle of how the soull and the person (and the boddy) can be related so that the soull might pass its specialness on to the person. (Classically, this new puzzle is known as "the mind-body problem," and it has spawned a truly wondrous variety of philosophical responses—from "interactionism" to "pre-established harmony."[8]) The appeal to "souls" urged on us by step (8) of our reasoning, in other words, is misconceived from the very outset. It is not the kind of appeal which could be an explanation of what puzzles us.

Another analogy may serve to drive the point home. Consider automobiles. Like people, automobiles are very different from, say, rocks. Of course, they are different in different ways. But not only might an automobile weigh 750 kilograms, be 3.6 meters long, be currently located in Detroit, and be composed of various elements in various proportions—as might a rock—an automobile is a self-moving entity. An automobile, but not a rock, can accelerate from 0 to 60 in twelve seconds, have a top speed of 85 miles per hour, get 35 miles per gallon on the highway, and transport people and cargo hundreds of miles in a day. Automobiles, in short, are special. Not only do they, like rocks, have banal b-properties, but they also have a large set of other properties, properties which mere rocks cannot have. Let us call these other properties 'v-properties' (short for 'vehicle-properties'). It does not take too much imagination, I suggest, to see how one might get into a frame of mind in which these facts about automobiles could begin to seem very puzzling. How, one might begin to ask, could one thing, an automobile, have both b-properties and v-properties?

And consider what happens when the general picture of the specialness of automobiles is brought up against the phenomenon of running out of gas. Do we not once again encounter in a moment a dramatic transition: from an operating automobile in all its specialness to an inert mass of metal and plastic—something which looks ever so much like the automobile which a moment ago was tooling along at a mile a minute; something, indeed, which is intimately related to the automobile which has just stopped running; but something which is not special at all. We confront a transition from a functioning vehicle to a mere object, a thing among things, to something which just sits there. The phenomenon of running out of gas brings the specialness of automobiles into sharp and vivid focus. It creates a demand for an account of the specialness of automobiles which will allow us to explain the vanishing of that specialness in running out of gas.

Now, what would it be like to attempt to explain the specialness of automobiles on the model of souls? Clearly, it would be to hold that automobiles were composite entities. One constituent of an automobile, of course, would be something which could have only b-properties. Call it a 'body-7'. In strict analogy to step (8) of the argument in the case of persons, however, we would also assert that

(8) Since an automobile can have both b-properties and v-properties, but a body-7 can have only b-properties, there must be something else which an automobile has that can have v-properties, but which is not a body-7.

We would advance a theory of automobiles, in short, which postulated or hypothesized two constituents—a body-7 and, say, a "vehicular soul." Of course, neither of the terms 'body-7' and 'vehicular soul' would admit of being understood in terms of our ordinary uses of such words as 'body' and 'vehicle', but, it would be urged, we should not see this as any objection to the theory. Rather we should let the theory itself teach us the meanings of 'body-7' and 'vehicular soul'. And then we would, finally, propose to explain the specialness of automobiles by appealing to the specialness of vehicular souls: An automobile is a self-moving entity because it contains a vehicular soul which is a self-moving entity.

Well, there is no need to multiply such absurdities any further. It is clear enough, I think, that the attempt to explain the specialness of automobiles—the interesting ways in which they differ from rocks—by postulating a constituent of automobiles, a "vehicular soul," which is what really differs from rocks in all those interesting ways, is fundamentally misguided. The crucial point for our purposes is that the attempt to explain the specialness of persons—the interesting ways in which they differ from rocks—by postulating a constituent of persons, a soul (or "soull"), which is what is really special, is fundamentally misguided in the same way. To the extent that what puzzles us about persons does pose an authentic problem, no postulation of souls could serve as a solution to it.

2.10: BEING AND DOING—
HOW WE RESEMBLE AUTOMOBILES

There is, to be sure, a point of disanalogy between the case of an automobile which runs out of gas and the case of a person who dies. A fuelless automobile, we may notice, is still an automobile, whereas a dead person, as we have already had occasion to remark, is not a kind of person but a thing of a different kind, a corpse or cadaver. This disanalogy, however, does not rest on any difference concerning specialness and the vanishing of specialness. What it turns on, rather, is the question of whether the vanishing of specialness is transient and temporary or permanent and irreversible.

We can, in fact, tighten up the analogy in either direction. If we wish to implicate automobiles in a vanishing of specialness which is not a change of condition but a change of kind, we need only refocus our attention from an automobile which has run out of gas to one which as been, as the common expression puts it, "totalled." Here the specialness of the automobile is irretrievably lost. A "totalled" automobile is beyond repair. And what we find is that, with an irreversible loss of specialness, our customary language indeed delivers up the picture not of a change of condition but of a change of kind. A totalled automobile is not a kind of automobile but a wreck or a hulk, the remains of an automobile—a linguistic verdict which exactly parallels the observation that a dead person is not a kind of person but a corpse, a person's remains.

If, on the other hand, we wish to preserve the person through a loss of specialness, it is sufficient to consider a merely temporary and correctable loss of specialness. One simple case is unconsciousness. Both consciousness and unconsciousness are conditions of persons, and an unconscious person, unlike a dead person, is a kind of person—in spite of the fact that an unconscious person fails to be special in many of the same ways in which a corpse fails to be special. Like a corpse, an unconscious person cannot think or perceive, feel or deliberate, remember or decide—although some of the special properties which separate persons from rocks are preserved uninterruptedly through a period of unconsciousness (much as a fuelless automobile with a live battery might still turn over when the ignition switch is thrown, something which no rock could ever do).

Parenthetically, the picture here may well be muddled by yet another, troublesome, linguistic appearance. For there is, in a manner of speaking, a kind of "dead person" which is a kind of person. What I have in mind is a person who, during the course of a surgical procedure, for instance, is said to have been, for a time, "clinically dead." "Clinical death" is the temporary cessation of so-called "vital signs." A person undergoes clinical death when, for example, heartbeat and respiration are momentarily suspended and then restarted through massage or electrical shock. A clinical death, in other words, is a reversible condition of persons, something which a person can and often does survive.

But what follows from this is not that persons can survive death, but that clinical death is not a kind of death. A clinical death is a traumatic event within the history of a living person. But it is not a kind of death, for the simple reason that a person undergoing a clinical death does not die. He survives. And so we are dealing here with another linguistic appearance. A clinically dead person is a kind of person but, for precisely that reason, a clinically dead person is not a kind of dead person. The phrase 'clinically dead' modifies the noun 'person' as a unit. It picks out a reversible, survivable condition of persons, a condition in which people resemble dead persons—that is, corpses—in important ways.

The phrase 'clinically dead person', in other words, behaves quite like the phrase 'apparently pointless remark'. There are not two kinds of pointless remarks, apparently pointless remarks and, perhaps, really pointless remarks. Rather, 'apparently pointless' modifies the noun 'remark' as a unit. An apparently pointless remark is not a kind of pointless remark, but a remark which resembles genuinely pointless remarks in important ways—a remark which one is tempted to mistake for a pointless remark. 'Clinically dead person' is like that. There are not two kinds of dead person, clinically dead persons and, perhaps, really dead persons. Instead, a clinically dead person is a person whom one is tempted to mistake for a dead person, that is, for a corpse, because of the important resemblances between persons in that unfortunate condition and genuine corpses. Clinical death, like unconsciousness, is a merely transient and temporary loss of specialness and, for that reason, not a sort of death at all but a mere manner of speaking, a temptation to linguistic illusion.[9]

Much more significant than such explicable disanalogies between fuelless automobiles and dead persons, however, is the central feature of the analogy upon which I have been trading. What the analogy brings into focus is a crucial difference between what I have been calling 'b-properties' and what I have been calling 's-properties'. It brings into focus the fact that what is special about persons is not, so to speak, what they are but rather what they can do.

The b-properties of an automobile relate to features of its structure—the sizes, shapes, weights, and compositions of its material parts, and the disposition of those parts in space. But the v-properties of an automobile, the properties which make automobiles special, do not relate to its structure. The v-properties of an automobile single out features of its performance—its acceleration, top speed, fuel economy, and load capacity. The specialness of automobiles, that is, is not a matter of what they are but of what they can do. And the crucial point we need to make now in order to advance in our discussion of persons is that the specialness of persons is also like that. It is also a matter of performances. What is striking about corpses is that, although they look like persons, are made of the same sorts of stuffs as persons, and, indeed, are intimately related to persons, for all that they can't do anything.

The special s-properties of persons may be loosely collected under the headings of 'life', 'motility', 'sentience', and 'rationality'. What is significant about such terms is that what they pick out are not qualities but powers. Life, motility, sentience, and rationality are abilities or capacities of persons. Life is the capacity to grow and reproduce; motility, the power of self-movement; sentience, the ability to perceive and to feel; and rationality, the power to reason, deliberate, argue, converse, plan, decide, and draw conclusions. To use some old-fashioned terminology, life, motility, sentience, and rationality are faculties which manifest themselves in various activities which are their exercises. It is these activities, however, which come first in the order of understanding. That is, the nouns 'life', 'motility', 'sentience', and 'rationality' are to be understood, not as bare labels for special or mysterious things, but in terms of their relations to certain verbs—'grow', 'reproduce', 'see', 'hear', 'feel', 'move', 'think', and the like. Like the v-properties of automobiles, in other words, the s-properties of persons are performance capabilities—powers, abilities, or capacities for certain activities. The specialness of persons, in other words, is a matter of their capability to engage in such activities—a matter, that is, of what people can do.

To say that a person is living, motile, sentient, or rational, then, is not to attribute a quality to a thing. Modifiers, we should remind ourselves, are not all of a piece. Not all adjectives stand for properties. These adjectives, in particular, do not stand for qualities or properties but rather for powers, capacities, or abilities.

Being alive, motile, sentient, or rational, in other words, does not resemble being, say, blue or spherical, but is rather more like being, say, magnetic or water-soluble. To say that something is a white, cubical piece of sugar or a silvery, cylindrical piece of iron is to say what something is. To say that something is water-soluble or magnetic, however, is to say something about its powers, abilities, or capacities—to dissolve in water or to attract bits of metal. Something is water-soluble just in case it can dissolve in water, and something is magnetic just in case it can move bits of ferrous metal in its vicinity. What comes first in the order of understanding, then, are the performances—the dissolving or the attracting and moving—and such adjectives as 'magnetic' and 'water-soluble' are to be understood in terms of their relationship to the appropriate verbs which indicate those performances.

And now I think we can both see and say more clearly why the postulation of souls as things in their own right which are possessions or constituents of persons could not in principle explain the specialness of persons. For now we see that what wants explanation is a performance capability (or set of performance capabilities), and we cannot in principle explain a thing's performance capabilities by denying that the thing in question is what actually has those performance capabilities. Just this, however, is what both the 'Having' Theory and the 'Team' Theory do, for, on either theory, what actually has the relevant performance capabilities turns out to be a soul, and on neither theory is a soul a person.

2.11: THE COLLAPSE OF A THEORY

Theory 3, however, does not suffer from this logical defect. Theory 3, we recall, held that

   T.3   A person is a soul.

And this 'Soul' Theory, we may also recall, was the only variant of body-soul dualism which allowed even the possibility that the history of a person might continue beyond that person's death. It might appear, then, as if Theory 3 were both logically and motivationally better off than either of its dualistic alternatives. What I want to argue next, however, is that quite the contrary is the case. The 'Soul' Theory is in actuality the most muddled of our various dualistic pictures of persons.

On both T.1 and T.2, the relation between a person and a soul is the same as the relation between a person and a body. Both soul and body are possessions of a person (T.1) or parts of a person (T.2). Theory 3, however, rejects this form of symmetry. According to T.3, a person is identical to a soul, but only temporarily inhabits or occupies a body. Now, once again, the term 'body' which occurs in our theory cannot be interpreted and understood according to any of our ordinary ways of speaking and thinking about bodies, as 'body-1' or 'body-2' or 'body-3' or 'body-4' or 'body-5'. Once again, we must view the theory as introducing a new, contrived sense of the term 'body'—I shall again write 'boddy'—which we are to allow the theory itself to teach us to understand. And among those teachings, of course, will be the assertions that a boddy can have only banal b-properties, that a boddy is temporarily inhabited or occupied by a soull (with two 'l's, for Theory 3 is what will teach us to understand this use of the word 'soul', if anything will. It is again not our idiomatic use, the one which contrasts with 'body-5'.), and that a boddy becomes a body-4 —a corpse—upon its abandonment by that soull.

So much, for the moment, for Theory 3's use of the term 'body'. What shall we say about the theory's use of the term 'soul' (i.e., 'soull')? A soull, the theory informs us, is something that can have special s-properties. The key question to ask, though, is whether a soull can have only s-properties. As soon as we put the question, however, we can see that either answer to it—yes or no—makes logical hash of the theory.

For suppose, first, that a soull can have both s-properties and b-properties. It will immediately follow that the postulation of soulls urged upon us by Theory 3 is totally pointless. After all, we evidently started with something which could have both s-properties and b-properties—a person, as we ordinarily, pretheoretically, think and talk about persons. It was puzzlement at the idea that one thing could have both special s-properties and banal b-properties which sent us off chasing souls versus bodies in the first place. But, even worse, this answer leaves us with a whole extra set of b-properties on our hands—the b-properties of the soull. We already have something of determinate size, shape, weight, color, density, location, and material composition in our story—the postulated boddy which becomes a corpse at death. If the soull now is also something with a determinate size, shape, weight, color, density, location, and material composition, what becomes of it at death? According to Theory 3, it departs the boddy. But if it does have the relevant sort of banal b-properties—properties which would render it observable, or at least detectable, if only by instruments (say, by reason of its tinyness)—then it ought to be something it would make sense to set out to observe or detect. It ought to be available to us, that is, not merely as a postulation or hypothesis but, at least in principle, as part of our empirical data.

It is, of course, a coherent and possible hypothesis that the things which we encounter as we go about our daily business that we take to be persons are only hosts or vehicles, occupied or inhabited or operated by another, very different, living organism—a parasite or a driver—and that it is these parasites or drivers which are really persons—indeed, that we are really such parasites or drivers. (A sort of universal "invasion of the body snatchers," I suppose.) This is indeed a coherent and possible hypothesis—but it is also a silly hypothesis. It is both pointless and groundless. If what a soull is supposed to be is a living organism of unknown genus, either parasitic upon *homo sapiens* (as tapeworms, for instance, are parasitic) or operating what we mistakenly take to be animals of the species *homo sapiens* (as an engineer operates a locomotive, which some primitive might mistake for a living creature)—if that is what Theory 3 proposes—then our verdict must surely be that there is no consideration at all which speaks in favor of the theory, and, what is more, that there are very good reasons indeed to reject it as false in fact.

But the alternative supposition, that soulls can have only special s-properties, is, if anything, even worse off. To begin with, when interpreted in this fashion, Theory 3 now also contradicts the data upon which it was supposedly based, the phenomenon which the theory was introduced to explain. For that phenomenon, we recall, was that persons manifestly do have both s-properties and b-properties. What Theory 3, understood according to this interpretation, requires us to say instead, however, is that a person is (i.e., is identical to) a soull, and that a soull cannot have both s-properties and b-properties. It follows, of course, that a person cannot have both s-properties and b-properties. Far from explaining what it was introduced to explain, then, Theory 3 implies, on this interpretation, the falsity of the very data which gives rise to it.

But that is not the worst of the theory's problems. Understood in this manner, in fact, the 'Soul' Theory is not just inconsistent with its motivating data, it is internally incoherent. The reason, to put it in a nutshell, is that there is no sense to be made of something's having only s-properties.

For s-properties, I have argued, are not qualities but performance capabilities. To ascribe s-properties to a thing, then, is to say something about what it can do. It will always make sense to ask, however, what the thing is which can do this or that. What, in other words, is the performer to whom these performance capabilities belong? The difficulty is that, on the present interpretation, Theory 3 precludes this question from having any answer.

If we say of a thing that it is magnetic or water-soluble, it is possible to go on to ask what it is which is magnetic or water-soluble. In the one case, the answer might be "a piece of iron, cylindrical in shape, 7 centimeters long, silvery in color, and weighing 2 ounces"; in the other, "a white, 5-gram cube of sugar." In each case, the answer to the question of what the performer is to whom those performance capabilities belong—what it is which has the powers, abilities, or capacities that interest us—is given by citing properties of the thing which are not themselves performance capabilities. And the answer must take this form, for to say that what it is that has these powers, capacities, and abilities is whatever it is that has those other performance capabilities would not be to tell us what something is but only to tell us more about what something—we do not yet know what—can do.

On the present interpretation, however, Theory 3 rules out any such answer to the question of what a soull is. What T.3 now tells us is that a soull can have only s-properties. Anything we can say about a soull, in other words, will be another remark about what soulls can do. What follows, unfortunately, is that the whole notion of a soull supplied by Theory 3 is exhausted by the notion of these powers, capacities, and abilities. The notion of a soull built into Theory 3, that is, collapses into the idea of a bundle or collection of such powers, capacities, and abilities which are not, however, the powers, capacities, and abilities of anything. It is, in short, the notion of a set of performance capabilities which have been logically disconnected from any idea of a performer which might exercise those capabilities. And that, alas, is an internally incoherent notion.[10]

2.12: . . . AND AN END
TO THEORIZING

I formulated this last, decisive, set of considerations in application to the dualistic picture supplied by Theory 3, the only interpretation of soul-and-body talk which appeared to offer even the hope of a possibility that the history of a person might continue beyond that person's death. But the dilemma with which I confronted the 'Soul' Theory is a perfectly general one. It is one with which any soul-body or mind-body dualism must come to terms.

Any dualistic picture of persons begins by sorting the characteristics ordinarily ascribed to persons into two groups—properties or features which could also be properties or features of a mere object, a corpse or a rock (banal b-properties), and properties or features which contribute to the specialness of persons (s-properties). The "body" spoken of in the dualistic account, then, is held to be something which can have only b-properties, and the "soul" or "mind" (or "soull" or "mindd") to be the subject to which s-properties are ultimately correctly attributable. Any dualism, consequently, leaves room for the question: But does a "soul" or "mind" have only s-properties? Either answer defeats the dualism.

If the answer is "Yes," then we are left with the absurd picture of a bundle of performance capabilities without a performer—a set of powers, abilities, and capacities which are not the powers, abilities, or capacities of anything. But if the answer is "No," then we are left with the gratuitous picture of a person as a composite or collection of physical entities, only some of which have the performance capabilities which we ordinarily ascribe to people as such—a theory which contradicts the very data that motivates it, which lacks any experiential ground or basis, and, worst of all, which pointlessly replicates in its notion of a "soul" or "mind" the idea that it was intended to render explanatorily intelligible, namely, the idea of one thing having both s-properties and b-properties.

It follows from this, however, that there cannot be a coherent soul-body (or mind-body) dualism at all. That is, there cannot be a dualism which is both consistent with its point of departure—the fact that persons have both s-properties and b-properties—and free from internal absurdities. But the possibility of formulating such a dualistic picture of persons, I have shown, is a necessary condition for even making sense of the idea that the history of a person might continue beyond that person's death. For, as we have seen, the only coherent monistic view of persons requires that a person's death be understood as a change of kind—the event of that person's becoming (changing into) a corpse—and therefore as an event which puts an end to the history of the person.

If the very intelligibility of the idea of an "afterlife" logically requires a coherent dualistic picture of persons, and if, as I have argued, we do not have, nor can we formulate, any coherent dualistic picture of persons, it follows, however, that we do not have, nor can we formulate, any intelligible idea of an "afterlife." It is not simply that we have no reason to believe that a person's history continues beyond that person's death. We cannot even make sense of the idea that a person's history might continue beyond that person's death. If it seems to us that we can make sense of that idea, then, we must be victims of an illusion.

What I have tried to show, of course, is that we are, indeed, victims of an illusion—a linguistic illusion (or, rather, a family of them). We regularly and systematically mistake linguistic appearances for linguistic realities.

Misled by surface grammatical forms, we mistake nominal objects seemingly referred to in idiomatic expressions for things in their own right. Misled by the uniformly adjectival appearance of modifiers, we mistake the ascription of performance capabilities to a thing for a description of the intrinsic character of something, the attribution of a qualitative nature. And finally, aided by these errors, we suppress the multiple ambiguities of such words as 'body' and allow our speaking and thinking about persons to be guided by mere homonymy, by sameness of spelling and sameness of sound. These are the confusions, I have argued, which, under the influence of the powerful picture of the specialness of persons, conspire to create the illusion that we already have—or, at least, can coherently formulate—an intelligible dualistic (soul-body or mind-body) view of persons, and thereby the illusion that we can make sense of the idea that a person's history might continue beyond that person's death.

CHAPTER 3

Bodies and Souls, II: The Limits of Imagination

3.1: AN IMPASSIONED OBJECTION

At this point, the ever-patient reader may well begin to feel just a bit annoyed with me. Let me supply him with a monologue:

> In your opening remarks, you promised to take us wandering down some little-used byways of thought and language. Well, by golly, you've sure kept that promise! I've followed you patiently past events, processes, and instantaneous events, through five senses of the term 'body', and over three kinds of dualisms—and you've managed to keep the angels dancing on the head of the pin the whole time. And where do you come out? You come out claiming that I can't even make sense of the idea that a person's history might continue beyond that person's death. Well, buddy, you've gotten things so twisted and tangled up that I can't tell you just where you've gone wrong—but you've sure gone wrong somewhere!
>
> You tell me that I can't make sense of the idea that a person's history might continue beyond that person's death. But nothing could be simpler! All that I need to suppose is that somebody dies and that, later, I meet him again. It might be in Heaven, I guess, but it doesn't have to be. Wherever I meet him, the fact that I do is enough to show that he's still around, that his history didn't come to an end with his death.
>
> And, listen, as far as souls and bodies or minds and bodies are concerned, I can easily imagine a person changing bodies. (You see it on science-fiction television shows all the time!) Now you go right ahead and figure out what sense of the word 'body' I'm using. I don't care. The fact that I can imagine it happening is good enough to show that it makes sense. And whatever it is that changes bodies, that's what I'm going to call "the soul." So there's at least one dualism that I can make sense of—and if that's what it takes to make sense of an "afterlife," then I can make sense of that, too.

I was right the first time. You philosophers aren't worth the paper your diplomas are printed on.

To which the proper, measured, Socratic response is: "Let's talk about it." Frankly, I don't think that one can "easily imagine" any of these things. I don't think that one can imagine them at all. If the reader will bear with me a while longer, perhaps I can convince him, too, that what he does so easily imagine isn't what he thinks he's imagining—and certainly not what he says he's imagining.

3.2: A BIT OF SCIENCE FICTION

To focus the issue, let us ask this: Just what does one imagine when one imagines "a person changing bodies"? In fact, let's make it even more dramatic. Let's imagine two people exchanging bodies.[1] Just what do we see depicted on science-fiction television shows? What does it look like?

Well, there are two chairs, aren't there? Over each chair there is a metal helmet, and each helmet is connected to a complicated electronic-looking box by a bundle of wires. Our two subjects—call them 'John' and 'Emma'—sit in the chairs, and the helmets are lowered over their heads. Switches are thrown, dials are turned, lights flash, meters register, an electrical hum is heard, and John and Emma suddenly slump forward in their seats. The machine is turned off and the helmets removed. And then, as John and Emma slowly resume consciousness, something very peculiar happens. The one who looks like John claims to be Emma, and the one who looks like Emma claims to be John. What is more, the one who looks like John begins behaving like Emma, and the one who looks like Emma begins behaving like John. And both of them appear to be very startled and somewhat confused by it all. "Aha!", we say to ourselves, "John and Emma have exchanged bodies. John is now in Emma's body, and Emma is now in John's."

Now I don't want to deny for a moment that this is a picture which we have learned to associate with the expression "John and Emma have exchanged bodies." But we have already had occasion to call into question the power of a picture to bestow sense or content upon a bit of language. Recall "There is an undetectable gremlin in my refrigerator." There, too, we found ourselves with a picture on our hands. What we discovered, however, was that the picture which we were able easily to construct in our imaginations wasn't—and couldn't be—a picture of what the words apparently said.

Perhaps the present case is actually similar to that one. Here, again, we have an easily imaginable picture associated with some fairly peculiar words. What we need to ask, however, is whether the picture which we can so easily construct in our imaginations is—indeed, whether it could be—a picture of what the words apparently say. And that, of course, requires that we have a clear idea of just what it is that the words do apparently say. Like it or not, in other words, we need to go back to asking those bothersome questions about language that we analytic philosophers keep insisting upon.

So let me begin with this question: Why do we associate these words with this picture? What is the point of putting words and picture together in this way?

3.3: ONE PICTURE, TWO STORIES

One point, clearly enough, is that we are trying to explain something. To simplify our discussions, let us call the person who looks like John (but claims to be Emma) after the experiment 'Jack', and the person who looks like Emma (but claims to be John) after the experiment 'Jill'. Then what we want to explain, surely, is why Jack, who looks like John and whom we would expect to behave like John, nevertheless claims to be, and behaves like, Emma, and why Jill, who looks like Emma and whom we would expect to behave like Emma, nevertheless claims to be, and behaves like, John.

The sentence 'John and Emma have exchanged bodies' is intended to supply the desired explanation. There are, in fact, two things to be explained, and the sentence 'John and Emma have exchanged bodies' aims to explain both of them. The first thing to be explained is why Jack claims to be and acts like Emma and why Jill claims to be and acts like John. The explanation which our sentence offers is quite straightforward:

> EXP 1A Jack claims to be and acts like Emma because Jack is Emma, and
>
> Jill claims to be and acts like John because Jill is John.

Having been offered this explanation, however, we immediately acquire a need to explain something else. If Jack is Emma, then why does she—that is, Emma—look like John? And, if Jill is John, then why does he—that is, John—look like Emma? This is where the talk of 'bodies' come in. The explanation runs:

> EXP 1B Emma looks like John because Emma is inhabiting John's body, and
>
> John looks like Emma because John is inhabiting Emma's body.

Now, rather than subject this supposed explanation to immediate scrutiny, let me instead offer an alternative explanation of our puzzling phenomena. Let me, that is, supply a different set of words which we might also associate with the same, easily imaginable, picture. Suppose that what the electronic machine with the metal helmets does is to induce an acute delusionary personality psychosis. What happens when two people are processed by this machine is that each emerges from the experiment mistakenly thinking himself to be the other. The machine works by impressing upon the brain of each person the pattern of electrical currents originally characteristic of the brain of the other, and the result of this procedure is a peculiar form of madness.[2] Each person begins to claim that, and act as if, he (or she) were the other—but, of course, both persons are mistaken, and both persons are quite mad.

If we associate this set of words with our easily imaginable picture, however, we get two quite different explanations of the striking phenomena with which we are confronted. It is most revealing to present them in the reverse order:

EXP 2B   Jack looks like John because Jack is John, and

Jill looks like Emma because Jill is Emma.

EXP 2A   John claims to be, and acts like, Emma because John is suffering from a particular kind of artificially induced insanity, and Emma claims to be, and acts like, John because Emma is also suffering from a particular kind of artificially induced insanity.

The moral which I wish to draw from the availability of this alternative mode of explanation concerns the way in which we describe what needs to be explained. On Story 2, the appearances of the two persons present no special problems. Of course, Jack looks like John. Jack is John. What is puzzling is why John is behaving so peculiarly. On Story 1, on the other hand, it is not the behavior which calls for a special explanation. Of course, Jack behaves like Emma. Jack is Emma. What is puzzling is why Emma suddenly looks so very different from the way she looked before the experiment began.

The point of focusing attention in this way upon the question of what needs explanation is to highlight the fact that even the picking-out of a description of the phenomenon which confronts us in our imaginary scenario requires a prior decision concerning the identification of the participants in our hypothetical experiment. That is, before we can ask what's happened to John and Emma, we need to identify John and Emma, to pick them out, to locate them, to determine who's who. Until we've identified John and Emma, we don't know what kind of phenomenon our picture is a picture of. We don't know, in other words, whether our picture is a picture of a machine which induces a radical change of appearance (roughly Story 1) or of one which induces a radical change of behavior and beliefs (roughly Story 2).

And so we are led to the question: How does one *identify* persons? How do we determine who's who? How can we establish who somebody is? Each of our stories about our easily imaginable picture presupposes a specific form of answer to this question. That is, each of our stories about the picture presupposes a theory of personal identity. To judge the cogency of the two stories, then, we must first inquire into the theories of person identity which underlie them. We need to look at what each story takes for granted about the identification of persons.[3]

The crucial point is that this question takes us out of the realm of pictures and imagination. It is not a question which could be answered by an appeal to the imaginability of something, because it is a question which we need to answer before we can judge whether we've succeeded in imagining what we set out to imagine (for example, "two people exchanging bodies").

That we can picture something in our imaginations goes without saying. The problem is that there are various descriptions of the something which we can more-or-less-easily imagine in this way. And which description correctly applies to that something—indeed, which description could correctly apply to it—does not go without saying. It is, rather, precisely a matter of saying—of what we can sensibly and justifiably say about what we can picture in our imaginations—and so it is not a matter which can be settled by a mere inspection of the picture itself.

What we need to look at is not our pictures but rather our practices, the ways in which we do—or could—identify persons. We need to look, in other words, at the considerations to which we appeal when we make such judgments as "This is John and that is Emma." What, then, are the considerations implicit in the two stories we currently have before us? What theories of personal identity do the two descriptions of our easily imaginable picture presuppose?

3.4: A LESSON IN CRIMINOLOGY

In the case of the second story—the one about the acute delusionary personality psychosis—the answer is relatively straightforward. The criteria of personal identity upon which we tacitly rely are the same as those upon which, for instance, the police and the law courts explicitly rely. If the police have a question about who's who, they will, for example, take fingerprints. If the fingerprints of some suspect—say, the man who calls himself 'Sam Smith'—match those of the wanted criminal—say, the notorious Elmer "Eggs" Benedict—the police straightaway conclude that the man who calls himself 'Sam Smith' is the notorious "Eggs" Benedict. Sameness of fingerprints is regarded in law as conclusive for purposes of identification. And something rather like that is being taken for granted in our second story. Jack not only has the same fingerprints as John, but, indeed, all Jack's "physical" characteristics (his banal b-properties) are identical to what John's were before the experiment. And so, in Story 2, just as in the law, we straightaway conclude that Jack is John. Since Jack thinks he's Emma, then, he is evidently suffering from some sort of madness. Our hypothetical machine must be a device for inducing a most peculiar form of insanity.

Now, to be sure, sameness of fingerprints is not logically conclusive proof of identity. There is no absurdity, incoherence, or self-contradiction in supposing that two people might be born with indistinguishable fingerprints or that a particularly ingenious plastic surgeon might succeed in altering the pattern of loops and whorls on somebody's fingers. To the best of our knowledge, this currently does not in fact happen, and so we in fact treat sameness of fingerprints as conclusive for purposes of identification. To the best of our knowledge, in other words, a person's fingerprints are an invariant characteristic of that person—unlike, for instance, his height, weight, hair color, or the shape of his nose. But there is no absurdity in supposing that—like height, weight, hair color, nose shape, and the like—fingerprints, too might change (or be caused to change) over time.

At a deeper level, then, what is decisive for personal identity in our second story is the continuous and uninterrupted existence of the thing which has these presumed-invariant fingerprints. What is tacitly viewed in Story 2 as logically decisive for the identity of persons is the continuous and uninterrupted existence of the thing of which fingerprints, hair color, height, weight, nose shape, and the like are (possibly changeable) characteristics. Underlying Story 2, in other words, is a view of persons which runs something like this:

A person is born in a certain place at a certain time. Subsequently, the person may undergo many changes. He may grow in height and gain or lose weight, dye his hair, have his nose bobbed, and even, perhaps, have his fingerprints surgically altered. But throughout all these changes, the person himself occupies and traces out a continuous path through space and time. He does not vanish and reappear, but rather exists during each subinterval of his life at locations regularly and systematically connected to his immediately previous locations.

To determine conclusively in point of logic, then, whether our suspect-in-custody "Sam Smith" in New York is the same person as our wanted-felon "Eggs" Benedict, who escaped last month in California, it would be necessary and sufficient to trace a continuous spatio-temporal path connecting today's New York "Sam Smith" with last month's California "Eggs" Benedict—to show, that is, that fleeing from pursuers last month in California and being taken into custody today in New York were two episodes in the uninterrupted history of a single spatio-temporal object. Sameness of fingerprints creates presumptive evidence that this is the case, since, to the best of our knowledge, fingerprints are invariant characteristics of such a single object—that is, characteristics which do not in fact change as the object follows its track through space and time.

In capsule form, then, on our second account, personal identity consists in what is often called "bodily continuity." The term 'body' here is used in the sense of 'body-1'—the physicists' sense of 'body' as a causally interactive thing in space and time. On Story 2, a person is a body-1, and the identity of a person across time is no different from the identity of any body-1 across time. It consists in the uninterrupted and continuous existence of that body-1 across time—its tracing out of an uninterrupted and continuous path through space and time between one of our encounters with it and the next.

3.5: A QUESTION OF IDENTITY

It is as clear as can be, however, that our first story—the one about "exchanging bodies"—cannot take the identity of persons across time to consist in the unbrokenness of some body-1's spatio-temporal path. The question is, then: What test for personal identity does Story 1 implicitly put in place of bodily continuity?

Well, what is it which creates even the presumption that Jack is not (as he appears to be) John but rather Emma and that Jill is not (as she appears to be) Emma but rather John? Evidently, it is the things that Jack and Jill do and say. The presumptive evidence that Jack is, despite appearances, Emma is evidently the fact that Jack believes himself to be Emma, and that he speaks and acts after the experiment in the ways in which Emma spoke and acted before the experiment.

Now, like fingerprints, however, such features of persons as beliefs, manners of speech, and characteristics of behavior are merely presumptive evidence of personal identity, not logically conclusive indications. To see this, it suffices to consider any classic case of "delusions of grandeur." It is perfectly possible to encounter a person who claims to be Napoleon, who speaks to us imperiously—perhaps even in somewhat archaic French—and who recounts his inglorious handling by the British, his defeat at Waterloo, his exile on Elba, and other such episodes from the history of Napoleon, comporting himself all the while very Napoleonically, his hand thrust under the lapel of his coat in that well-known and characteristic fashion. In this instance, however, we would not, I suspect, have even a slight inclination to suppose that the poor wretch is Napoleon. Instead, we would surely conclude that we were in the presence of a madman, a megalomaniac, of a rare and striking sort. For Napoleon, as we all know very well, is long since dead and entombed.

But if beliefs, speech, and behavior are merely presumptive evidence of personal identity across time in the way that general appearance and even fingerprints are merely presumptive evidence of personal identity across time—for all of these characteristics, both physical and psychological or behavioral, can and often do change dramatically across time—what then would be, on the view of personal identity implicit in Story 1 (about "exchanging bodies") a logically decisive indication of personal identity across time? What plays the equivalent role in the first story to bodily continuity in the second story? What is it, that is, the determination of which would be logically conclusive, both necessary and sufficient in point of logic, to secure a decisive identification of Jack as Emma or, for that matter, of our possible lunatic as Napoleon?

If we were to attempt to proceed at this point in strict analogy to our discussion of Story 2, we would need to find something analogous to a body-1 to which all of these changing psychological and behavioral characteristics could be ascribed but which itself existed in continuous and uninterrupted fashion between one of our encounters with it and the next. The catch, however, is that there is no such thing to be found.

What we encounter from time to time are bodies-1, some of which are persons.[4] We carry on conversations with them, work and play with them, teach them and learn from them, and so on. To say that it is these bodies-1 to which psychological and behavioral characteristics are to be ascribed is, of course, to revert to our previous criterion of person identity, the criterion of bodily continuity. But we are searching for an alternative to that criterion. We could, of course, ascribe these behavioral and psychological characteristics to the person. But it is the person whom we are trying to locate and identify. What we need to find is some continuant which we could keep track of as something other than a person, the uninterrupted existence of which we could then use to identify the person as, in Story 2, we used the uninterrupted existence of a body-1—traced merely as a body-1, that is, through space and time—to determine the identity of the person. But there is no such thing to be found.

We might, of course, attempt to invent such a thing. We might say that—just as in Story 2 it is the continuous and uninterrupted existence of a body-1, tracked merely as a body-1, through space and time which is decisive for the identity of persons—so in Story 1 it is the continuous and uninterrupted existence of a soul (or soull), tracked merely as a soul, which is decisive for the identity of persons. The criterion of personal identity in our first story would be "soul continuity," as the criterion of personal identity in our second story was bodily continuity.

The difficulty with this line of attack, of course, is that we haven't the vaguest idea what it would mean to "track a soul merely as a soul." If souls mark out continuous and unbroken paths through space and time, then they just are bodies-1—physical things—(however "rarefied" they might be), and we have gotten nowhere. We have simply postulated a mysterious additional physical thing, for which we have neither any evidence nor any use. But if souls do not mark out continuous and unbroken paths through space and time, then how could we track them merely as souls? The problem of determining whether we have encountered the same soul again will be absolutely indistinguishable from the problem of determining whether we have encountered the same person again. A soul is, of course, supposed to be the thing to which our psychological and behavioral characteristics are primarily ascribed, but to take those characteristics as logically conclusive indicators of sameness of souls across time is to abandon our search for a continuant which we could track independently of tracking it as a person. For the soul would then become a superfluous postulaton. We could as well and as easily directly take similarity of psychological and behavioral characteristics to be logically conclusive indicators of sameness of persons across time. We could, that is, adopt the view that our poor lunatic must in point of logic actually be Napoleon. But that, I think, is not a course which is likely to appeal to many. (What, for example, shall we say about the next such lunatic?)

The point is that we do have criteria for tracking bodies-1 through space and time merely as bodies-1. When the question arises of whether some person—say, "Sam Smith" in New York today—is the same as some otherwise describable person—say, "Eggs" Benedict in California last month—then, we have the option of retreating to criteria which do not depend upon the identifications of persons as persons. We can undertake to determine whether fleeing from prison in California last month and being taken into custody in New York today are episodes in the history of a single body-1, something which we can trace through space and time—and through a vast variety of changes of size, shape, hair color, weight, and even fingerprints—without first determining whether it is this person or that whom we are tracking. And we can therefore use the results of this investigation to settle the question of whether the person whom we have now tracked simply as a body-1 from California's escape last month is or is not the "Sam Smith" whom we have in custody in New York today.

We do not, however, have any analogous criteria for tracking such supposed continuants as souls simply as souls. When the question of whether "Sam Smith" is or is not the notorious "Eggs" Benedict arises, then, given that we have abandoned the criterion of bodily continuity, we are left without any criteria at all to fall back on. There is no logically simpler position to which we can retreat. All we can do is to regard behavioral and psychological characteristics as themselves logically adequate to settle the question of who's who. But to do this is to fly in the face of the fact that beliefs, behavior, tastes, inclinations, and the like can change—that is, that one person can have different psychological and behavioral characteristics at different times—just as much as height, weight, hair color, nose shape, and even fingerprints can or could change.

We need, therefore, to give up the notion that in our first story about John and Emma—the one which has them "exchanging bodies"—we are relying on any criterion of personal identity which allows us to decide questions about who's who by tracking some continuant as something other than a person and then using the results of that investigation to settle the question concerning the identities of our two persons. But if Story 1 does not view the identity of a person across time as resting upon the uninterrupted existence of some continuant across time, how are we to think of personal identity in connection with our first story? What is being taken for granted in Story 1 which would allow us to identify Jack as Emma and Jill as John, the pair of identifications which the story of "body exchanging" obviously presupposes?

3.6: A VISIT TO THE CINEMA

Well, let's try an analogy. Suppose that we are attending a double feature movie. Two films are being show, say *Jowls II* and *Moon Wars*. Midway through *Jowls II*, I am struck by a nicotine fit and retreat to the lobby for a cigarette. Chatting with the usherettes, I lose track of the time. Some time and several cigarettes later, then, I come wandering back into the darkened theater and, of course, some movie is playing on the screen. What I want to know, however, is whether it is the same movie I walked out on. Is this still *Jowls II*, or has *Moon Wars* already begun? Here, then, is a problem of film-identification analogous to the problem of person-identification which was exercising us a moment ago.

In this case, however, my question is not one which it would be appropriate to address by looking for some continuant which I could track as something other than the film *Jowls II*. I could, of course, go up to the projection booth and determine whether the same strip of celluloid is uncoiling through the projector as was uncoiling when I left, but while that discovery might be sufficient to settle the question about which film is now showing, it is hardly necessary. (It might not even be sufficient. The two films may have been spliced together on one reel!) For it might have been the first reel that was being projected when I left and the third reel which is being projected now—but still the same film, *Jowls II*. Its being the same film showing on the screen does not depend upon its being the same strip of celluloid uncoiling through the projector. Nor does it depend upon the continuous and uninterrupted existence of any body-1. While I was in the lobby, the theater management, for some bizarre reason, might have not only changed reels but also replaced the projector, lowered a new screen, and installed new speakers—but for all that, it could still be the same film, *Jowls II,* that is now up on the screen as was running when I stepped out for a smoke. The question of whether it is the same film, in other words, is not one which we can settle by retreating to tracing some continuant as something other than *Jowls II*. What we need to trace is *Jowls II* itself.

What, then, is necessary for it to be the same film playing when I return as was playing when I left? What is necessary, surely, is that the episodes now being projected on the screen are suitably related to the episodes projected on the screen earlier. They need to be further developments of the same plot. They need to be related to each other in the way in which different scenes of a single story are related to each other. And that is to say that they need to be connected to earlier episodes in the story, not by something outside the story, but by a chain of successive episodes within the story. This, however, gives us another way of thinking about persons.

We've been looking for something analogous to a wire—a single, unbroken something which stretches through time upon which various psychological and behavioral episodes could be hung like so many paper lanterns. But perhaps the identity of a person across time is more like a chain. There is no single, unbroken something which stretches through time but only the various psychological and behavioral episodes themselves, which fit into one another like successive links, that is, which are connected together in the way in which successive episodes of a story or film are connected together. It is the internal connections between episodes of a story or film—relations of character and plot from scene to scene—which make them episodes of the same story or film. Why, then, could it not be the internal connections between psychological and behavioral episodes in the history of a person which make them episodes in the history of the same person?[5]

Here we have a conception of personal identity which does allow us to tell Story 1 about John and Emma. Just as a story can be continued from book to book, or a film can be continued from reel to reel, so, too, a person could be continued from body to body—that is, from body-1 to body-1. The way in which we would identify Jack as Emma following our little experiment would be by discovering that the psychological and behavioral episodes in Jack's history after the machine was shut off were suitably (internally) connected or related to the psychological and behavioral episodes in Emma's history before the machine was turned on.

3.7: TWO FORMS OF LITERARY UNITY

We have arrived at a conception of personal identity across time which holds that, for example, in order for our suspect-in-custody "Sam Smith" to be the same person as the escaped criminal "Eggs" Benedict, it is both necessary and sufficient in point of logic that the psychological and behavioral episodes in "Smith's" history today and those in Benedict's history last month be suitably connected by an unbroken chain of successive intervening episodes, each appropriately internally related to preceding and succeeding episodes. Let us call this, in contrast to the criterion of bodily continuity, the criterion of psychological connectedness. The question now becomes: What internal relations between successive psychological and behavioral episodes are necessary and sufficient in point of logic to make them episodes in the history of a single person?

The analogous question concerning a book, for example, would be this: What internal relations of style, plot, characterization, and the like between two volumes are necessary and sufficient in point of logic to make them two parts of a single literary work, rather than, say, a pastiche of similar works? Such questions are often difficult and intricate tasks for literary scholarship. Was this or that book completed by some author before his death, or were the concluding chapters added afterwards by his son or his secretary? Did this or that playwright actually compose the work as we have it, or is the last act an extraneous accretion? From time to time, a literary scholar will be called upon to face such a question in the course of his studies, and then begins a delicate and complicated hermaneutic investigation, often drawing even on such arcane statistical matters as letter-counts and the average length of words. That is, the scholar will attempt to determine by internal clues alone, let us suppose, whether the earlier and later parts of the manuscript are products of the same hand, or whether, rather, some talented mimic has added material to an already extant, perhaps incomplete, manuscript.

Having said this much, however, it becomes clear that no amount of such internal evidence is or could be decisive in point of logic to guarantee the desired literary unity. The reason, quite simply, is that all such internal evidence is functioning here merely as a more-or-less plausible indicator of something else which would be conclusive in point of logic—sameness of authorship. The unity of a work of literature in this sense—call it "authenticity"—in other words, logically depends upon the identity of something external to the work of literature, namely, upon the identity of the person(s) who composed the various parts of the work which we have before us. Since, however unlikely or difficult it may be in fact, it is possible in point of logic (that is, not self-contradictory or incoherent) to suppose that a second person might successfully mimic the style of some author, even down to the tiniest minutiae of letter frequencies and average word-lengths, it follows that no amount of such internal, literary evidence can ever conclusively settle the question of single authorship. The internal connections among successive episodes of a story, in other words, can be convincing evidence of the unity of the work—in the sense of its authenticity—but such connectedness is not that in which the authenticity of the work logically consists.

What we need as an analogy to the criterion of psychological connectedness for the identity of persons, then, is not this sort of unity of a literary work—sameness of authorship, authenticity—but rather a purely literary unity—a unity in which the internal evidences of style, plot, and characterization are themselves logically sufficient to settle the question of the work's literary unity—call it the work's "integrity"—irrespective of the number of authors who may have contributed to its composition. The difficulty now becomes, however, that this sort of literary integrity is, alas, not identity.

Suppose, for example, that the author of "The Lady or the Tiger?" had composed two endings for his story—one in which it is the lady whom the suitor finds behind the chosen door and another in which it is the tiger. (We can disregard the fact that either of these stories would have been of a quality inferior to that of the carefully open-ended actual version.) What we would then have would be two stories—call them "The Lady!" and "The Tiger!"—which were exactly alike up to the moment at which the suitor opened the door. Each of these stories would have the appropriate sort of literary unity. Each climactic scene would be suitably internally connected in terms of plot, style, and characterization to the scenes which had preceded it. Each story, in short, would possess the requisite literary integrity. But, in spite of that, they would be two stories, not, for example, one story twice told. "The Lady!", although similar (up to a point) to "The Tiger!" would not be identical to (one and the same story as) "The Tiger!" Of course not. For one thing, it would have a different ending. (And what is more, as any good literary critic will explain to you, the early scenes of "The Lady!" would often have significances radically different from the early scenes of "The Tiger!", even though recounted in the same words, since the early parts of a literary work need to be interpreted in light of its concluding scenes.) While internal connectedness is logically decisive for literary integrity, then, literary integrity is not a form of identity, since the same (opening) scenes and episodes can enter into two nonidentical literary works, both of which have the requisite sort of integrity.

3.8: A DECISIVE DILEMMA

These observations concerning the unity of a work of literature—whether it be a unity of authorship ("authenticity") or a purely literary unity ("integrity")—transpose readily into a set of observations concerning the adequacy of psychological connectedness as a criterion of personal identity across time. They confront the proposed criterion of psychological connectedness, in fact, with an irresolvable dilemma. In briefest form, the dilemma runs roughly as follows:

Either the criterion of psychological connectedness stands to the question of personal identity as internal literary evidence stands to the question of literary authenticity (singleness of authorship)—in which case psychological connectedness cannot, in point of logic, be the ultimate criterion of personal identity, but instead presupposes some other criterion (e.g., bodily continuity) for which it serves merely as a probabilistic indicator,

or the criterion of a psychological connectedness stands to the question of personal identity as internal literary evidence stands to the question of literary integrity (the unity of theme, plot, and characterization of a work of literature)—in which case psychological connectedness cannot, in point of logic, be a criterion of personal identity across time at all.

The internal relatedness of psychological and behavioral episodes, in other words, is demonstrably either inadequate to secure conclusive answers to questions concerning who's who or else irrelevant to such questions. It follows that psychological connectedness cannot be, in the needed sense, a criterion of personal identity at all. If psychological connectedness is relevant to personal identity at all, then, it is only as more-or-less convincing evidence, not as a logically adequate, decisive, or conclusive criterion. If however, psychological connectedness is taken to be a logically adequate, decisive, and conclusive criterion of something, that something cannot be personal identity across time.

3.9: THE GLUE OF MEMORY

Let me illustrate this dilemma by exhibiting it in connection with one specific, traditionally proposed form of psychological connectedness—the "glue of memory." The idea behind this proposal is quite straightforward. If, at some time, a person remembers having done something at an earlier time, then the person who remembers having done that thing must be the same person as the person who did that thing. If, for instance, "Sam Smith" today in New York remembers escaping from prison a month ago in California, then "Sam Smith" must be one and the same person as (identical to) the person who did escape from prison in California a month ago, namely, "Eggs" Benedict. And if, for instance, Jack, following the operation of our machine, remembers having sat down a few moments earlier in the chair now occupied by Jill, then Jack must be one and the same person as (identical to) the person who did sit down in that chair a few moments earlier, namely, Emma.

To bring this proposal into contact with our dilemma and thus demonstrate its failings, all that we need do is remind ourselves that the word 'remember' admits of a certain slippage. Probably the most common use of the word is to indicate success, so that, for example, someone's misremembering something would not count as a case of his remembering something. To remember something in this sense, it is not sufficient that one merely have the experience of something's occurring to one in that special memoryish way—that one have that characteristic feeling of recalling or recollecting something. It is necessary, in addition, that what occurs to one in this special, characteristic way be correct.

Less commonly, however, we use the word 'remember' simply to indicate this characteristic experience, and we set questions of correctness to one side. In this sense, misremembering something would be a case of remembering something. All that is required here is that one's experience be a memory experience—as opposed, for instance, to a perceptual experience or an imagining.

If we are being careful, then, we will distinguish between (actually) remembering—which connotes success or correctness—and (merely) seeming to remember—which comments on the character of one's experience without implying correctness or success. Let us call the characteristic experience of seeming to remember something an experience of "seemingly remembering" or, for short, "S-remembering." We can then say that someone actually remembers something just in case he or she S-remembers it and is right. Some cases of S-remembering, then, are cases of actually remembering—namely, the correct or successful cases of S-remembering—and others—the incorrect or unsuccessful ones—are not.

We can now ask which sense of 'remember' is being invoked in our proposed "glue of memory" version of the criterion of psychological connectedness. Is it actual remembering that is required to secure personal identity across time or only S-remembering? Each answer corresponds to one horn of our dilemma.

Suppose, first, that it is actual remembering which is being proposed as decisive, in point of logic, to secure personal identity across time. That is, suppose that Jack, who certainly S-remembers having sat down a few moments earlier in the chair now occupied by Jill, will be the person who did sit down in that chair a few moments earlier—namely, Emma—just in case Jack actually remembers having sat down in that chair at that time.

Interpreted in this way, the "glue of memory" proposal is eminently plausible. Since actually remembering something implies correctness, if Jack actually remembers being the person who sat down in Jill's chair a while ago, then Jack is the person who sat down in Jill's chair a while ago. Since that person was Emma, it would follow that Jack was (identical to) Emma—the conclusion presupposed by our first, "exchanging bodies" story.

But does Jack actually remember being the person who sat down in Jill's chair a while ago? Alas, to answer this question, we need to know two things: First, whether it seems to him that he remembers this (that is, whether he S-remembers it); and second, whether he is right (that is, whether he is the person who sat down in Jill's chair a while ago). All that we in fact know, however—and, more importantly, all that Jack in fact knows—is the first of these two things. We and Jack both know that he S-remembers being the person who sat down a few moments earlier in the chair now occupied by Jill. We know, and Jack knows, that it seems to Jack that he (actually) remembers having sat down a few moments earlier in that chair. Jack takes himself actually to be remembering this. It is, as far as he is concerned, just as if he actually remembers it. But none of this is sufficient, in point of logic, to guarantee that he does actually remember it—that is, to guarantee that he is right.

Our poor lunatic, after all, S-remembers having commanded the French troops at Waterloo. It seems to him that he (actually) remembers it. He takes himself actually to be remembering it. It is, as far as he is concerned, just as if he actually remembered commanding the French troops at Waterloo. But none of this is sufficient to guarantee that he does actually remember it—that is, to guarantee that he is right. And, indeed, he is not right. He merely seems to remember having lived through various episodes in the life of Napoleon. The fact of the matter, however, is that he is insane. His S-memories are only symptoms of his particular form of insanity.

For us to determine whether what Jack S-remembers is correct—and, more importantly, even for Jack to determine whether what he S-remembers is correct—we (and he) would need to be able to appeal to some criterion of personal identity independent of Jack's S-memories. To determine whether Jack's S-memories are actual (correct or successful memory experiences), we—and even Jack—would need some way of finding out whether what Jack S-remembers having been the case was indeed the case—that is, whether Jack indeed is the person who, a few moments earlier, sat down in the chair now occupied by Jill. Since we all know that that person was Emma, then, we need some way of determining whether Jack is (identical to, one and the same person as) Emma. If he is, then his S-memories are correct; they are actual memories. But if he is not, then his S-memories are incorrect; they are merely seeming memories.

But an independent criterion of personal identity, a way of determining whether Jack is or is not identical to Emma, is precisely what we do not have! That was what the appeal to the "glue of memory" was supposed to equip us with. We can get such an independent criterion, of course. We can, that is, retreat to the criterion of bodily continuity. Jack's S-memory, we may conclude, is correct (an actual memory) just in case the body-1 which Jack now is continuously connected in space and time to the body-1 which sat down in the chair now occupied by Jill as our experiment began. But if we do this, if we retreat to the criterion of bodily continuity, then our conclusion will not fit Story 1 (about "body exchanging") but rather Story 2 (about "machine-induced insanity"). For the body-1 which is Jack is not connected in space and time to the body-1 which was Emma, but to the body-1 which was John. Jack, in other words, merely seems to remember having sat down a few moments earlier in the chair now occupied by Jill. It was, however, Emma who actually did that, and, according to the test of bodily continuity, Jack is not Emma but rather John. Thus Jack is incorrect, and his S-memories are not actual memories but mere seeming-memories. Our experiment, alas, has driven John mad.

The point here is a very simple one. Since people's memories are generally and for the most part reliable, the fact that someone S-remembers something is a pretty reliable indicator that what he S-remembers was indeed the case. In particular, if someone S-remembers having been the person who did something, then that is pretty good evidence that he is, in fact, the person who did it. But, and this is the catch, it is not logically conclusive evidence. For people can and do misremember various things. It can and does sometimes merely seem to someone that he remembers something. And, sadly, people can and do sometimes go insane—with or without mechanical or chemical assistance. In particular, then, the fact that someone—for instance, Jack—S-remembers being the person—for instance, Emma—who did something does not settle the question of whether he is the person who did that thing. It is only more-or-less convincing, defeatable evidence of personal identity, but not a logically adequate, decisive criterion. Using S-memories as evidence of personal identity, therefore, presupposes the availability of some other, independent, ultimate criterion of personal identity (e.g., bodily continuity). And that is the first horn of our dilemma. If S-memories are relevant to personal identity at all, they are not so in point of logic but only in point of fact, as more-or-less reliable indicators, rather than as logically adequate conclusive criteria.

If, on the other hand, we supposed that S-memories alone, questions of correctness aside, should be treated as conclusive criteria of something, as adequate in point of logic decisively to settle some question, then that question cannot be the question of who's who, the question of personal identity. To see this, it is sufficient to recall that there can be many lunatics, all of whom seem to remember having lived through the events of Napoleon's life. If S-memory-connectedness were sufficient to make any of these poor wretches identical to Napoleon, then, it would be sufficient to make all of them identical to Napoleon—and thus to make each of them identical to (that is, one and the same person as) all of the others, a conclusion which is simply incoherent (self-contradictory, logically absurd), for several people cannot, in point of logic, be one person.

This, of course, is only the lesson we learned long ago from Alvin, Amos, and Ambrose: No relation which multiplies entities can preserve identity across time. The reason, quite obviously, is that two things are not one thing. If x is identical to (is one and the same thing as) y, and x is identical to (one and the same thing as) z, then y is identical to (one and the same thing as) z. If Ned's S-remembering being Napoleon were enough to guarantee that he was (identical to, one and the same person as) Napoleon, then Norbert's S-remembering being Napoleon would be enough to guarantee that he was (identical to) Napoleon—and then it would follow that Ned is (one and the same person as) Norbert, which is absurd.

Similarly, what our machine can do to John, it could also do to Jerry. All we'd need is another chair and another helmet, and Jerry, too, could have simultaneously impressed upon his brain the pattern of electrical impulses characteristic of Emma's brain at the moment the experiment began. We could produce, in other words, a Jack-2 who, like Jack, talked and behaved in an Emma-like fashion and, indeed, also took himself to be remembering having done the things which Emma, in fact, earlier did. It follows immediately, then, that Jack cannot be identical to Emma. For if Jack were

Emma, then so would Jack-2 be Emma (and why not Jack-3, Jack-4, and so on?). But just as two things are not one thing, two (three, four . . . .) people are not one person.[6]

And that is the second horn of our dilemma. S-memory-connectedness might be a conclusive, logically adequate criterion of something, but it cannot be a conclusive, logically adequate criterion of personal identity across time. For S-memory-connectedness is a relation which can multiply entities—two persons can be S-memory connected to one person, as Jack and Jack-2 are to Emma or Ned and Norbert to Napoleon—and thus it cannot be a relation which preserves identity.

3.10: THE OBJECTOR ANSWERED

And now where do we stand? Well, we began this latest discussion, you will recall, with an objection. Earlier I had argued that the very possibility of a person's history continuing beyond that person's death presupposed that one could make coherent sense of a dualistic view of persons—a view of persons according to which persons are not bodies (i.e., bodies-1, spatio-temporal things caught up in causal interactions and having determinate "trajectories" through space across time), but rather something else—minds or souls—standing in some relation to bodies-1, the bodies-1 which become bodies-4, that is, corpses. And I had also argued that one could not, in fact, make coherent sense of a soul-body or a mind-body dualism. I argued, indeed, that it was only by engaging in a kind of "doublethink" which traded on linguistic illusions generated by surface grammatical forms of speech that one could suppose that one's dualistic talk embodied a view of persons on which it might be true that a person is not a body-1.

Now our objector responded to these arguments with the claim that he, at least, could easily make coherent sense of a dualistic view of persons since he, at least, could easily imagine "a person changing bodies"—that is, one and the same person "affiliated" at different times with two distinct bodies-1. A particularly dramatic case of "a person changing bodies" would be "two persons changing bodies—by exchanging bodies," and it was in this form that I undertook to examine our objector's claim.

What I have just finished arguing is that, despite his insistence, our hypothetical objector cannot "easily imagine" what he claims to be able to imagine—"a person changing bodies." I have not for a moment, of course, denied that he can easily imagine something. Indeed, I have given detailed descriptions of something easily imaginable. What I have argued, however, is that "two persons exchanging bodies" cannot be a correct description of what we were imagining. Analogously, and for the same reasons, then, "a person changing bodies" will not be a correct description of the simpler, less dramatic case which our objector claims to be able easily to imagine.

The reason that "two persons exchanging bodies" cannot be the correct description of the case we have sketched and imagined (the case of John and Emma) is that this description presupposes that there is a way of identifying persons which is logically independent of the identification of bodies—that is, logically independent of the tracking of bodies-1 through space and time. But there is no such independent criterion of personal identity. The only candidate for such a criterion is some form of internal relatedness of successive psychological or behavioral states or characteristics across time, but any such appeal, I have shown, either itself presupposes some such purely "physical" criterion as bodily continuity or else is simply irrelevant to the question of who's who.[7]

Our objector, then, while he can certainly imagine something, cannot imagine what he says he can. His failure, however, is not a failure of imagination. He does not fail to imagine what he says he can because, for example, his powers of visualization are too meager. What he fails to do, in fact, is to talk sense about what he indeed visualizes with consummate ease. He fails to do this because he does not recognize that there are preconditions which must be satisfied if what he says about his imagined cases is to make sense—and because he does not undertake to investigate whether or not those preconditions can, in point of logic, actually be satisfied.

It is precisely that investigation which belongs to analytic philosophy, as I am in this book understanding "analytic philosophy." It is that investigation, indeed, which I have just concluded. And the finding was negative. We cannot make sense of "two persons exchanging bodies" (or of "a person changing bodies") because we cannot, in point of logic, have a criterion of personal identity across time which is independent of the spatial continuity of bodies (bodies-1) across time.

If this is the case, however, then the further possibility which our objector claimed also to be able to imagine—the possibility of encountering a person who has died (either on earth or "in Heaven")—will also demonstrably be incoherently described, and thus also no intelligible possibility at all. For such a case, too, would require that one be equipped—at least theoretically and in principle—with a criterion for establishing who it is that one has encountered, a criterion independent of bodily continuity (since the only body-1 which one might attempt to track has become a corpse and lies decaying in the ground). There would need to be a way of determining whether this person, whom one has just now met (on earth or "in Heaven") is indeed identical to (one and the same person as) one's deceased relative or friend, the person one knew formerly ("in life"). But, as I have demonstrated, even in principle there can be no such independent criterion of personal identity across time, no criterion independent of the tracking of a body-1 through space and time.

Once again, then, it follows that what our objector can "easily imagine" cannot be what he says he can imagine. And, here too, it is not his imagination which has played him false, but rather his description. It is not that he has failed to imagine something. Of course he can imagine something! It is only that the description which he supplies for what he imagines—"meeting again a person who has died following that person's death"—is not a coherent description, and thus not a correct description of what he imagines nor, indeed, of any possibility.

3.11: . . . BUT NOT SILENCED

Once again, then, we have failed to make coherent sense of the supposed possibility that a person's history could continue beyond that person's death. Our imaginative objector, however—although perhaps a bit chastened—is by no means finished. What he now proceeds to say, let us suppose, goes something like this:

> Well, I have to give you this much: You philosophers are as clever as you are perverse. I wouldn't have thought it possible, but you've gotten me thoroughly confused about whether I can imagine two people exchanging bodies or meeting a friend or relative after he's died.
>
> But listen, all of the problems which you've raised about what I can imagine, all of the knots you've gotten me tied up in, come from the fact that we're trying to figure out who someone else is. Maybe then I do have to use what you call a 'criterion of personal identity across time'. Well, I may not know who someone else is, but I sure know who I am! And that's enough to do the trick.
>
> I still claim that I can imagine a person changing bodies. But that's not because I can imagine someone else changing bodies. Maybe you're right. Maybe I can't really do that. But I can imagine myself changing bodies! There's obviously no problem with that. I can, for instance, perfectly well imagine myself falling asleep in one body and waking up in another—or even, like poor Gregor Samsa in Kafka's "Metamorphosis," waking up in the body of a giant cockroach. And I don't need to 'track a body-1 through space and time' in order to know who I am!
>
> OK. Now suppose that what happens isn't that I fall asleep in one body and wake up in another but, for instance, that I start out to undergo heart surgery in one body but die on the operating table. That body is buried as a corpse. Meanwhile, however, I have gotten into another body—as I simply discover when I regain consciousness in that other body. And I don't need any 'criterion of personal identity' to discover that. I know who I am. And there it is! My history extends beyond my death! Why, I might even attend my own funeral. So a person's history can continue beyond that person's death. At least mine could—and if mine could, then so could everybody else's.
>
> What do you have to say to that, smart guy?"

The chastening effect of our earlier discussions, I notice, has not had very much staying power.

3.12: MORE SCIENCE FICTION—A MEDICAL MIRACLE

Once again, then, we are called upon to imagine something—this time, however, in the first person. Well, let's do it.

I have, let us suppose, just suffered a series of rather nasty heart attacks. Now I find myself in the hospital, awaiting radical surgery. My chances, the doctor informs me, are, unfortunately, not very good, but their chief neurosurgeon—a brilliant fellow—has only quite recently developed some incredible new techniques which, should worse come to worse, could, as a last resort, be called into play. One way or another, then, I may yet pull through.

The fateful morning arrives. Garbed in green robes and masks, the attendants wheel me into the operating room. The surgeons and nurses gather around the table. The anesthetist prepares her instruments. I am instructed to count backwards from 100. Somewhere in the middle I lose consciousness. The last thing I see is a green-masked figure bending over me, silhouetted against the lights.

When I regain consciousness, I am once again lying in the bed of my now-familiar private hospital room. My first thought is "I made it! He pulled me through!" Slowly my head clears, as the last effects of the anesthetic wear off. I struggle to sit up. "Lie still," a voice orders me. "Doc? How'd it go?" My surgeon is sitting in the chair by the side of my bed. "Not very well, I'm afraid," he answers me. "We had to take some pretty drastic steps. I'm afraid you're in for a bit of a shock. Look." He holds up a mirror. Reflected in it, I see a wholly unfamiliar face! I raise my arm and look at my hand. But it is not mine! My hands are short-fingered and muscular, but this hand is delicate and long-fingered. "Doc?" I ask. "Do you remember my telling you that our chief neurosurgeon had developed some new techniques?" he says. "Well, I'm afraid we had to use them. Your old body was in pretty bad shape. We just couldn't patch it up, it turned out, so we gave you a new one. It's rather a shock, I know. But look at it this way. You're now in perfect health."

This familiar science fiction can be—and has been—indefinitely elaborated, of course. Detailed descriptions could be given of my old appearance and my new one, of my continuing reactions and adjustments to my startling situation, of the reactions and behavior of my family, co-workers, and friends, and so on. Once again, in other words, the picture which our objector asks us to construct in our imaginations—each of us for himself—is perfectly clear. In some sense, I can easily imagine losing consciousness in one body and regaining consciousness in another, and so, I don't doubt, can you. The question is, however: In what sense? We have the picture, but now we need to say something about it. We need to settle on a description of this picture. We can, each of us for himself, easily imagine something quite shocking happening to us. But what is it that is supposed to have happened to me? More precisely, what does it make sense to say has happened to me?

The point I wish to make here is that shifting from imagining something in the third person—something happening to someone else—to imagining something in the first person—something happening to oneself—has not succeeded in moving the question of mind-body or soul-body dualism out of the realm of questions about language. In either case, we need to discover what we can sensibly and coherently say about what we can more-or-less easily visualize or imagine. We need to locate a description of what we imagine happening which is logically admissible, that is, which makes sense. Only then will we be entitled to raise the question of whether our ability to imagine this or that—now in the first person—does, in fact, give aid and comfort to any "dualistic" view of persons, that is, to any view of persons which would allow us to make coherent sense of the supposed possibility that a person's history might continue beyond that person's death.

Very well. We have a case before us. My surgery has had some dramatic and unexpected side-effects. What, then, is supposed to have happened to me? What, indeed, does it make sense to say has happened to me? That is our next order of business.

3.13: WHY COMPLICITY MATTERS

What, then, does it make sense to say has happened to me? The first thing to notice, I think, is that, despite the first-person character of our present imaginative exercise, what it makes sense to say of me is not independent of the opinions and behavior of others. What primarily differentiates the present case from the case of John and Emma, in fact, is that the present story presupposes agreement on the part of other people—my surgeon, various nurses, members of my family, friends, acquaintances, and so on—in identification of the patient in the recovery room as identical to (one and the same person as) me. There is, in other words, complicity of identification already built into what we are, each of us for himself, supposed to be imagining.

Suppose however, that such complicity were lacking. Suppose that the surgeon said nothing in the recovery room about dramatic new neurophysiological discoveries and techniques, but rather professed total astonishment at my insistence that I was an analytic philosopher, professor at such-and-such a university, husband of such-and-such a woman, father of so-and-so many children, and so on. Suppose, that is, that the surgeon denied emphatically that I was who I thought I was, and that his emphatic denials were echoed by other members of the hospital staff, by the people I took to be my colleagues at the university, and by the woman I firmly believed was my wife. Instead, all of these people insisted that I was, say, Phil Wirestringer, a linesman for the telephone company, and that judgment was also echoed by Wirestringer's co-workers and friends, and by Wirestringer's wife, who acted distraught and hysterical, unable to comprehend what had happened to her dear husband. "He went into the hospital for heart surgery, and now look at him! He can't even remember who I am. He can't even remember who he is! He thinks he's some kind of professor. My God, what have you done to my Phil? What am I going to tell the children?"

Well, what should she tell the children? What does it make sense to tell the children, to conclude has happened in this case? I, of course, continue to insist that I know who I am—Rosenberg the philosopher, not Wirestringer the linesman. And that, indeed, is how it seems to me. But in this case, lacking complicity, what are my insistences worth? The fact that I continue to assert that I am not a telephone linesman named "Wirestringer" but rather a philosopher named "Rosenberg" obviously shows something about me. But what does it show?

Well, haven't we met this case before—in the third person? For our poor lunatic, we recall, insisted quite emphatically that he knew who he was—namely Napoleon—and he was both shocked and aggravated by the fact that nobody else was prepared to acknowledge what, to him, was quite obvious—namely that he was Napoleon.

In that case, however, the correct conclusion for us to draw—the conclusion that it made sense to draw—was quite unproblematic. The poor wretch was insane. And in the present, first person, case, the conclusion that it makes sense to draw is equally straightforward. My surgery has, somehow, quite inadvertently, resulted in my becoming insane. It has, somehow, induced in me—that is, in Phil Wirestringer, for that is who I in fact must be—the most peculiar delusion that I am a philosopher named Rosenberg, professor at such-and-such a university, married to such-and-such a woman, and so on. I, of course, will deny that I am insane, just as our poor Napoleonic lunatic will continue to deny that he is insane—but these denials, in each case, are only further symptoms of the particular brand of delusionary madness with which each of us is afflicted, for, in each case, our lunacy consists, primarily, in the fact that neither of us knows who he actually is.[8]

The moral of this story is that identity is a public matter. I may have "privileged," first-person knowledge of many things—what I believe, what I like and dislike, whether my foot hurts, and even who I *think* I am. But it does not follow from this that I have privileged knowledge of who I *actually* am—and, as our case of the Napoleonic lunatic clearly demonstrates, I in fact do not. I can, indeed, be as wrong about who I am as I can be about who Jack or Jill is. The fact that, following my surgery, I believe myself to be Rosenberg the philosopher and S-remember teaching at the university and the like no more implies that I am Rosenberg the philosopher and actually remember these things than the corresponding facts about Jack's belief and S-memories following the experiment implied that he was Emma or those about the lunatic's beliefs and S-memories implied that he is Napoleon.

The question of who's who, that is, is not a question about subjective certainties but rather a matter of telling a logically coherent story about intersubjective data. My personal convictions enter into this story, however—to the extent that I make them public—only as more data, as phenomena which need to be accommodated into the story of who's who in a way which maximizes overall logical coherence. And, as we have seen, in the absence of confirmation by such criteria of personal identity as bodily continuity—more generally, in the absence of any objective, public grounds for complicity with my first-person self-identifications—the story which does thus maximize logical coherence, the only story which, in the last analysis, it makes sense to tell on such an occasion, is not a story about "body changing" or "soul migration" but rather a story about madness, delusions, false beliefs, and insanity.

If poor Mrs. Wirestringer wants her answer to make sense, then, that is what she must tell the children. "I'm afraid something very bad has happened to Daddy. He's very sick, so sick that he's forgotten us. He doesn't know who he is any more, and it may be a very long time before he gets well again."

3.14: OF PERSONS AND PERSONAS

Our current imaginative exercise, however, is not such a sad story about madness and delusions, but rather a story about first-person self-identification with complicity. Here surgeon, wife, friends, and all agree with me that I am Rosenberg the philosopher. They agree, indeed, in spite of the fact that all the various aspects of my appearance (height, weight, hair and eye color, posture, skin tones, vocal inflections, and even fingerprints) have somehow undergone radical changes. Here, indeed, my surgeon claims to have given me a new body, to have "installed" me in a body other than the body with which I entered the surgical theater. The question now becomes: Are we all correct? Or, better: Is there a way of enlarging upon the imagined scenario in which it both makes sense to say and is true that, following the surgery, I am still Rosenberg the philosopher but now equipped with a new body?

I think that, surprisingly, there is—but that it is not a story which gives any aid or comfort to the sort of dualism needed to make sense of the proposal that a person's history might continue beyond that person's death. In a moment, I will want to argue for this claim in some detail. It will simplify the exposition, however, if I first make a small detour and introduce one new, auxiliary, notion which will prove useful to us in what follows.

What I need is a term which designates what Jack (after the experiment) and Emma (before the experiment)—or what Napoleon and our lunatic—do have in common. Jack and Emma, for example, have a great deal in common. They share certain beliefs—including beliefs about who they are (although Jack's belief about who he is, namely Emma, is, as we have discovered, a false belief)—certain S-memories, certain abilities, capacities, and capabilities (both Emma before the experiment and Jack after it, let us suppose, can play the violin and speak fluent Serbo-Croatian), certain inclinations and dispositions (both, let us suppose, are short-tempered but quick to forgive), and certain likes and dislikes (say, a weakness for butter brickle ice cream).

Now it happens that we have no convenient term in common use which covers this complex of beliefs, seeming memories, abilities, inclinations, desires, preferences, and traits of character. 'Personality' is probably about as close as we can come, but 'personality' customarily adverts just to temperament and character and only infrequently, if at all, to beliefs and

S-memories, for example. Let me, therefore, introduce the artificial term 'persona' as a label for the whole complex. Just as a person's personality consists, typically, of his inclinations, dispositions, character, and temperament (so that, for instance, a person may be said to have a shy or outgoing, irascible or forebearing, optimistic or pessimistic personality just in case the person himself is shy, outgoing, irascible, forebearing, optimistic, pessimistic, or whatever), so, too, a person's persona will consist of all of what we earlier called his 's-properties'—not only such traits of character as those which contribute to his personality, but also occurrent beliefs, active convictions, desires, apparent memories (S-memories), plans, goals, intentions, and the like as well.

With this new term at our command, we can say fairly briefly, for example, what our experiment with John and Emma accomplished. What our machine turned out to be was a "persona exchanger." That is, the effect of our machine's operation was that John's persona after the experiment was indistinguishable from Emma's persona before the experiment, and conversely. Our lunatic, too, admits of an easy redescription in these terms: Although not Napoleon, he has acquired (or is afflicted with) Napoleon's persona. That is, the lunatic's present persona is exactly like what Napoleon's persona (most likely) would be, were Napoleon still alive.

We must, of course, be cautious in our use of this new technical terminology, since a persona, of course, like a personality, is merely a nominal object, not something in its own right which could be literally "transferred" from person to person. The only things-in-their-own-right in our stories remain the persons themselves, and talk about personas simply abbreviates talk about those persons' beliefs, S-memories, desires, preferences, plans, inclinations, abilities, and temperaments at various times. Two people can have "the same persona," then, only in the sense that they can have exactly similar or indistinguishable personas. That is, they can believe all the same things, seem to remember all the same things, want all the same things, prefer or intend all the same things, behave in the same ways, have the same talents and abilities, and so on.

Normally, of course, persons and personas match up. There is no logical reason, however, why they could not come apart and, indeed, sometimes they do. The most familiar cases of such dissociation can be found in certain rare forms of psychosis. *The Three Faces of Eve* is perhaps the best-known example. Here we had one person who was discovered to manifest, at various times, three different—although interrelated—personas ("Eve White," "Eve Black," and "Eve Gray"). The case was finally resolved, as I recall it, through the therapeutic integration of elements of these three personas into a fourth persona—different in some respects and similar in others to each of the three originals—which restored a stable one-to-one relationship of persona and person.

What I have "privileged" knowledge of is precisely my current persona. I know better than anyone else can know, that is, what I now believe—including who I think I am—what it now seems to me that I remember, my current likes and dislikes, plans, preferences, desires, and inclinations. But, as we have just seen, a persona is not a person. That is, sameness of persona does not imply identity of persons, nor does a multiplicity of personas imply that we are dealing with different persons. The reason, again, is that no relationship which allows multiplication of entities can preserve identity. Two people—Napoleon and a lunatic, for instance—can have the same persona (that is, can have indistinguishable beliefs, S-memories, etc.), and one person (Eve, for instance) can, at various times, manifest different personas. It follows in point of logic, then, that sameness of persona (say, before and after surgery) can be, at best, only defeatable evidence of personal identity across time (before and after surgery) but not a logically conclusive criterion of such identity. My "privileged" knowledge of my current persona, therefore, does not give me an equally privileged knowledge of who I in fact am—that is, of which person I in fact am. More importantly, my testimony concerning who I am is only testimony about (and evidence of) my current persona and thus cannot, by itself, supply a logically decisive basis for someone else to arrive at a correct judgment concerning who, indeed, I am.

If there is complicity with my self-identifications, then—and if the shared judgment of my surgeon, wife, co-workers, and friends is to be, in point of logic, correct—that complicity must be groundable, at least in principle, on something other than my first-person testimony. There must be some other facts about the case—known to my surgeon and acquaintances or, at least, discoverable by them—which would be adequate in point of logic to settle the question of whether I actually am who I think I am. And this observation brings us to the next crucial question in our investigations.

So far, I have said only that, somehow, I have "gotten into another body," and my surgeon has said only that he has, somehow, "given me another body." We do not yet know, however, whether either of these claims even makes sense. To determine that, what we need to know are precisely the other, missing facts of the case. What, in other words, is supposed to have happened in the operating room? That is, what are we supposed to imagine that the brilliant neurosurgeon actually did?

3.15: THE "PERSONAGRAPH"—
HOW TO MAKE A NEW PERSON

Well, one thing which the brilliant neurosurgeon might have done was to make use of a variant of the machine which we earlier applied to John and Emma. His dramatic breakthrough, in other words, might have consisted in the development of techniques for recording the transient electrical patterns of a person's central nervous system at a moment of time and then "playing them back" into the "blank brain" of a "surplus body"—grown, we can suppose, in a giant test tube at Acme Body Farms, Inc. What our brilliant neurosurgeon might have devised, in short, is a machine for recording and playing back the neuro-electrical configurations of a person's nervous system which are (causally) responsible for that person's having a specific persona. Even more compactly, he might have devised a "personagraph."

But if that is what our brilliant neurosurgeon is supposed to have done, then, as we have already seen, it is just wrong to conclude that the person who wakes up in the recovery room is identical to (one and the same person as) the person who lost consciousness on the operating table. For the brilliant neurosurgeon, enamored of his new technique, could just as easily have ordered five or six assorted test tube bodies from Acme Body Farms, Inc., and, in a fit of enthusiasm, played back his personagraph recording into each of them. We would then have five or six people waking up in five or six recovery rooms, each of whom claimed emphatically to be me. Since each of those people would bear the same relationship to the person who lost consciousness in the operating room (namely, me), if any of them were right about who he actually was, then all of them would be right about it, which is absurd—for five or six people cannot, in point of logic, be one and the same person. It follows, then, that none of these people actually would be who he thinks he is, and, since all of these people would think that they were me, it follows, too, that none of these people actually would be me.

But when we are concerned about what it makes sense to say in some specific situation, the fact that the neurosurgeon didn't actually order and "imprint" five or six bodies, but only one, makes no difference at all. It is sufficient, from the standpoint of logical coherence, that he could have. For the claim that the one person waking up in the one recovery room has to be me is based upon exactly the same facts that the identical claim would be if advanced by five or six people following an attack of neurosurgical overenthusiasm. The claim of that one person, therefore, is logically and evidentially no better off and no worse off than any of those five or six identical claims would be. If the facts on which the five or six "copies" could base their several claims to be identical to me are not, in point of logic, adequate to render those claims correct, then, (and we have seen that they are not), neither are those facts adequate to render it correct that the one person awakening in a recovery room following a "personagraph imprint" is identical to (one and the same person as) me. It follows that, if what the brilliant neurosurgeon did in the operating room was to use his newly developed personagraph for the first time, then all of us—surgeon, friends, co-workers, wife, and the person in the recovery room himself—are wrong to conclude that that person in the recovery room is me (the person who lost consciousness on the operating table).

The curious fact of the matter, indeed, is that—in this instance—the person who wakes up in the operating room isn't *anyone*. More precisely, he isn't anyone who existed prior to the neurosurgeon's machinations. He's a brand new person, and his history begins with his coming to consciousness in the recovery room. Now there is nothing myserious about new persons coming into the world. It happens all the time. What is odd about this case is that, whereas normally a new person does not come already equipped with a fully developed persona, this new person does. And, what is more, he comes already equipped with a persona which is "continuous" with the persona of a previously existing person who has only just died.

Such a new person would be very intimately related to that just-dead person with whom his persona was, in this way, continuous—more intimately related, in certain respects at least, than any child to his or her parents. In the unlikely event that test tube bodies and personagraph imprints were to become widespread within our culture, we should need to —and undoubtedly would—evolve customs and concepts for dealing with persons who are related, in this intimate fashion, as "predecessor" and "successor." But we would need to evolve such customs and concepts. We do not already have them. In particular, we must not allow ourselves to be seduced by the intimacy of the evisioned relationship and the oddity of the imagined case into supposing that such a phenomenon would fall under a concept which we do already have—the concept of personal identity. For that, as I have just finished arguing, would be a logical error. However unique and intimate the relation between "predecessor" and "successor" persons may be, it is not identity. They would not be, as a matter of logic, one and the same person.

3.16: BODY TRANSPLANTS— THE LIMITS OF PLASTIC SURGERY

But, of course, our brilliant neurosurgeon might also be supposed to have done something quite different. Instead of being a method for recording and playing back transient electrical configurations of a person's central nervous system, his new technique might instead be a unique, rapid, and foolproof method of nerve-splicing. Faced with radical and irreparable failure of my circulatory system, then, what he might have done, in other words, was briskly to remove my brain (transient electrical configurations and all) from my skull and install it in the empty cranial cavity of a surplus test tube body from Acme Body Farms, Inc., from which the brain had been removed and discarded—promptly and deftly splicing all the trailing nerves from my brain to the appropriate connections with the balance of the test tube body's sensory and neuromotor systems.

To discover what we ought correctly to say about this case, it is useful to consider a variety of intermediate possibilities. There are many unproblematic ways in which I could lose consciousness on the operating table and wake up later in a recovery room radically altered in appearance. Suppose, for example, that the original purpose of the operation was not cardiac surgery but rather extensive plastic surgery. I undertook the operation precisely in order to have my appearance dramatically altered. In this case, too, I would wake up in the recovery room to confront in the mirror a face which, let us suppose, was also wholly unfamiliar to me (my plastic surgeon being a secretive sort of fellow). Here, however, there would be no question about the identity of the person in the recovery room. That person would, quite unproblematically, be me. Reshaping of noses, strengthening of chinlines, raising of cheekbones, hair transplants, and the like are all things which can be done to a person without raising any questions concerning the identity of that person before and after the operations.

Nor would it have made any difference to questions of identity if my plastic surgeon had, say, amputated my limbs on the operating table and grafted new arms and legs, different in shape and size, to my torso. Here, too, the person who resumed consciousness in the recovery room would, unproblematically, still be me. Extensive skin transplants would also have made no difference. Nor would questions of identity have arisen if various of my internal organs—heart, lungs, liver, pancreas, and the like—had been replaced at the same time, whether by equivalent organs from some donor or by mechanical substitutes (prostheses). Such things, too, can be done to a person without imperiling the identity of that person before and after the operations.

The question now arises: Just how much can be done to a person before serious questions concerning the identity of a person before and after certain operations logically come into play? Now I do not think that there is an absolute, definable boundary to be erected here, for I do think that this is an empirical (matter-of-factual) question and not a logical or conceptual one. But I think that we can draw on logical and conceptual dependencies and relationships in order to determine how an approximate answer to it might be discovered.

The logical point upon which we need to draw is this: While continuity of a persona across time is not sufficient, in point of logic, to guarantee personal identity across time, discontinuities between the persona of some person at an earlier time and that of some person at a later time are sufficient, in point of fact, to raise the question of whether we are dealing with one and the same person at both times. Of course people's personas do change across time—people mature; they "settle down"; their opinions change; they learn things and forget things; and so on—and so we are clearly dealing here with a matter of degree. In general, however, the more serious and sudden such discontinuities of persona appear to be, the more pressing the question of whether this person is actually our former acquaintance or really someone else (an imposter, a lunatic, or the like) becomes. We may recall that it was just such a radical discontinuity of persona between John (before the experiment) and Jack (after it) that led us to raise the question of whether Jack was actually identical to John (as he turned out to be) or rather one and the same person as Emma, with whose former persona his postexperimental persona was largely continuous.

The question of just how much can be done to a person before serious questions concerning the identity of a person before and after certain operations arise, then, is basically the question of how much can be done to a person before serious and sudden discontinuities of persona between the patient in the operating room and the patient in the recovery room emerge. And we already know enough, in general, to give a rough and ready answer to this question. In general, we can avoid introducing such discontinuities of persona into our surgical scenarios just so long as, in our fiddling with the patient, we leave the brain largely alone. To put it another way, just as the heart turned out to be the organ of a person's circulation and the lungs to be the organs of a person's respiration, so, too, the brain has turned out, as a matter of fact, to be the organ of those complex functions and capacities (thought, memory, temperament, desire, and so on) which are constitutive elements of a person's persona.

There is another useful way in which we can look at this little thought experiment. Consider the analogous question: How much can be done to an automobile without seriously altering or impairing its mechanical functioning? Here the answer will run something like this: We can replace the tires, reshape the fenders, put new glass in the windows, install different headlights, and so on. In general, we can avoid introducing serious alterations or impairments of a car's mechanical functioning just so long as, in our fiddling with the automobile, we leave the engine and drive train largely alone. In familiar terms, we can make all kinds of alterations to the chassis, but we had better leave the works as they are.

The general form of our question, in other words, is approximately this: How much fiddling can we do with the structure of a thing before we start seriously modifying or interfering with its mode of functioning (its mode of operation)? And it is questions of this sort which allow us to discover—to determine empirically or experimentally—how much and what parts of the overall structure of some thing to allocate to its "chassis" and how much and what parts to allocate to the "works." Of course, what counts as "chassis" and what counts as "works" will vary according to which modes of functioning or operation we focus on in our question. It is in this way that we pick out the various "systems" which make up a complex functioning whole—the electrical system, cooling system, and so on of an automobile, for instance.

As it is with automobiles, so, too, is it with persons. We pick out various organic systems of a person—circulatory system, respiratory system, and the like—by determining what parts of the body (that is, body-1) we can fiddle with without affecting the corresponding organic functions of the person—circulation, respiration, and the like. And it is in roughly this way that, for instance, a cardiovascular or gastrointestinal surgeon arrives at his rough division of a person into "chassis" and "works" or, as it is more commonly put, into "body" and "internal organs."

The notion of a body at issue here is that of a body-3—a "chassis" or "body shell." The question of how much of the body-1 to allocate to the body-3 and how much to allocate to the "works," in other words, is just the question of how much of the body-1 can be reworked without affecting the functions upon which the chassis/works distinction is based in any particular case.

In the case currently before us, the functions of a person which interest us are not such organic functions as respiration, circulation, digestion, and locomotion, but rather those functions (abilities, capacities, and capabilities) which contribute to that person's persona—cognition, perception, desire, memory, volition, deliberation, sensation, and the like. These are commonly called "mental" functions, but we must be careful not to take the verbal distinction between two classes of functions—"mental" and "organic"—to imply a difference of subject. It is one and the same thing—the person—which breathes, digests, moves, thinks, remembers, perceives, deliberates, and so on.[9]

The distinction between two classes of functions—"mental" and "organic"—is not grounded in a distinction of functioning entities—"souls" or "minds" versus "bodies"—but rather in an appreciation of the ways in which those bodies-1 which are persons are interestingly different from those which are rocks or carrots or fish or dogs or apes. The "specialness" of persons, we have already seen, is not a matter of what they are but of what they can do. And just as a person's ability to breathe or to walk can be altered or impaired by damage to or modification of some parts of a body-1—lungs or legs—so, too, that person's "special" abilities to perceive, believe, desire, deliberate, choose, and remember can be altered or impaired by damage to other parts of the same body-1—eyes or brain, for instance.

The distinction between "mental" and "organic" functions, in short, is not a distinction between two kinds of entities—"mental" and "physical" —for "mental" functions are just as "physical" as organic (biological) functions. They are all abilities, capacities, or capabilities of a physical organism—that is, of a body-1 having a determinate trajectory through space and time and causally interrelated to other such spatio-temporal bodies-1—and all causally dependent upon the structure and condition of that physical organism.

To return, then, to our brilliant neurosurgeon, what he might have done, we can now say, was to have installed my "works" (my brain) into a new body-3. He might, in short, have given me a body transplant (that is, a body-3 transplant). And now it makes perfect sense to say that I wake up in the recovery room in a "different body." It is not, however, that I am a "soul" which has somehow been "transferred" from one body-1 into another body-1. Rather, I wake up in the recovery room in a new and different body-3, in a new "chassis."

It is important to understand here precisely why it is I, and not someone else, who wakes up in the recovery room—precisely why, that is, personal identity here tracks with sameness of the brain. It is not because there is any logical or conceptual connection between the concept of a person and the concept of a brain. It is because there is a logical or conceptual connection between the concept of a person and the concept of an entity having a persona, and because we have discovered, not in point of logic but as a matter of fact, that the brain is the organ of those functions which constitute a person's persona, that is, the part of the body-1 upon which those functions are primarily causally dependent.

The reason that personal identity is preserved in spite of a replacement of one body-3 by another, then, is simply that this contrast between "chassis" and "works" is drawn already *using* the concept of personal identity. The notion of a body-3 which we are making use of in this discussion just is—"by definition," as it were —the notion of that part of a person (i.e., of a body-1) which can be reworked (modified or replaced) without generating substantive questions concerning personal identity across time, that is, the notion of that part of a person (body-1) which can be reworked without introducing any serious discontinuities into that person's persona. This turned out—empirically, experimentally, as a matter-of-fact—to be, roughly, the whole of the organism (body-1) exclusive of the brain. But there was nothing in the logic of the case to demand that it would turn out that way. In point of logic, it could have turned out that the liver, for instance, and not the brain, was the organ of those functions which constitute a person's persona and was causally responsible for the continuity of that persona. (This is, apparently, what the ancient Greeks believed. The brain, on their view, was an organ whose function was to cool the blood.) Had that been so, then the description "waking up in a different body-3" would not have applied to the present example. I would, instead, have died on the operating table—about the time that my liver ceased to function.[10]

3.17: THE TRIUMPH OF CRIMINOLOGY

Our hypothethical objector's contentious appeal to his imagination has again borne fruit—but not quite the fruit which he had hoped to feast upon. As in the case of John and Emma, our objector can, of course, easily and vividly imagine something. But, once again, what he can so easily and vividly imagine is not exactly what he says he can imagine.

Here, however, we can coherently adopt more of his description of the case than in the preceding example. For, as we have seen, we can make coherent sense of the notion of losing consciousness on the operating table and waking up in the recovery room "in a different body," whereas we could not, analogously, make coherent sense of the notion that John and Emma—the two persons—had "exchanged bodies." We can only make coherent sense of our objector's description, however, if what we mean by 'a different body' is different from what he wants to mean by 'a different body'. For our objector still thought that his ability to imagine what he could, indeed, imagine supported a "body-soul" (or "body-mind") dualism. He thought that he could imagine waking up in a (wholly!) different body-1, and his term 'body' was intended to contrast with 'soul' or 'mind'—with some kind of "nonphysical" thing or stuff.

I have argued, however, that, although he can certainly imagine something, that cannot, in point of logic, be the correct description of what he successfully imagines. What he can imagine, however, is waking up in a different body-3. But a different body-3 is not a wholly different body-1, but only a partially different body-1. 'Body-3' does not contrast with 'soul' or 'mind' but rather, in this instance, with 'brain'. It is not a contrast between two kinds of entities—"physical" and "nonphysical"—but rather a classification of one kind of entity—a classification of bodies-1 that are (physical) parts of a composite body-1, which is grounded in a prior classification of the modes of functioning (abilities, capacities, and capabilities) exhibited by that composite whole. It is, in short, a contrast between "chassis" and "works," but that sort of contrast is drawn wholly within the domain of the "physical."

The ultimate criterion of personal identity, in other words—whether of the identity of other persons or even of oneself across time—once again turns out to be, in point of logic, bodily continuity, that is, the tracing out of a continuous trajectory through space and time by a body-1. What our latest imaginative exercises have shown us, however, is that not all of a body-1 need be equally relevant to questions of personal identity.[11]

While a person is not identical to a persona—since one person can have many personas and two or more people may have indistinguishable personas—there is a logical or conceptual connection between the concept of a person and the concept of an entity having a persona. This connection is revealed, among other things, by the fact that the emergence of sudden or serious discontinuities in that cluster of beliefs, S-memories, desires, competences, and the like which constitutes some person's persona gives rise to substantive questions concerning the identity of persons across time. Such questions are resolved, however, not by further elaboration or investigation of personas as such, but, in point of logic, by tracing the source or origin of such discontinuities to their causal roots.

When discontinuities of persona give rise to questions of personal identity, in other words, these questions are resolved by determining whether the manifest discontinuities are a consequence of damage to or modification of a single spatio-temporally continuous body-1 or rather a reflection of the fact that we are dealing with different parts of the histories of several spatio-temporally distinct such bodies-1. They are resolved, that is, by an empirical, causal investigation. This causal investigation, however, may very well lead us to focus only upon some parts (e.g., the brain) of a composite organism, while spatio-temporal discontinuities introduced into other parts of that organism (e.g., legs, lungs, liver) by transplantation or replacement turn out to be a matter of indifference to us.

3.18: CLOSING THE QUESTION

And now we have reached an important milestone in our study of death. It would be well, indeed, to pause for a moment and mark it with a sort of monument. What we have discovered and demonstrated is that we cannot pry the notion of a person loose from the notion of a living organism, that is, of a body-1 (an entity having a determinate trajectory through space and time in causal interaction with other such spatio-temporal entities) which possesses a variety of interesting and special abilities, capacities, and capabilities.

The significant corollary of this result is that we cannot make coherent sense of the supposed possibility that a person's history might continue beyond that person's death. A person's death is an event which brings that person's history to an end, for what a person is, is, so to speak, a uniquely competent living organism. There is no possibility that a person's history might extend beyond that person's death—not for the reason that, for instance, such a happening would be "contrary to the laws of nature" (like "antigravity" or spaceships which travel faster than the speed of light), but because we cannot even describe such a supposed happening without misusing language, mistaking linguistic appearances for linguistic realities. We cannot coherently state the supposed possibility that a person's history might continue beyond that person's death.

It is important to appreciate that this is a genuine discovery, and not an arbitrary bit of legislation. Let me offer an analogy. The impossibility of a person's history extending beyond that person's death is similar to the impossibility of there being a four-sided triangle. In the phrase "four-sided triangle," we set two concepts together which separately cause no problems. There is nothing mysterious about four-sided plane figures and nothing mysterious about triangles. Put them together, however, and it turns out that one is talking a kind of nonsense. For there is, in point of logic, no way of picking out a triangle (in fact, in theory, or even in our imaginations) apart from picking out a three-sided figure, and, of course, to speak of a four-sided, three-sided figure is to speak nonsensically.

Analogously, in the phrase "a person's history continues after that person's death," we set two concepts together which separately are similarly unproblematic. What we need to focus upon, however, is the identification of one person on two separate occasions which is built into the phrases "a person's history" and "after that person's death" (that is, after one and the same person's death). Here, too, it is the combination of the concepts which produces a subtle sort of nonsense. For, as I have extensively argued, there is no way of picking out a specific person on two separate occasions (e.g., before and after death)—in fact, in theory, or even in our imaginations—apart from tracing the history of a particular body-1 (a living organism or a functionally selected part of a living organism). There is no problem about picking out episodes in the history of some person following a person's death. The difficulty comes when we try to describe what it would mean to pick out episodes in the history of the same person who has just died after that person's death. For we would then need a way of identifying persons across time which does not depend upon tracking a living organism or functional part of a living organism through space and time—and we no more have, nor can we have, such a method of identification of persons than we have, or can have, a method of picking out triangles which does not depend upon counting sides and reaching the answer "three."

When we put the phrases "a person's history continues" and "after that person's death" together, then, it turns out that we emerge talking a kind of nonsense. Since the identification of persons across time is a much more complicated business than the identification of some plane figure (real or imagined) as a triangle, the incoherence of this manner of speaking is subtler and more difficult to detect than the incoherence of "four-sided triangle," but it is no less logical and conceptual incoherence for all that.

The matter was further complicated, however, as we have seen, by a variety of longstanding and traditional efforts to make the notion of "life after death" make sense, some of which have gotten built into easily misinterpreted, commonplace, idiomatic expressions, thus, for instance, "has a (muscular) body" and "has a (generous) soul." But all such "theoretical" dualisms, we saw, failed equally to be coherently statable. In each case, we confronted a linguistic difficulty—nominal objects (mere manners-of-speaking) being mistaken for things in their own right, for example, or judicious blurring of the multiple ambiguities of terms such as 'body'. And the same proved true of efforts to make the notion of "life after death" make sense by exercises of the imagination, that is, to secure an "imaginative" dualism by visualizing such supposed events as two persons "exchanging bodies" or oneself "waking up in a different body." Here, too, the difficulties proved to be linguistic. While it was easy enough to visualize or imagine something, the only coherent and intelligible descriptions of what was thus visualized or imagined proved incompatible with the sort of dualism needed to make sense of "life after death."

We can therefore bring this movement of our study to a close with a definite conclusion:

> The expression "a person's history continues after that person's death" does not formulate a possibility, that is, it does not even venture a hypothesis which might prove to be true or false.

As befits a study in analytic philosophy—as I am here understanding that discipline—this is a conclusion about what it makes sense to say (and, therefore, about what it makes sense to think). It is, in fact, the discovery of an empty expression. And that, of course, we have seen before—long ago. An exactly parallel conclusion, in other words, would be:

> The expression "an undetectable gremlin lives in my refrigerator" does not formulate a possibility, that is, does not even venture a hypothesis which might prove to be true or false.

The principal difference here is only that, whereas no one has ever seriously supposed that the expression "an undetectable gremlin lives in my refrigerator" did formulate a hypothesis which might turn out to be true or false, lots of people have supposed that the expression "a person's history continues after that person's death" formulates a hypothesis which might turn out to be true or false and have, indeed, claimed that the hypothesis which the expression supposedly formulates was in fact true. Since such herculean efforts have been traditionally dedicated to making the latter expression make sense, clearing away the muck and clutter of "immaterial souls" took quite a bit longer than clearing away the "undetectable gremlins."

But the job is now done. There is simply no sense to be made of "life after death" or "survival of death" or "a person's history continuing after that person's death." And so we are at last in a position to being doing what, after all, we set out so long ago to do—to think clearly about death.

That, then, is our next order of business. What remains to be said about death after the litter of incoherent views, muddled theories, and nonsensical descriptions has been cleared away?

INTERLUDE

An Agenda
for Further Discussion

It will be useful to pause to develop a sort of agenda for the remainder of this study. So far, we have addressed ourselves, surprisingly enough, to only one question—the question which the person who asks "Is there life after death?" intended to be asking. Our results have been, in essence, negative. If the intended question does admit of a yes-or-no answer, then the answer is "No"—for, in that case, the question amounts to some variant of the silly question "Is a corpse still a living organism?" If, on the other hand, the intended question is equivalent to the question "Does—or could—a person's history continue after that person's death?" then, as we have seen, the question does not admit of any answer, yes or no. For, in that case, the questioner is presupposing that one can make coherent sense of "a person's history continuing after that person's death" and that, we have seen, we cannot do.

The sentence "A person's history continues after that person's death," we have discovered, is a sort of subtly disguised nonsense, a linguistic deception. It appears to be perfectly in order, but, as I have shown, it actually does not even express a possibility. It formulates no hypothesis which might prove true or false. The question "Does, or could, a person's history continue after that person's death?" does not admit of any answer, then, not because there are some facts which we would need to know in order to answer it and which we do not know, but because it is only apparently a question. It is, so to speak, a "counterfeit" question—something which looks like a question—but it can no more be answered than, for instance, a counterfeit passport could expire, that is, could lose a validity which it never possessed in the first place.

But while some variation on "Is there life after death?" has, perhaps, always been the chief "philosophical" question concerning death, it is by no means the only "philosophical" question about death. What I propose to do in the balance of this study, then, is to use our hard-won insights concerning death and persons to address some of these other "philosophical questions." These questions can be arranged, more or less, under four main headings:

A. The nature of death

B. The recognition of death

C. The ethics of death

D. The significance of death

A. Under the heading "the nature of death" we find a question which is an immediate consequence of the negative results which we have already reached. For those results imply, among other things, that death cannot be what Plato, for instance, said it was: "the separation of the soul from the body." More generally, death cannot be the dissolving of a relationship between two things (like the breakup of a marriage, for example) for the simple reason that a living person is not such a composite of two related things in the first place. Such a dualistic view of persons, we have seen, cannot even be coherently stated. We can make neither "theoretical" nor "imaginative" sense of it.

But if death is not "the separation of the soul from the body," then what is it? What happens to a person when he dies? This is the question of the nature of death. To answer it, we shall need to investigate the nature of life as well. Death is, after all, "the end of life"—more particularly, "loss of life." But just what is it that comes to an end when life (not, let us notice, "a life", that is, a history) comes to an end? Just what is lost when life (again, not "a life") is lost? In short, just what is it that differentiates a living organism from its remains, from a corpse? These questions concerning the nature of life and death will be our first order of business in what follows.

B. Once we are reasonably clear about what happens to a person when he dies, we can sensibly ask and answer the logically next question: How does one determine that it has happened? This is the question of the recognition of death. In medical and legal contexts, it becomes the question "How does one fix the moment of death?" that is, "When is a person dead?"

The question has an important parallel at the other end of life, of course. That is, we can not only ask when a person's life ends but also "When does a person's life begin?" The distinction which we have already marked between "life" (a condition) and "a life" (a history) will prove crucial here, for as we have seen in the case of our amoebae, there are other ways for a life to end besides death and, analogously, other ways for a life to begin besides birth. There is, in fact, a large and complex family of questions to be sorted out here. Sorting them out will require us to become clear about certain conceptual matters which have so far been left alone—for instance, the relations between the concept of a person and the concept of a human being. And what we will find, to anticipate a bit, is that the concept of a person is a concept of quite a different kind than the concept of this or that sort of living organism—of a carrot or a fish or a dog or an ape or, for that matter, of a human being.

 C. This distinction of kinds of concepts will be an essential prologue to our addressing the traditional, central, ethical questions concerning life and death. We will, in fact, be looking at three such questions—euthanasia or "mercy killing," "allowing to die" versus the artifical prologation of life, and "rational suicide." Not surprisingly, it will turn out that our investigations have implications for moral questions arising at the other end of a person's history as well, for questions concerning abortion and "the right to life." The principal thesis which I shall wish to advance in this connection is that these are not theoretical questions, calling for a discovery, but instead practical questions, calling for a sort of decision. And, although I shall insist that such decisions are not arbitrary but can be more or less sensible or reasonable and, thus, that some decisions can be better than others, I will argue that this sort of sensibleness or reasonableness is not a matter of "fitting or not fitting the facts." For what is essentially at issue in the difficult cases will turn out to be questions about how to fix the scope of the concept of a person—and the concept of a person is not the kind of concept the scope of which is delimited by "scientific discoveries" but rather precisely by our "moral practices."

 D. Finally, I shall turn from such third-person concerns with life and death—questions about how it is appropriate to regard and to treat others—to the matter of the first-person significance of death. Do we, as Heidegger claimed, live "toward our deaths"? Is there, as Socrates proposed, an attitude toward death which especially befits a "true philosopher," that is, a "lover of wisdom"?

 We humans, it is frequently asserted, are the only creatures who are conscious of their own mortality. Like fish and dogs and apes, we, too, will die—but, unlike fish and dogs and apes, we know that we will die. With equal frequency, however, it is also asserted that no one can conceive of or imagine or genuinely contemplate her own death. While we know in some sense that we will die—for we know that all men are mortal and that we, too, are but men—we cannot, it is often claimed, appropriate this "abstract impersonal fact" as a "concrete personal reality."

 Our discussions of the significance of death must finally rest upon some reasoned judgment concerning these matters. How do we stand with respect to our own deaths? Does each of us genuinely know that she will die? If so, how does she know? Is the human consciousness of human mortality based somehow in a special first-person, subjective, awareness of mortality, or is the fact that all men are mortal (oneself included) of a piece with the fact that all ravens are black? And can we genuinely conceive of or imagine our own deaths?

 The significance of death, the appropriate attitude toward one's own prospective death, depends upon the answers to such questions. And that will be our last order of business in this study. When I have finished with it, I will have said, at least, all that I have to say about the contributions which the "new" philosophy—my "linguistic," "analytic" philosophical method—can make to the question of death. Surprisingly, it will turn out to be quite as much—and as little—as any "classical" philosophy has had to say about death. But there is, after all, only so much which can sensibly, rationally, and coherently be said about death. And if "analytic" philosophy has any special virtue, it is that it insists on locating and marking that boundary—the limits of what it makes sense to say and to think—and then, unlike some "classical" philosophies, on remaining resolutely within it.

CHAPTER 4

Death and Personhood: Conceptual Preliminaries

4.1: ON THE NATURE OF LIFE AND DEATH

Death is the end of life. More particularly, death is the loss of life. To understand the nature of death—what death is—then, we need to understand the nature of life—what life is. Life, of course, is a condition. The handiest dictionary, indeed, informs me that life is

> the condition that distinguishes animals and plants from inorganic objects and dead organisms.

And it goes on to add that this condition is manifested by "growth through metabolism, reproduction, and the power of adaptation to environment through changes originating internally."

Life, then, is the condition which differentiates living organisms from "inorganic objects"—for instance, rocks—and "dead organisms"—that is, corpses or the remains of organisms. My convenient dictionary goes on to tell me how this condition is manifested, that is, how it shows itself in the world and, thus, how its presence might be recognized. But it does not tell me what this condition is, that is, in what it consists. It does not tell me, that is, what it is which differentiates living organisms from rocks and corpses. Just that, however, is what we want to find out next.

Notice that we are dealing here with life, a condition, and not with a life, a history. The end of life, we have seen, is necessarily also the end of a life. That is, a person's history necessarily comes to an end when that person dies. We can make no sense, I have argued, of the notion that a person's history might continue beyond that person's death. (And the same holds true, of course, for living organisms other than persons.) But the converse relationship does not obtain. The end of a life is not necessarily the end of life.

There are other ways for a life to come to an end than by a death. This, too, we have already noted. The life (that is, the history) of an amoeba can come to an end by division, and the history of a caterpillar by metamorphosis into a butterfly, for example, and in neither case does anything die. A life ends, but no life is lost. Life, so to speak, is conserved through these changes of number or of kind.

But life is not conserved through the change of kind which is death—the change from, for instance, a living person into a corpse. In that instance, life itself, as it were, and not just a life, is lost (comes to an end). What we need to ask, then, is what is lost in the passage from living person to corpse. How, that is, is a living person different from the corpse which, upon death, that person becomes?

Well, one thing at least is now clear. The loss of life is not a loss of substance. That is, life is not a kind of stuff which "leaks out" or "departs," however much this primitive notion may have gotten built into our customary ways of speaking. A living person is an intricate structure of elements—primarily atoms of carbon, hydrogen, oxygen, and nitrogen— or, perhaps better, an intricate structure of structures . . . of such elements. The atoms compose molecules which compose cells which compose tissues which compose organs which, finally, compose the total organism.

The distinction between "organic" and "inorganic" matter, in other words, is not the distinction between two distinct kinds of stuffs but rather the distinction between two ways in which stuffs of the same kinds—atoms of various elements—can be arranged or structured. The synthesis of urea in 1828 erased once and for all any "metaphysical" distinction between organic and inorganic substances. The concept of "organic chemistry" lost its necessary (logical or conceptual) connection to the concept of life, and "organic chemistry" became simply a label for the study of carbon compounds which, because of carbon's knack for building up long and intricate chains, turned out to be in fact pervasive substantial constituents of the living organisms which are so dear to us.

The difference between a living organism and a corpse, however, apparently cannot consist simply in the way in which their constituent material elements are structured or arranged, for surely, one might protest, the arrangement of the material constituents of a fresh cadaver is essentially the same as the arrangement of the material constituents of the living organism shortly before that organism became that corpse. Just as in a living organism, the atoms in a fresh cadaver compose molecules which compose cells which compose tissues which compose organs which, finally, compose the nonliving whole.

But here, I think, we come upon our essential clue. For it is important that we have selected a fresh cadaver for our material and compositional investigations. With the passage of time, this organization of structures of structures in a corpse rapidly begins to break down. Unless special precautions are taken, a fresh cadaver will fairly quickly begin to decay—that is, to come apart, through various interactions with its environment, into its constituent elements (which are then taken up into combinations with other elements present in the immediate environment). It is precisely this, however, which does not happen to the still-living organism.

What primarily differentiates the still-living organism from the fresh cadaver, in other words, is not that the material elements of which each respectively consists are differently structured, organized, or arranged (although, in detail, as we shall see in a moment, they must be), but that the corpse lacks an ability, a capacity, or a capability which the still-living organism still has—the ability, capacity, or capability to preserve its intricate material organization through ongoing (physical, chemical) transactions with its environment. The difference between a still-living organism and a fresh cadaver, in short, is not so much a matter of what each (materially) is, but rather of what each respectively can or cannot do.

Like the "specialness" of persons, then, the "specialness" of living organisms in general is properly located in the realm of abilities, capabilities, capacities, and competences. It is a classic failing and confusion in human history that we so frequently attempt to account for a striking or impressive feature of the things we encounter by, in essence, postulating some special entity (a nonphysical "soul" or "mind," an *élan vital*, or something equally mysterious) to "explain" it. We attempt to turn abilities which we cannot otherwise account for into things or stuffs or forces—about which we can then say, however, only that they are whatever it is that accounts for the abilities.

What is almost universally the case, however, is that the abilities, capacities, and competences of a thing are properly to be accounted for, not by the presence of some mysterious and extraordinary constituent thing or stuff, but by the way in which the perfectly ordinary constituent things or stuffs which compose the talented original are structured or arranged—by the organization and modes of functioning or operation of perfectly ordinary material constituents. It is the shape of an airplane's wings, for example, which accounts for its ability to get off the ground—not some antigravitational materials or an "aeronautical soul" which "strives for the heights."

So, too, is it with living organisms. Any physical (spatio-temporal) thing is in continuous causal interaction with its environment. And every physical thing is a more-or-less intricately organized arrangement of physical constituents. There are, then, two possible trends or tendencies which a physical thing might exhibit over a series of causal transactions with its environment. It might change in the direction of less structure and organization, that is, it might tend toward a loss of its initial intricate internal arrangements. Or it might preserve its initial organization and structure or even tend in the direction of greater and more intricate arrangements of constituent elements. Things of the first sort, to introduce a bit of jargon, are "entropic." Things of the second sort, I shall call "syntropic."

Living organisms are syntropic. Rocks and corpses are entropic. That is the key difference. It is a difference in ability, capability, capacity, or competence—in what living organisms and nonliving things can respectively do. A living organism has the ability or capacity to preserve or even increase its structural organization through causal transactions with its environment; a rock or a corpse lacks this ability or capacity. Left to their own devices, rocks erode and corpses decay. Left to their own devices, living organisms do neither. Instead, they take in matter and energy from their environments and organize it into molecules, cells, tissues, and organs. The condition of life is this syntropic capacity or ability. And that is what is lost when life (not: a life) is lost.

That tells us, too, what death is. It is not "the separation of the soul from the body." It is the loss of syntropic capacity or ability—the loss of a (purely physical) ability to do something.

Whether a complex and intricately organized arrangement of material constituents is syntropic or entropic does not depend upon its being "inhabited" by a mysterious thing or stuff (a "soul") or its being "pervaded" or "animated" by some mysterious "life force," but upon how its material constituents are, in detail, structured, organized, or arranged. Just as the surfaces of an airplane's wing are arranged precisely to transform lateral thrust into vertical lift, so, analogously, the organs, tissues, cells, molecules, and —ultimately—the atoms of which a living organism is composed are arranged precisely to transform incoming matter and energy (in the form of food, water, sunlight, and the like) into more cells, tissues, and organs (which is called "growth"), and—ultimately—even into more living organisms (which is called "reproduction").

It is a fact, however, that this self-preserving, self-organizing organization of material constituents is fragile and imperfect. The causal processes upon which syntropic capacities depend are relatively fine-tuned. And so a living organism can lose its syntropic abilities—either suddenly, through damage or injury which disrupts essential structures and arrangements, or gradually, through the cumulative effect of random entropic processes occurring within the organism. And that is what death is—in the one instance, a violent death and in the other, a natural death of old age. Death is the loss of syntropic capacity or ability—the loss of an organism's power to do something.

And that is the answer, too, to the first question on our agenda—the question about the nature of death.

4.2: HOW TO RECOGNIZE A CORPSE

Death is the loss of syntropic capacity or ability. More precisely, an organism dies when it loses its power to preserve and sustain its self-organizing organization permanently and irreversibly. That is to say, death is to some extent a matter of "the state of the art."

We have already seen that the notion of "the (instantaneous) moment of death" is a kind of idealization or linguistic fiction. What we encounter are instances of clearly living organisms—entities whose syntropic capacities are not in question—and clear instances of corpses—entities whose environmental transactions are all plainly entropic—and a gray area of transition between the two which admits of continuously narrowing "bracketing" up to a point. That is, we can find nested series of increasingly shorter intervals which span the (idealized, fictional) "moment of death" in the sense that the entity which we encounter at the beginning of each such interval is (still, barely) a living organism and the entity which we encounter at the end of each such interval is (only just, freshly) a corpse. The "moment of death" itself, however, is available to us only as the ideal limit of such a series of nested intervals—that is, only as something thought and not as something experienced—for we do not, and could not, encounter an "interval of zero duration."

How narrowly we can in practice draw such spanning intervals around the ideal "moment of death" obviously depends upon how finely we can monitor the structure and functioning of the organism in question. "Fixing the moment of death," in other words, is to some extent a matter of our technological capacity to register minute changes within an organism. But we should not be seduced by this observation into supposing that an increasingly refined medical technology of measurement would automatically lead to increasingly precise approximations to some actual punctiform "instant of death," for there is no such "fact of the matter" to serve as the outermost boundary of technological precision.

Suppose, for example, that our techniques of monitoring had increased in precision to the point that we were able to register microevents within an organism of durations on the order of a millionth of a second on a cell-by-cell basis. Rather than allowing us a more precise determination of "the moment of death," such exquisitely delicate technology would rather, on the contrary, lead to an increase of indeterminateness. For these refined measurements would only serve to reinforce and confirm what we already know—that syntropic capacity is lost gradually and piecemeal. Individual cells and groups of cells lose their syntropic abilities singly and to a certain degree. There is no one individual cell which the heart, lungs, liver, kidneys, or brain cannot do without, and the extent to which the loss of syntropic capacity by this or that collection of cells impairs the functioning of this or that organ will be a function of which other collections of cells might previously have lost such capacities and, more generally, of how this or that group of cells relates from time to time to the totality of the organism to which it belongs.

What an exquisitely refined technology of measurement would drive home, in short, is that we are dealing—in the transition from living organism to corpse—with a statistical continuum. Microevents within the organism have only probabilistic influences upon overall, global, syntropic capacities, and such global capacities, in turn, fall off gradually from the dynamic growth of infancy to the purely entropic environmental transactions of a corpse.

The logical point which needs to be stressed here, then, is that there is nothing more to be discovered about an organism which is relevant to "fixing the moment of death." To put the point epistemologically, we will, in principle, never be in any better position to determine when an organism dies than we already are right now. For our de facto measurement technology is already sufficiently fine tuned to yield all the information about the structure and functioning of an organism which could, in principle, be useable for that purpose.[1]

The reason that this is so, to put the point in briefest form, is that the question concerning "the moment of death" is not a theoretical scientific question but, primarily, a practical legal question. The "moment of death" needs to be "determined" as a condition for further proceedings—filling out death certificates, giving permission for organ donations and transplants, embalming, cremation or burial, and the like. The only reason that "the moment of death" is important is that there are things which one is allowed to do to corpses—dissect them, remove their parts, embalm them, burn or bury them—which one is not allowed to do to living organisms, most especially to persons. And what is needed to convey such license and permission is not an arbitrarily fine microdetermination of the momentary state of some organism but rather a clear and unmistakeable sign (or cluster of such signs) that the entity in question has lost its overall, global, syntropic capacity or ability permanently and irreversibly.

What counts as such a clear and unmistakeable sign will also vary according to the state of our medical technology—not the technology of measurement and registration, in this instance, but the technology of intervention and resuscitation. A hundred years ago, prolonged absence of respiration or the cessation of heartbeat were perfectly reliable indicators of permanent and irreversible loss of syntropic capacity. Nowadays, however, stopped hearts can be restarted, and both heartbeat and respiration can be sustained by electromechanical aids. Many of what were unmistakeable indications of death, in other words, have been downgraded to the status of "acute traumas" or, to remind ourselves of an expression we looked at earlier, to the status of "clinical death." Our current interventionist technology, however, is ineffectual in cases of loss of brain functions. It is consequently customary nowadays to fix "the moment of death" at the time when detectable brain activity ceases.[2] There is nothing in the logic of the case to dictate this criterion rather than some other criterion or complex of criteria, however. Rather it is—currently—a fact that the absence of measurable cortical activity is a reliable sign or indication of a loss of autonomous global syntropic capacity which, given the present state of medical technology, is permanent and irreversible.

4.3: SOME DIFFERENT KINDS OF KINDS

I have just argued that "fixing the moment of death" is primarily a practical, rather than a theoretical, matter. There are things which one is permitted to do to a corpse that one is not permitted to do to living organisms, especially persons. "Fixing the moment of death" is essentially a question of settling upon criteria for granting the right and license to such conducts, such doings.[3]

This shift of focus from theoretical and scientific questions to practical and moral questions marks our transition from a discussion of the nature and recognition of death to a discussion of the ethics and significance of death. In order to proceed further, however, it will be necessary to lay some fairly extensive groundwork. In particular, I shall need to articulate and defend a certain rather complicated thesis about the concept of a person.

Rather than straightaway stating and arguing for my thesis, however, I shall begin by filling in some of the background. Let us, therefore, forget about persons and death for a moment and, instead, talk about the notion of a kind of thing or entity.

What I specifically want to look at are the various sorts of criteria to be met for a thing or entity to correctly be said to belong to a certain specific, determinate kind. Let me abbreviate this a bit by speaking of "criteria of belongingness."

Consider, for example, the kind "sugar cube," that is, those things or entities which are sugar cubes. What criteria does a thing need to satisfy in order to be a sugar cube? The answer, of course, is childishly simple. In order to be a sugar cube, a thing must be (a) made of sugar and (b) roughly cubical in shape. These are the criteria of belongingness for the kind "sugar cube." They are what I shall call "structural" criteria. What counts, in the case of the kind "sugar cube" is the structure of the thing—what it is made of and how, specifically in what shape, the stuff it is made of is put together.

The criteria of belongingness for the kind "magnet," in contrast, are not structural but, let me say, "functional." What is required of a thing in order for it to be a magnet is not that it be made of any particular substance nor that it have any particular shape, size, color, and so on. What is required is that it have a certain performance capability. In order to be a magnet, a thing must have the ability or capacity to attract bits of iron. Whether or not something is a magnet does not depend upon what it is made of but only upon what it can do. That is why there can be ceramic magnets, steel magnets, and Alnico magnets, and why there can be bar magnets, horseshoe magnets, and circular magnets. It is performance capabilities, not material composition or shape, which are the criteria of belongingness for the kind "magnet."

Structural criteria and functional criteria, however, by no means exhaust the options available to us here. The kind "product of Denmark," for example, is determined by genetic criteria of belongingness. In order for a thing to be a product of Denmark, it is necessary neither that it be made of any particular materials nor that it have any particular size or shape nor that it have any special performance capabilities. What is required is that a specific genesis or origin—in this case, a specific geographical origin. In order for a thing to be a product of Denmark, what is necessary is that the thing be produced in Denmark. Structural and functional considerations are here simply beside the point.

Consider now the kind "sibling." What criteria does a thing need to satisfy in order to be a sibling? Well, it needs to have a brother or sister, of course. But what does that mean? It means that it needs to be a child of parents who have another (living) child. This looks like another instance of genetic criteria of belongingness, but it isn't quite. What is important here is not the particular genesis but rather the relation of co-genesis. In order to be a sibling, a child must stand in a specific relation to some other child—namely, the relation of having the same origin (i.e., the same parentage). The kind "sibling," in short, has what I shall call "relational" criteria of belongingness.

Rather than speaking of sorts of criteria of belongingness, of course, we can take the shortcut of using different sorts of criteria as labels for different sorts of kinds. Thus, for example, we can say, in this abbreviatory idiom, that "sugar cube" is a structural kind; "magnet," a functional kind; "product of Denmark," a genetic kind; and "sibling," a relational kind.

To be sure, not all kinds of things or entities have criteria of belongingness which are as clean-cut and tidy as the examples we have been considering. In particular, various natural kinds will typically be determined by a variety of different sorts of criteria of belongingness. Thus, for instance, something's being a common domestic cat—a member of the biological species *felis catus* (or *felis domesticus*)—will depend upon a complex interplay of structural, functional, genetic, and relational criteria of belongingness. Indeed, biological taxonomics is such a subtle and complicated business that it is quite as much an art as it is a science. Species lines may initially be roughly drawn by using purely structural (anatomical) criteria, but a precise and fully adequate determination will need to take into account evolutionary ancestry, breeding populations, fertility of offspring, geographical distributions, and numerous other facts and factors which it is the business of a qualified taxonomist—and, fortunately, not an analytic philosopher—to know about. A biological species is a structural cum functional, genetic, and relational kind, and such criterial complexity infects the notions of even such simpler natural kinds as, for example, the various chemical elements.

Even taking into account these dimensions of complexity, however, we have not yet begun to cover the ground. There is, in fact, a whole other family of criteria of belongingness which we have not yet even caught a glimpse of, and, correspondingly, a whole other family of sorts of kinds which we have yet to discuss. That, indeed, is what I want to talk about next.

4.4: LICENSED DRIVERS AND LEGAL CITIZENS

Consider, to begin with, the kind "driver's license." What criteria need a thing satisfy in order to be a driver's license? The question is a puzzling one. It seems clear enough that structural criteria of belongingness are not what we need here. It may be the case that driver's licenses are typically small rectangular pieces of paper or cardboard or, perhaps, plastic, but there is nothing about the kind "driver's license" which requires this. A driver's license could equally well be a bit of metal looking like a Phi Beta Kappa key, or even a number tattooed on a person's forehead.

Nor do functional criteria of belongingness seem to be to the point here. To be sure, a person typically needs to be able to do certain things in order to obtain a driver's license. But there is nothing which a thing needs to be able to do in order to be a driver's license. It is not the performance capabilities of the bit of plastic-laminated cardboard in my wallet which make it a driver's license. My plastic-laminated Social Security card has the same performance capabilities, and it is not a driver's license.

We could continue in this vein for quite a while, of course, but it ought, by now, to be clear that we are looking in the wrong sort of place. What, after all, is a driver's license? To put the answer into a nice compact formula: A driver's license is something which is recognized as signifying that its bearer has a certain legal status. Specifically, it is something which is recognized as signifying that its bearer is a licensed driver. To get a handle on the kind "driver's license," then, let's take a look at the kind "licensed driver."

What criteria does a thing—a person—need to satisfy in order to be a licensed driver? There are lots of wrong answers. To begin with, a person does not need to be able to drive. True, the typical licensed driver is able to drive, but someone who yesterday was able to drive and who today, in consequence of a stroke, let us suppose, has been left paralyzed and thus unable to drive may still be a licensed driver. Such a person, to be sure, was able to drive. But consider someone who, although unable to drive, successfully bribes the licensing examiner into issuing him a valid driver's license. If the matter ever becomes public, the license will probably immediately be revoked, of course, but, until it is, our briber remains a licensed driver. It begins to look like the best we can do here is to go around in a circle: A licensed driver is simply a person who is the bearer of a valid driver's license. But I think that we can do better than that.

The problem is that we are looking for some matter of fact. But being a licensed driver is not a matter of matters-of-fact. A licensed driver need not be a person who can drive or even ever could drive. A licensed driver is a person who has the legal right to drive. Being a licensed driver is not a matter of matters-of-fact but a matter of rights. "Licensed driver," in short, is a legal kind.

"Licensed driver," of course, is only one among many legal kinds. Other familiar examples include "registered voter," "property owner," and "citizen." In each case, some thing's belonging to this or that legal kind is a matter of rights and obligations or responsibilities. A licensed driver has the right to drive certain sorts of vehicles over public roads and the obligation or responsibility to comply with the laws regulating such activities, that is, with the traffic ordinances. A properly owner has rights of use and disposal for, for instance, a piece of real estate and, correlatively, for example, the obligation or responsibility to pay the relevant ad valorem taxes. Similarly, a citizen is just any entity which is the subject of certain rights and entitlements (e.g., to vote, to run for public office, to have a trial by jury) and of certain obligations, duties, and responsibilities (e.g., to obey the law, to serve in the armed forces, to pay taxes).

Let me pursue the case of the kind "citizen" for a while. The Emperor Caligula, you may recall, made his horse a citizen (indeed, a senator) of Imperial Rome. Given the way that Imperial Rome was organized, curiously enough, he had the right and the power to do so. ("Emperor," too, is a legal kind!) When he did so, the horse became a citizen (and a senator) of Imperial Rome. That is, the horse immediately acquired certain rights (e.g., the right to vote in the Roman Senate). Of course, the poor beast quite obviously lacked the capabilities needed for exercising the rights which it had thereby acquired, but having rights is no more a matter of exercising rights than being a licensed driver is a matter of being able to drive. The two are not, to be sure, unrelated, but the ability to exercise a right is not, for all that, a condition of having it.

Citizenship is what I shall call a "bestowed status." The matter is a little complicated, but important. Let me belabor the case for a while.

Consider a nation—let's call it "Alphabetia"—which is just getting started. How does that happen? Interestingly enough, it happens more or less in this way: Some people get together and start it. Getting it recognized, of course, is a different matter. They may need to fight a successful revolution to accomplish that. But let us suppose that there are no problems about recognition by other nations. What I am interested in is the status of citizenship within our new nation, Alphabetia, abstracting for the moment from international questions.

The way in which a group of people start a new nation is by laying down some specifications. For example, our founders need to lay down some specifications about what the rights and obligations of a citizen of Alphabetia will be. They will also need to lay down some specifications about how Alphabetia will be governed, for the point—or, at least, one point—of having a government is that there be structures and institutions charged with securing and guaranteeing the rights of the citizens and with enforcing their correlative obligations. And, obviously, our founders will need to lay down some specifications about who will be the citizens of Alphabetia, that is, about who will be the subjects of those rights and obligations which it will be the job, at least in part, of the Alphabetian government to protect and enforce.

A typical set of specifications of who will be citizens of Alphabetia looks something like this: First, and necessarily, the founders need to specify that they themselves will be citizens of Alphabetia. Next, they need an initial stock of citizens. Here geographical criteria are usually used. It is specified that all persons (or all white persons, or all black male persons, etc.) residing in such and such a territory as of such and such a date will also be citizens of Alphabetia. Here, again, an opportunity for many complications arises. If the duties of an Alphabetian citizen—e.g., to pay taxes—thereby accruing to some of these folks significantly outstrip their new rights—e.g., to elect representatives to the governing body which sets the tax rates—it might take some convincing, even military convincing, to get them to accept their new citizenship. Thus we might find ourselves with another war on our hands which, depending upon who wins it, will get written up either as another successful revolution or rebellion or as a civil war. In what follows, I want to abstract from such complications as well. Things are already complicated enough.

Once an initial stock of citizens has been established, however, there will need to be some specifications for the creation of new citizens. Here, again, things can get complicated, but there will basically be two ways in which a person can become a citizen of Alphabetia—automatically or voluntarily. A typical specification of the first sort would be that a person is automatically a citizen of Alphabetia if one (or both) of her parents was a citizen at the time of her birth, or if she was born within the geographical boundaries of the nation. Voluntary citizenship, in contrast, typically requires the performance of certain acts ("naturalization proceedings"). A person may need to qualify—for instance, by a period of residence in Alphabetia or by demonstrating an adequate knowledge of Alphabetia's history, laws, and form of government—and she may need to publicly accept the status of a citizen—for example, by "swearing allegiance" to Alphabetia and "renouncing" any other nationality.

The crucial point to all this is that the existence of any Alphabetian citizens requires the existence of a community of persons who count themselves and each other as Alphabetian citizens. This "counting as" is a matter of conduct. The members of such a community count themselves and each other as Alphabetian citizens precisely by acknowledging in practice that each member of the community, oneself included, is the subject of certain rights and entitlements and of certain duties, responsibilities, and obligations—including the obligation to acknowledge and protect the rights and to support and enforce the obligations of others whom one counts as Alphabetian citizens.[4]

It is in this sense that citizenship is a bestowed status. The matter is complicated by the fact that, in a nation which is a going concern, persons become citizens automatically, in virtue of satisfying certain matter-of-factual conditions. There is a sense, in other words, in which one can "discover" that some person is a citizen of Alphabetia. What one can literally discover, however, is only that someone in fact satisfies the conditions for automatic Alphabetian citizenship—e.g., that his birthplace fell within a certain geographical area. This counts as "discovering" his Alphabetian citizenship, however, only because there exists among a community of people who count themselves and others as Alphabetian citizens the practice of automatically granting and protecting certain rights to and imposing and enforcing certain obligations upon all persons who happen to be born within that geographical area.

Once such practices are in place, in other words, it will in fact be the case that all persons born within geographical area X will be citizens of Alphabetia. But it does not follow from this that the concept of a citizen of Alphabetia is, even in part, identical with the concept of a person born in geographical area X. The concept of a citizen of Alphabetia is the concept of a member of a legal kind—that is, of an individual subject of the rights and responsibilities which are criterial for Alphabetian citizenship. But the concept of a person born within geographical area X is the concept of a member of a genetic kind—that is, of an individual having certain origins. These two kinds, legal and genetic, are connected, if at all, not logically or conceptually, but merely as a matter of certain practices. The easiest way of seeing this is by noticing that, although a person cannot alter his place of geographical origin, it may well be the case that he can be "stripped" of his Alphabetian citizenship, have it "revoked," and be "exiled" or "banished." Alphabetian citizenship, then, remains a bestowed status—a legal status, rather than a natural or matter-of-factual condition—even though it is a status which is bestowed automatically upon any person who in fact satisfies some natural or matter-of-factual condition.

By now, you are probably wondering what all these ruminations on citizenship have to do with persons and with death. Well, it turns out that they have quite a bit to do with persons and with death. For they enable me to formulate a central thesis. What I want to argue next, indeed, is this: Like citizenship, personhood is a bestowed status. Now there is, of course, a difference. But the difference is only that, whereas the existence of citizens was a matter of the existence of a community of beings who counted themselves as citizens—that is, acknowledged, protected, and enforced in practice certain civil rights and civic duties—the existence of persons will be a matter of the existence of a community of beings who count themselves and each other as persons. And this "counting as" will also be a matter of acknowledging, protecting, and enforcing certain rights and responsibilities, not now civil rights and civic responsibilities, but rather those which are (somewhat misleadingly) called "human" rights and the cluster of obligations and responsibilities which are collected under the heading "respect" for persons. To put the point in a nutshell, the thesis for which I now propose to argue is that "person" is an ethical kind.

4.5: CONTRA ARISTOTLE

The position which I am taking here parts company with a venerable philosophical tradition. Man, Aristotle is supposed to have said, is a rational animal. If we interpret this as a "definitional" remark, what it amounts to is the thesis that the concept of a person is the concept of a member of a functional kind. As we have already seen, the concept of a rational being is the concept of a being which has the ability or capacity to do certain things—for example, to speak, reason, deliberate, decide, theorize, learn, and so on. In Aristotle's sense of "rational," in short, the rationality of some entity is a matter of its performance capabilities. "Rational being," like "magnet," is a functional kind.

I have replaced Aristotle's "rational animal" with "rational being" in the conviction that what Aristotle was after was the "specialness" of persons. As we have seen, however, this "specialness" is a matter of performance capabilities (in contrast, for instance, to its being a matter of the possession of some special thing, a "mind" or "soul"), and there is nothing in point of logic to prevent some nonanimal—a machine, say—from having and manifesting the same performance capabilities. (Even if, per impossible, a "mind" or "soul" were required for rationality, there would be nothing other than good taste to prevent some deity from issuing one to, say, a machine.) Of course there aren't any rational machines yet, and perhaps there never will be. But since what is criterial for belonging to the kind "rational being" is the possession of a family of performance capabilities, there is no reason, in principle, that there couldn't be.[5] In such a case, indeed, we might see an Aristotelian insistence that 'person' be limited to rational animals as a kind of prejudice or bigotry—"protoplasmic chauvinsim," if you will—of a piece with insisting that only male animals or pink-skinned animals could be persons. A rational machine would be "special" in exactly those relevant ways that a rational animal is "special," and what it is made of—protoplasm or metal—or how it originated—birth or manufacture—should be no more important than what color or size it is or where it originated.

The position which I am taking, however, disagrees with the (implicit) Aristotelian thesis that "person" is a functional kind. One reason that I disagree is that there seem to be clear cases of persons who do not possess the appropriate performance capabilities constitutive of rationality. Included in this group, for example, would be the newborn infants who do not possess the abilities and capacities characteristic of rationality because they haven't developed them yet, and certain comatose or brain-damaged individuals who do not possess these performance capabilities because they have lost them (or even, in the case of genetically brain-damaged individuals, because they never did or could develop them). All of these individuals in fact do not belong to the functional kind "rational being." They cannot do the things which a being must be able to do in order to belong to that kind. But I think it is pretty clear, nevertheless, that newborn infants and certain comatose or brain-damaged individuals are counted as persons. What I conclude, then, is that 'person' does not label the functional kind "rational being."

As matters now stand, I think, only human beings—that is, organisms of the species *homo sapiens*—get counted as persons. There are still no machines which pose a serious question about or challenge to this exclusivity; the Martians or what have you haven't landed yet; and, while certain dolphins and chimpanzees do have their casual advocates, their case has yet to be pressed with any seriousness. So, in fact, only human beings get counted as persons. And for most of us, I think, all human beings get counted as persons.

It has not, alas, always been so. There was a time when only those human beings who, for instance, spoke the right language got counted as persons. The others were dismissed as "barbarians"—"subhuman" creatures whose "language" was only a collection of guttural grunts. Or, with greater poignancy, there was a time not so long ago when only beings who had white skin or "Aryan ancestry" got counted as persons. The ones with black skin or the wrong ancestry were regarded more or less as mere animals—suitable for buying and selling, like draft horses, or, tragically, for mass extermination in the interests of "racial purity."

Nowadays, however, for most of us, all and only human beings get counted as persons. This "counting as" is, again, a matter of practice. To count some being as a person is, I claim, to acknowledge in practice that it is the subject of certain rights—the so-called "human" rights—and, correlatively, to accept in practice one's own obligation and responsibility to respect and protect those rights. It is to agree that there are some things which it is not permitted that one do to this entity—buy it or sell it, for instance, arbitrarily lock it in a cage, or shoot it. To count some being as a person, in short, is to grant to that being the sort of respect and treatment due persons, to acknowledge it as having a certain ethical or moral standing.

Some entity becomes a person, on this view, by being counted as a person by members of a community of individuals who count themselves and each other as persons. And this "counting as" is, again, a matter of acknowledging, protecting, and enforcing certain rights and responsibilities—the so-called "human" rights of all community members, oneself included, and the correlative obligation and responsibility to respect, protect, preserve, defend, and enforce such rights. Just as "citizen" or "licensed driver" or "registered voter" is a legal kind for which being the subject of civil rights and civic duties is criterial, in other words, so similarly "person" is an ethical kind for which being the subject of "human" rights and the moral duties of respect is criterial.

4.6: HUMAN BEINGS, RATIONAL ENTITIES, AND PERSONS

What complicates and obscures the fact that "person" is an ethical kind are the different ways in which the concept of a person interacts with two groups of natural or matter-of-factual conditions. The kind "person," that is, is intimately, although differently, related to two other kinds. What we need to do in order to sort all this out is to distinguish clearly among three concepts:

(H) The structural (cum genetic, relational) concept of an animal belonging to the biological species *homo sapiens*

(R) The functional concept of an entity possessing the "special" performance capabilities of intelligible speech, cogent thought, reliable memory, purposive action, and the like

(P) The ethical (moral) concept of a being who is the subject of rights which one has an enforceable obligation to acknowledge and respect and of enforceable obligations which include the reciprocal acknowledgement and respect of parallel rights and obligations in others

I shall say that (H) is the concept of a human being, (R) of a rational being, and (P) the concept of a person. In our customary thought and practice, these three logically distinguishable concepts are closely interlocked. In the paradigmatic core cases, indeed, they all apply to the same entities. That is, a clear or paradigmatic example of a person is a paradigmatic example of a mature, biologically normal, human being which, in turn, is a paradigmatic example of a competent and functioning rational being. It is outside of this core of clear cases, however, that things begin to get conceptually interesting—and confusing. The reason is that there is a certain subtle tension between what I shall call our "implicit moral theory" and our moral practice.

Our implicit moral theory posits a connection between (P) and (R). Very roughly, it is because some entity is a rational being that it is a fit subject of those rights and responsibilities which are constitutive of personhood. Only a rational being is, so to speak, equipped to exercise or acknowledge (its own and others') rights and to accept or enforce (its own or others') obligations. For the practices or conducts in which such exercises, acknowledgements, acceptances, and enforcements consist are one and all rational practices and conducts—doings which are actualizations and manifestations of the performance capabilities collectively constitutive of rationality.

The connection between (P) and (R) recognized by our implicit moral theory is rather like the connection between being a licensed driver and being able to drive. In theory, being able to drive is a necessary condition, a requirement, of being a licensed driver. One needs, in some sense, to demonstrate one's entitlement to the rights of a licensed driver and one's competence to fulfill the correlative obligations of licensed drivers, and the way in which one does this is by demonstrating one's ability, capacity, or capability to engage in the relevant driving performances. In theory, in other words, the legal status "licensed driver" ought to accrue only to members of the functional kind "qualified driver." In practice, however, the two kinds do come apart. Some licensed drivers are not able to drive, either because they have lost the ability to drive or because they obtained the legal status of licensed driver in some illegitimate way.

The relation between (P) and (R) is like that. Our implicit moral theory holds that the (ethical) status "person" ought to accrue only to members of the functional kind "rational being." (And, what is more, I think, that it ought to accrue to all of them. It is immoral—indeed, reprehensible—to deny some rational entity its "human" rights on such "irrelevant" grounds as that it has the wrong skin-color, religion, ancestry, or sex.) In practice, however, (P) and (R) also come apart. Our moral practice, in fact, is to couple (P) and (H). That is, we bestow the status of personhood automatically on all and only human beings—irrespective of their actual performance capabilities. We count all newborn human infants, however helpless, as persons, and we count brain-damaged, retarded, aphasic, paralyzed, and comatose human beings as persons, again however impaired their actual performance capabilities may in fact be.

The connection between (P) and (H), in other words, is rather like the connection between being a citizen of Alphabetia and having been born in geographical region X. The legal status of citizenship is bestowed automatically upon all individuals born in the relevant geographical region, irrespective of their actual abilities to exercise the rights and fulfill the obligations and responsibilities of an Alphabetian citizen.

It is in consequence of this moral practice that the collection of persons (acknowledged persons) is in fact coextensive with the collection of human beings. But this fact (if it is a fact) does not show that the concept of a person, (P), is identical to the concept of a human being. It may also be a fact (I have, indeed, read that it is) that all and only those organisms with a liver are organisms with kidneys. But this fact—if it is a fact—would not show that the concept of an organism with a liver is identical to the concept of an organism with kidneys. It would not show, that is, that there couldn't be organisms which had a liver but no kidneys or kidneys and no liver. And similarly, the fact (if it is a fact) that all and only human beings get counted as persons does not show that there couldn't be persons (machines or Martians) who were not human beings nor, crucially, that there couldn't be human beings who were not (or even who shouldn't be) regarded as persons.

For our moral practices, such as they are, ought to be justified—or at least, in principle, justifiable—on the basis of our moral theory. Moral practices, that is, ought to be rational practices—i.e., practices for which one could, in principle, give cogent moral reasons. If we ask why, in other words, we should acknowledge only human beings as persons, there ought to be an answer which calls our attention to the right sort of connection between human beings and rational beings, and if we ask why we should acknowledge all human beings as persons, there ought again to be an answer in terms of our (implicit) moral theory, an answer of the same sort. To see whether there are such answers, then, what we need to look at is the relationship between the structural (cum genetic, relational) kind "human being" and the functional kind "rational being," that is, the connection between (H) and (R).

What we find when we do this, however, is that there is no conceptual connection between (H) and (R) at all. All of the rational beings that we in fact know of, to be sure, happen to be animals of the biological species *homo sapiens*. But since the concept of a rational being is the concept of an entity having certain performance capabilities, there is no reason in point of logic that it couldn't be otherwise. When we ask, then, why we should limit personhood—à la Aristotle—only to human beings, our implicit moral theory yields no answer at all. For that moral theory couples the having of "human" rights and the duties of respect to the ability, capacity, or capability to engage in those rational conducts and practices which are exercises of such rights and acceptances of such responsibilities. Counting only human beings as persons, while it is a moral practice which is in fact reasonable in the present circumstances, appears not to be a moral practice which is justifiable theoretically or in principle.

On the other hand, the question of why we should count all human beings as persons fares somewhat better. The answer, however, is not that all human beings are rational beings. As we have seen, this is not in fact the case. There are newborn humans, brain-damaged humans, and comatose humans, for example, all of whom de facto lack the performance capabilities constitutive of rationality. In each of these cases, however, we can still offer some justification in principle for our moral practices. We can argue that the entities to whom we extend the status of personhood in this way, while not themselves rational beings, nevertheless do stand in some special relationship to rationality or to entities which are rational beings. A newborn human infant, for example, is a potentially rational being—unlike, for instance, a newborn dog or fish. And a brain-damaged or comatose human being may be a formerly rational being and even, depending upon the state of future medical technology, a being whose rational capabilities might someday be restored. Most significantly, however, all of these nonrational human beings are, in point of fact, the offspring of beings who are both human and rational persons.

Just as Alphabetian citizenship may be automatically extended to all individuals who are the offspring of Alphabetian citizens, independent of the inability of a newborn infant to exercise the rights and fulfill the obligations of an Alphabetian citizen, in other words, so, too, the ethical or moral status of personhood may be—and, indeed, is—automatically bestowed upon all individuals who are the offspring of acknowledged persons, independent of their abilities to exercise the rights and fulfill the obligations of a person as such. The ethical status of personhood, in short, is transmitted across the matter-of-factual relationship of parenthood. The parent-child relationship is given a special moral status vis-à-vis the concept of a person.

There are a variety of good (theoretical) moral reasons for doing this. One, for example, is that human parents are generally concerned about the treatment of their offspring. Respect for this parental concern is part of the general respect due those parents as acknowledged persons and, thus, arguably part of the family of responsibilities belonging to the concept of a person. Another reason, of course, is that membership in the biological species *homo sapiens* at birth is a pretty reliable indicator of the eventual development of those rational capacities which are conceptually connected to the ethical kind "person."

More central than either of these reasons, however, is the fact that human beings as a species form a homogeneous breeding population. This fact suffices to render any subdivision of the collection of human beings into persons and nonpersons on structural—e.g., racial—grounds morally arbitrary. Racial interbreeding, for instance, produces a continuum of, say, skin colors, in which any cut—conceptually disconnected as it must be from considerations of rational capabilities—becomes no more defensible on moral grounds than any other. Analogously, the development of rational capabilities in individual organisms is also a matter of degree and gives rise to a parallel continuum. The young human being does not acquire rational competences suddenly and all at once, but gradually and piecemeal. Any cut in this continuum which supposedly marked the boundary between nonpersonhood and personhood, then, would be, like a cut in the continuum of skin colors, morally arbitrary and, to that extent, morally indefensible. The only theoretically justifiable moral practice in this case, then, is to recognize human beings as persons, that is, as fit subjects of "human" rights and objects of the respect due persons, from birth on. (This is not to deny, however, that developmental facts about the gradual acquisition of rational capabilities do yield legitimate moral grounds for constraining the full exercise of "human" rights—e.g., to self-determination—by immature members of the species. An analogous case is the differential granting of legal rights and responsibilities up to an "age of majority," a practice which is rationally defensible in spite of the fact that the selection of an "age of majority" is, within certain limits, somewhat arbitrary.)

While there are no good reasons in principle to limit the ethical status of personhood only to human beings, then, (although in fact only human beings are, as far as we know, currently viable "candidates" for that status), there are good moral reasons for extending this ethical status to all human beings, irrespective of their actual rational performance capabilities. And yet, although there are good moral reasons for doing this, there do not seem to be any conclusive moral reasons for doing this. It is, in other words, a question on which reasonable individuals can—and sometimes do—differ. And this observation, indeed, brings us to the threshold of our discussion of the ethics of death.

4.7: A FEW FINE POINTS . . .

Before proceeding to the topic of the ethics of death, however, I need to repair several oversimplifications which have been with us since the outset of this study. They arise, in essence, from one fact: In the earlier sections of my discussion, I have used the term 'person' not only as a label for the ethical kind "person," but also as a blanket term to cover the natural kind "human being" and the functional kind "rational being" as well. While no actual distortions of substance in fact resulted from this practice, some potentially significant matters of detail were, indeed, blurred, and it is probably worth our time to pause for a moment and unblur them.

I wrote, for example, that the "specialness" of persons consisted in their having certain performance capabilities—the abilities or capacities, for instance, to experience, to reason, to communicate, to remember, to learn, to plan, and to deliberately act. This is not false, but it is potentially misleading. It is not false because those persons who are "special" are so by virtue of also belonging to the functional kind "rational being" and, as we have seen, the possession of certain performance capabilities is criterial for a thing's belonging to that (functional) kind. It is misleading, however, insofar as it suggests, first, that all persons are "special" in just these ways—a conclusion which the examples of newborns, the brain-damaged, and the comatose have shown to be false—and, second, that being "special" in these ways is criterial for belonging to the ethical kind "person"—a thesis against which I have just argued.

Again, in defending the thesis that death is a change of kind, I wrote that a person becomes a corpse, which is not a person. This claim, too, is not false—but it, too, has the potential to mislead. For we are now in the position to see that it collapses into a single thesis two quite different sorts of considerations. One of these turns on matters which are, so to speak, criterial for or "definitional" of death, while the other, in contrast, takes note of certain moral practices which come into play as a consequence of death. Death, to put the point briefly, is a change of natural kind which both rests upon a functional change in performance capabilities and has ethical consequences.

What, in the first instance and speaking literally, changes into or becomes a corpse upon its death is a member of the natural kind "human being." A human being, we recall, is a member of the biological species *homo sapiens*. Like all biological species, *homo sapiens* constitutes what is basically a structural kind, whose criteria of belongingness, however, also has genetic, relational, and functional elements. The functional components of the criteria of belongingness for the natural kind "human being" are what we particularly need to focus on here. The key point is that they include those syntropic performance capabilities, criterial for life, in the loss of which death, as an event, consists.

To put it compactly, one requirement which an entity must satisfy in order to belong to the biological species *homo sapiens*—and thus to the kind "human being"—is that it be an animal, and one requirement which an entity must, in turn, satisfy in order to belong to the kind "animal" is that it be a living organism. A being which has permanently and irreversibly lost syntropic capacity, then, and which consequently no longer is a living organism, is therefore also no longer a member of any biological species and, in particular, also no longer a human being. What such a being is, in fact, is only the remains of a member of some biological species—in particular, the remains of a human being. The remains of an animal are, to be sure, intimately related to the animal whose remains they are—but this intimate relation is, once again, not identity. It is, in point of fact, a relation which is generated or brought into being precisely by a change of kind. The corpse or remains of an animal are what that animal has changed into or become.

To say that the corpse of a human being is not a person, however, is to make quite a different sort of remark. It is, roughly, to say that, although all human beings are persons—that is, our (justifiable) practice is to count them as members of the ethical kind "person"—this moral or ethical status is not transmitted across the (unique, special, intimate) relationship which obtains between a human being and the corpse which, upon its death, it changes into or becomes.

The interesting observation now is that it could be. Just as Caligula's horse could be a citizen and a senator of Imperial Rome, although lacking the performance capabilities required to exercise the rights and fulfill the obligations of Roman citizenship and senatorial office, so, too, the corpse of a human being could be counted as a person. That is, our moral practice could be that of treating corpses as subjects of the full range of "human" rights and duties of respect, even though a corpse is incapable of the rational performances required to exercise those rights and fulfill those responsibilities—indeed, incapable of any performances whatsoever. Although it would be an exceedingly odd thing for us to do, in other words, just as we do automatically bestow personhood upon the offspring of persons, we could also automatically grant personhood to the remains of persons.[6]

I think that there have been—and perhaps there still are—cultures and societies in which this was, indeed, the customary practice. Ours is not one of them. Nevertheless, it is instructive to notice that we do, in practice, assign some special moral status to the corpse of a human being. This is shown, for example by the fact that it is possible to *desecrate* a person's corpse. Although there are many things which one is morally permitted to do to a corpse that one is not permitted to do to a living human person, it is not the case that one is morally licensed to do anything at all to a person's corpse. Ethically speaking, one may burn a corpse or bury it, for example, but one may not, in contrast, mutilate it or eat it. Like human beings, then, the corpses of human beings are due a certain respect—although not, of course, the full measure of respect for "human rights" due a (living) person.

The permanent and irreversible loss of syntropic capabilities which is the death of a living member of the species *homo sapiens*, then, is a functional change which constitutes a change of natural kind—from a human being to the remains of a human being—and which, in consequence of our moral practices, also results in a simultaneous change of ethical kind—from a person to a person's corpse (for, as we have just seen, "person's corpse" is itself an independent ethical kind, characterized by certain rights of treatment and duties of respect of its own).

There are, of course, good moral reasons for coupling this particular functional change automatically to a change in ethical or moral status, just as there were good moral reasons for coupling membership in the natural kind "human being" automatically to membership in the ethical kind "person." The essential point is that the permanent and irreversible loss of syntropic capabilities on the part of a human organism entails the permanent and irreversible loss of any and all rational performance capabilities as well. Since our implicit moral theory acknowledges a conceptual connection between rationality and the rights and duties criterial for personhood (analogous to the connection which ought to obtain between being a qualified driver and being a licensed driver), the moral practice of withholding the full measure of such rights and duties from entities which have suffered a permanent and irreversible loss of functional capabilities—in consequence of which indeed, they no longer even belong to a natural kind any of whose members possess rational capabilities—is a morally justifiable practice (just as revoking the license of a person who will never again be able to drive is a legally justifiable practice).

It is important to appreciate the force of this last remark. The point is not simply that the remains of a human being aren't themselves a rational being. The crucial point is that such remains no longer belong to the natural kind "human being" at all, a natural kind whose members could also belong to the functional kind "rational being." Withholding the ethical status of "person" from human remains—despite the fact that they are the remains of what was a rational living organism—is thus as morally justified, to take an absurd example, as withholding the ethical status of "person" from a croissant—despite the fact that it will be eaten by a rational living organism—for a corpse is no more a kind of entity which could itself be a rational being than is a croissant.

It is for this reason that the special relationship between a human being and its remains differs significantly from the special relationship between a human being and its offspring in its capacity to transmit the moral status of personhood. The offspring of human beings are also human beings and, thus, although they themselves lack at birth the rational performance capabilities which our implicit moral theory conceptually links to the ethical status of personhood, they do belong to a natural kind, "human being," members of which paradigmatically do possess such rational performance capabilities. The remains of human beings, however, are not also human beings. It thus makes moral sense to withhold automatically in the latter case an ethical status which is automatically bestowed in the former, even though the relationship between human beings and their remains is every bit as "unique" or "special" or "intimate" as the relationship between human beings and their offspring. Only human beings have human children—and only human beings become human remains.[7]

4.8: . . .AND A WORD ABOUT DEATH CERTIFICATES

We can now profitably return one last time to the claim that "fixing the moment of death" is not a theoretical or scientific question but rather a practical, legal, and moral question. What is at issue in such proceedings, we can now say with more precision, is the establishing of a determinate ethical status, the settling of a question of some entity's ethical kind—"person" or "person's corpse." And this, in turn, makes it clear why "fixing the moment of death" is not a theoretical or scientific matter, for ethical status—what is criterial for belonging to this or that ethical kind—is not, as we have seen, determined by the satisfaction of any matter-of-factual conditions but is entirely a question of moral practices. An entity becomes a person by being counted as a person by members of a community who count themselves and each other as persons. While this requires, to be sure, that such community members by and large themselves possess the performance capabilities constitutive of rationality, it does not require that the entity upon whom personhood is thus bestowed itself possess such rational capacities, any more than Caligula's horse needed the abilities requisite for its casting a vote in order to become a senator of Imperial Rome.

The question which confronts a panel of experts trying to settle upon decisive criteria for "fixing the moment of death," then, is not: Does the loss of these or those functional capacities imply the loss of the moral status of personhood? For no matter-of-factual observations of the functional capacities of some entity imply anything about membership in some ethical kind all by themselves—that is, apart from extant moral practices. The question confronting such a panel is the much more difficult one: Would the practice of withdrawing the full ethical status of personhood from an entity which manifested loss of syntropic capacity in this or that particular way be a morally justifiable or morally defensible practice? And, while an answer to this question turns upon the answers to many matter-of-factual, theoretical, and scientific questions, this is not itself a theoretical or scientific question but rather a practical and moral one—a question of the justifiability or defensibility of some specific conducts or doings.

As I argued a moment ago, there are considerations which can be adduced in support of the claim that the practice of withdrawing the ethical status of personhood from human remains is morally justifiable and defensible. The total and irreversible loss of syntropic abilities or capacities entails a loss of membership in the natural kind, "human being," to which, at present, all and only acknowledged persons belong. Since such a loss of life also entails the permanent and irreversible loss of all rational performance capabilities as well, there is nothing in our (implicit) moral theory to suggest the contrary practice or transmitting the status of personhood across this change of natural kind and extending the boundaries of the ethical kind "person" beyond the collection of human beings to encompass human remains as well. The prima facie moral case for withdrawing personhood from corpses, in other words, is undefeated by competing moral principles or arguments—and that is enough to show that the practice which it recommends is morally justifiable.

Matter-of-factual criteria for "fixing the moment of death" are thus needed only to secure the conclusion that a permanent and irreversible loss of syntropic capabilities (a loss of the sort which entails a change of natural kind) has indeed occurred. Since what is ultimately at issue in such a determination is a question of moral or ethical standing, however, what are needed in the way of criteria are not considerations which address theoretical niceties but rather criteria which yield moral certainty. For our overriding commitment to protect and enforce the "human" rights of persons demands that, if we err, we err only on the side of conservatism. Fixing "the moment of death" too early—and thus treating some still-living human persons as if they were mere corpses—has morally deplorable consequences. Fixing "the moment of death" too late—and thus treating some human remains as if they were living persons—does not.

It follows that what are wanted by way of criteria for "fixing the moment of death" are clear and unmistakeable signs of a complete, permanent, and irreversible loss of syntropic capabilities, not a detailed, moment-by-moment determination of the transient microstates of the dying entity. And it follows, too, that there is nothing more to be discovered about the "moment of death." Our technologies of measurement are already sufficiently advanced to yield determinations finer than could ever be useable to arrive at a verdict about loss of syntropic capacity with any greater moral confidence than we can already presently attain.

I add here, parenthetically, a remark about the so-called "death certificate." On the view which I have just been presenting and defending, a death certificate does not, essentially and primarily, testify to any matter-of-factual occurrence. A death certificate is rather more like a driver's license. Just as a driver's license is something which is recognized as signifying that its bearer has a certain legal status, so, similarly, a death certificate is something which is recognized as signifying that the entity for whom it is issued has a certain moral status (and, therefore, also a certain legal status). It signifies that the entity for whom it is issued belongs to the ethical kind "person's corpse" rather than the ethical kind "person"—and that it is therefore morally and legally permissible to treat that entity in practice as human remains, rather than human beings, are treated.

In theory, of course, a death certificate ought to be issued for some entity only if that entity has satisfied the matter-of-factual conditions regarded as criterial for a total and permanent loss of syntropic capabilities, just as in theory a driver's license ought to be issued only to individuals who have demonstrated their competence to drive (by passing certain tests, for example). But a death certificate is no more a report that such matter-of-factual conditions have been satisfied than a driver's license is a report that a person has passed his driving tests. Rather a death certificate signifies that the entity for whom it has been issued has a moral and legal status which is only legitimately awarded to beings which do satisfy the appropriate matter-of-factual conditions, just as a driver's license signifies that its bearer has a legal standing which is only legitimately awarded to persons who have passed the requisite tests—whether or not the matter-of-factual conditions have actually been satisfied or the driving tests actually passed. A legal document can testify to certain matters of fact if legitimate—but no document can testify to its own legitimacy.

CHAPTER 5

Values and Rights:
Moral Preliminaries

5.0: THE PROJECT AND THE STRATEGY

Using the apparatus of linguistic, logical, and conceptual distinctions that we have developed, it is now finally possible to begin to say something about those topics which are the main foci of most contemporary discussions of the ethics of death—euthanasia, the artificial prolongation of life, and the rationality of suicide or, as they are often tagged, "mercy killing," "allowing to die," and "death with dignity." What it falls within the province of analytic philosophy to do here, however, is not to recommend any answers to these disputed questions. Rather, my attempt here will be only to provide a framework of concepts and distinctions in terms of which such disputes may be usefully structured. I shall try, that is, to attain a certain measure of clarity about what the questions in fact are, about what sorts of matters are here at issue, and about what sorts of considerations would be relevant to resolving points genuinely in dispute. (And sometimes, of course, it may turn out that there are no points genuinely in dispute, and, in such a case, we will arrive at what can be called an "answer," that is, at a way of putting the supposed question behind us and ceasing to be plagued by it.)

To put it slightly differently, my purpose here is chiefly to provide a framework for making sense of contemporary reflections on the ethics of death, not definitively to resolve disputed questions or to mediate disagreements or to recommend any specific policies or practices. I will be concerned primarily with the conceptual interplay between moral and matter-of-factual convictions. To this end, we will require a grasp, not only of specific facts, but also of the values which interact with those facts. I shall therefore undertake, first, to offer a brief exposition of what I have been calling "our

126

implicit moral theory"—that is, an unfolding of a family of moral concepts and principles which, I shall argue, implicitly underlie not only our actual moral practices but also our debates over the justifiability of specific practices.

In conducting this exposition, I will be advancing various moral theses concerning rights, freedoms, and values. I want to make it clear, however, that I will not be arguing for these diverse moral theses. Although I do believe them to be eminently defensible, I will not, on this occasion, be defending them. What I will be claiming, on the other hand, is that it is this morality, this system of values and principles, which is more or less explicitly reflected in our undisputed moral practices and more or less explicitly presupposed in disputes over the ethics of euthanasia and the artificial prolongation of life, and that it is therefore in terms of this morality that the various conflicting stands on these issues should be structured and understood. My exposition, in other words, is intended to equip us with the outlines of a moral point of view which in some sense is our (fairly widely subscribed to, tacitly held) moral point of view–a morality which is in itself plausible; which arguably makes coherent sense of our moral practices in those instances where such practices are themselves relatively clear, widespread, and not seriously in dispute; and which renders intelligible the specific views and arguments that we in fact find advanced in those instances where our moral practices are unsettled and subject to disagreement and debate.[1]

Finally, following this exposition, I shall argue that, if we understand our moral practices as arising from and intended to be justifiable by appeals to the principles of this (implicit) moral theory, then we can usefully reconstruct the various conflicting positions, arguments, and considerations advanced in discussions of the ethics of death in a way which brings out what is essentially at issue and what is only peripherally relevant (if at all) to the points in dispute.

5.1: A CONTINUUM OF COMPETENCES

What will chiefly concern us when we return to the topic of death will be the connections between ethical principles, on the one hand, and the competences of some entity—its powers, abilities, and capacities—on the other. A reasonable first step, then, is to explore the structure of relationships obtaining among various of these capabilities in and of themselves. And what we discover first is that, considered in the order of causal dependency, the functional capabilities of living organisms form a rough continuum.

At one end of this continuum we find life itself, that is, the self-sustaining syntropic powers of an entity to preserve and increase its structural organization (upon which these functional capacities, in turn, themselves causally depend) through a variety of transactions with its environment. This syntropic capability, in turn, is itself causally requisite for the various functional capacities which cluster under the heading "sentience." These capacities range from marginal cases of mere sensitivity to external stimuli (exhibited, for example, by a plant which turns tropistically to follow the sun) across the sort of sensory awareness of its surroundings exhibited by a dog or cat or bird all the way to the full-fledged conceptually structured experiences of a normal mature human being. Finally, causally dependent upon such sentience, we have a collection of rational capabilities which is itself structured as a family of continua of competences—of communication (from mere signaling to conversation and disputation), of action (from mere goal-directedness to the intentional execution of elements of a complex, deliberately conceived plan), and of intelligence (from the mere environmental appropriateness of behavior across the ability to learn from experience all the way to capacities for abstract conceptualization and the construction of instrumentally effective explanatory theories).

These functional capabilities, of course, overlap, and each of them is itself a matter of degree. But, by and large, they do form something of an evolutionary progression of increasing functional complexity, echoing roughly the classical "Great Chain of Being"[2]:

. . . . . LIFE					. . . . . SENTIENCE
viruses,	algae,	ferns,	carrots,	sunflowers,	insects

		. . . . . RATIONALITY		
fish,	horses,	dogs,	apes,	human beings

Now what is basically at issue both in questions concerning the artificial prolongation of life and in questions concerning euthanasia is how it is morally (and legally) permissible to treat human beings who are suffering from various kinds and degrees of functional impairments, that is, from diminished capabilities. A normal mature member of the species *homo sapiens* possesses well-developed versions of all three sorts of functional capabilities—the syntropic capacities characteristic of life, the responsive capacities characteristic of sentience, and the complex behavioral and interactive capacities constitutive of rationality—as well as many other capabilities, e.g., the power of self-movement (motility). Any of these functional capabilities, however, may be impaired, to a greater or lesser degree, independent of any of the others.

Organic damage or damage to the autonomic nervous system, for example, can result in an impairment of syntropic capabilities while leaving sentient and rational functions intact. A human being, for instance, may lose the capacity for such subfunctions of overall syntropic capability as respiration, circulation, or the elimination of toxic waste. In such a case, it becomes unable to sustain life on its own—that is, it loses independent or autonomous syntropic capability.

There was a time, of course, when such functional impairment inevitably resulted in—and thus was tantamount to—a complete loss of life, that is, permanent and irreversible loss of all syntropic capability. An increasingly sophisticated interventionist medical technology, however, has rendered many of these functional impairments to syntropic capacity correctable con-

ditions. That is, we have become capable of constructing interactive systems—human being + iron lung, human being + pacemaker, and human being + dialysis machine, for example—which possess as systems the full syntropic capacities lacked by their human components considered in isolation. It is in such instances that we speak of "artificially aided" respiration and circulation, for example, and, more generally, of "artificially sustained" life.

Again, damage specific to sensory organs or systems can result in impairments of sentient capabilities which leave both syntropic and rational functioning undisturbed. Such cases of impaired sentience range from mild examples of bad eyesight or poor hearing—again more or less correctable by the use of eyeglasses or hearing aids—to total and irreversible losses of whole subcapacities of sentience, as in cases of blindness and deafness which lie outside the reach of current medical technology.

Finally, damage to portions of the brain and various sorts of genetic deficiencies can result in impairments of rational capacities which leave both syntropic and sentient functioning essentially intact. Here, too, we find a range of cases and a continuum of degrees, encompassing, for example, various sorts of aphasia and agnosia and various levels of what is somewhat unfortunately called "mental retardation."

The causal dependencies upon which the progression sketched above rests, then, are revealed clearly only in cases in which the loss of functional capacity is global and complete. While a profoundly retarded or, say, autistic individual (or, for that matter, a perfectly normal insect or fish) may lack all rational capabilities although undergoing no impairment of sentience, the converse is not true. A complete loss of sentience—as, for instance, in the case of an individual in profound coma—entails as well a complete loss of those functional capabilities constitutive of rationality. And, analogously, while such a nonsentient comatose individual (or, for that matter, a perfectly normal carrot or fern) may retain a full measure of undisturbed syntropic capabilities, the complete loss of syntropic capacity of course entails a complete loss of both rational and sentient functional capabilities as well—and, indeed, as we have seen, a loss of the status "living organism," that is, a change of (natural) kind.

5.2: FOUR KINDS OF RIGHTS

What is important for our present discussions is the fact that our implicit moral theory attaches values to these various functional capabilities and, what is more, it attaches these values (roughly, more or less, with exceptions, and with some individual and cultural variance) "from the top down." What this means, to formulate the point more usefully, is that, generally and for the most part, the more such functional capabilities an entity (of a kind) possesses and manifests, the greater the scope and strength of the rights which that (kind of) entity enjoys, and the more compelling our moral responsibility not arbitrarily to abrogate those rights in practice but, instead, to acknowledge, respect, support, further, and enforce them.

The sort of rights which are important here are what I shall call "passive rights"—the rights of a being to be regarded and treated in certain ways. Passive rights are not rights to do something but rights to have something done or not to have something done to or for the entities whose rights they are. What I shall call "active rights," in contrast, are precisely rights to do something. An active right is a right which can be exercised in conduct by those beings who have it. A passive right, on the other hand, is a right to be respected by others. It is not exercised in the conducts of the being whose right it is, but rather exercised—or, perhaps better, reflected—in the conducts of those others who have the moral duty to respect it. An active right enhances its bearer's freedom of action. A passive right, however, constrains the actions of others vis-à-vis its bearer. It sets moral boundaries to what they must do for or may do to its bearer, and it implies a moral obligation binding upon those others not to transgress such boundaries.

This distinction between active and passive rights must be carefully separated from another, the distinction between what I shall call "positive" and "negative" rights. A newborn infant, for example, has a right to have certain things done for it—to be fed, clothed, sheltered, cared for medically, and so on. Correlatively, the parents of such a newborn incur a moral obligation to respect these rights, that is, to do these things or to see to it, as best they can, that someone does them.

A normally developed human adult, in contrast, has none of these rights vis-à-vis any specific other persons. There is no one in particular who is morally obligated to feed, clothe, shelter, and provide medical care for such an individual. A normal adult, however, nevertheless does share with a newborn infant certain rights not to have various things done to it—not to be tortured, deliberately injured, incarcerated, sold into slavery, or killed, for example—and everyone else has a correlative obligation to respect these rights. That is, everyone has severally a moral duty not to do such things to this (or to any other) person, and a responsibility to see to it—as best they can—that no one else does them to anyone else either. All of the rights which I have just been enumerating are passive rights—rights to be respected by others, rather than rights to be exercised by their bearers—but the rights exclusive to the newborn infant are primarily positive—that is, they enjoin positive action on the part of specific others—whereas the rights shared by the adult and the infant are essentially negative—that is, they enjoin others in general to refrain from various conducts.[3]

5.3: A PHENOMENOLOGY OF MORAL PRACTICE

It is negative passive rights which our implicit moral theory correlates (roughly) with functional capacities. Such rights are thus most extensive in the case of rational beings. Indeed, the negative passive rights which our moral theory couples with possession of that cluster of functional capacities constitutive of rationality just are (a large portion of) those distinctively "human" rights, the having of which is criterial for belonging to the ethical kind "person." As we have already remarked in the cases of the adult and the infant, these rights include a broad set of protections from threats to one's or-

ganic integrity (torture, willful injury, imposed starvation, and, of course, death) and a broad set of protections from arbitrary constraints on independent action (slavery or summary imprisonment, for example).

When we move down the scale of functional complexity to merely sentient and nonrational beings, however, what we find is—again generally, but with exceptions—a systematic narrowing of these rights. Thus, for example, unlike human beings, pets and livestock may, morally speaking, legitimately be bought and sold and arbitrarily kept confined in pens, cages, or corrals. And while torture and deliberate mutilation are still morally proscribed, the deliberate killing of merely sentient animals is widely morally condoned, although with a variety of reservations and restrictions. The killing of animals for food is widely regarded as morally permissible—vegetarians and orthodox Hindus being notable exceptions to this practice—but the wanton killing of animals is almost universally looked upon as morally unacceptable conduct, while killing for such "marginal" purposes as sport occupies a grey area somewhere in between. In all cases, however, there is a moral demand that the animals in question be put to death "humanely," and even the most enthusiastic of sport hunters recognize some moral obligation to try for a "clean kill" and to track down and "finish off" animals which they have only wounded.[4]

The urgency of such strictures, however, falls off fairly dramatically as we move down the scale of functional complexity. The arbitrary killing of snakes and frogs, for instance, evokes little of the moral censure attaching to similar practices with respect to, say, squirrels and rabbits. Hunting for sport may be morally suspect, but sport fishing is surely less so. Many ideological vegetarians who exclude meat and poultry from their diets on moral grounds have no compunctions about using fish and seafood as sources of protein. And it is a rare person indeed who feels any moral qualms about swatting a disturbing fly or mosquito or poisoning the cockroaches infesting his kitchen.

When we drop below the level of sentience, to plants for example, a whole dimension of moral considerations simply falls away. There is, as far as I know, no one who has ever advocated that corn or tomatoes be harvested "humanely" or who would urge a farmer to go back and "finish off" the wheat stalks which his inefficient reaper had only "wounded." Nor do we find expressions of moral outrage–or even reservations–at the wanton slaughter of bacteria which results from the use of antibiotics.

These, then, are our moral practices. What we must ask next is: What does the acceptability of these practices reveal about our moral principles? To put it another way, what values are we furthering or protecting by circumscribing our actions in the world in these ways?

5.4: TWO KINDS OF INTRINSIC VALUE

All of these observations fall into place, I believe, if we think of our implicit moral theory as acknowledging two sorts of intrinsic value—a (positive) center of intrinsic worth and a (negative) center of intrinsic disvalue. By speaking of "intrinsic" value, I mean to call attention to the fact that our implicit morality treats some things as good or bad "in themselves," not as means to some further good or bad ends (which would be "instrumental" value). The negative passive rights which I have been enumerating, I want to suggest, function within our moral practice instrumentally as protections or guarantees of freedom with respect to matters of intrinsic value—the positive freedom to actualize in the world whatever is of intrinsic worth and the negative freedom from the actuality of whatever would be of intrinsic disvalue.

When we ask, then, what it is which is implicitly regarded, positively or negatively, as being of intrinsic value, one of the answers seems to be relatively straightforward. The one thing which is (most widely, implicitly) regarded as "bad in itself," I think, is pretty clearly suffering. The causing of suffering appears to be something for which one may always demand a moral justification. And while imposed suffering can sometimes be justified on moral grounds (as, for instance, "the lesser of two evils"—an undesirable means to the end of preventing the occurrence of something even more undesirable), its being in this way sometimes a right thing to do (morally permissible) in no way makes it a good thing to do (morally desirable). Other things being equal (as, alas, they almost never are), suffering is something which one has a permanent and standing moral obligation to attempt to minimize.

It is much less obvious, however, what it is that our implicit moral theory regards as being of positive intrinsic value, that is, of intrinsic worth. I want to propose a candidate for this status, one for which I will argue, however, only more or less indirectly, by attempting to show that my hypothesis concerning intrinsic worth indeed makes sense of much of our moral practice and moral reasoning which otherwise would be puzzling, opaque, and sometimes even unintelligible. To put the hypothesis briefly, what I propose is that the one thing which is (most widely, implicitly) regarded as "good in itself " is the exercise of moral autonomy, that is, the deliberate actions of a being in pursuit of what it believes (rightly or wrongly) to be the morally right thing to do.

This hypothesis has the virtue of explaining very simply why it is that the negative passive rights accorded in practice to rational beings are so much more extensive than those accorded to merely sentient beings—a practice which would be at least puzzling if all that were ultimately at stake in our implicit morality were the values attaching to pains and pleasures.[5] Only a rational being, however, could actualize in its conduct instances of the exercise of moral autonomy. That is, only a rational being could act for reasons and, thus, only such a being could do what it does because it believes, (rightly or wrongly) that is the morally right thing to do.

The hypothesis also has a second virtue to commend it. It explains as well our characteristic interest in the epistemic and motivational states of an agent whose conduct is being subjected to moral scrutiny. We may deplore the consequences of some action as disastrous or laud them as beneficial, but our moral assessment of the agent does not turn solely on the nature of those consequences. What we need to know to appraise the agent's moral status is whether those consequences were foreseen or intended. We need to know his reasons for doing whatever it was that he did—whether he knew or believed that those disastrous or beneficial consequences could result from his conduct and whether he desired or intended those consequences to take place—and we assign moral praise and blame on the basis of our assessment of those reasons, commending (or at least excusing) the agent who acts (however ineptly) out of good will and in the interests of moral rectitude and censuring (or at least dismissing) the agent who acts (however beneficially) out of narrow self-interest and greed.

If I am basically correct in my proposal, then, ethical protection from arbitrary constraints on independent action (slavery or summary imprisonment, for example), common to the rights of both adult and infant but lacking in the case of merely sentient animals, should be thought of as being morally justified essentially as guarantors of the freedom to act for moral reasons, that is to say, as guarantors of the very possibility of realizing a situation of intrinsic worth through such action.

Both rational and merely sentient beings, however, are capable of suffering, and thus both rational and merely sentient beings share negative passive rights to freedoms from the deliberate and arbitrary imposition of such suffering. The protections from torture, mutilation, starvation, and the like which are embodied in these rights should be viewed in this light as guarantors of the freedom from arbitrarily imposed suffering, and should be understood as morally justified essentially on the grounds that they thereby decrease the likelihood of realizing a situation of intrinsic disvalue in the world.[6]

5.5: WHY LIFE ITSELF IS NOT A VALUE

The understanding of the fundamental value structure of our implicit moral theory at which we have arrived has immediate and important consequences concerning the moral status which that theory assigns to the condition of life itself (that is, to an organism's independent syntropic capabilities). The crucial point is that the condition of life does not itself have the status of an intrinsic good. If I am correct, in other words, our most widespread and customary implicit morality is not an ethics of "reverence for life" (as such). The value, if any, which attaches to the functional capacities criterial for life, then, is instrumental value. Life itself is morally important to us, not as a matter of intrinsic worth (or, for that matter, disvalue), but as an indispensable condition of realizing either intrinsic worth or intrinsic disvalue in the world. The syntropic functional capabilities criterial for life, as things now stand, are causally necessary prerequisites of both rationality and mere sentience—and thus of both the very possibility of the exercise of moral autonomy and the very possibility of suffering.

This outlook is confirmed by, and in turn explains, the almost universal moral indifference attached to the treatment of merely living organisms, e.g., plants. Although life is, in the world as we know it, a causally necessary condition of both rationality and mere sentience, it is a sufficient condition of neither. The mere presence of life in entities of a kind which otherwise possesses neither the further capacity for suffering nor the capability of autonomous action (even potentially), then, ought properly to be without moral import—and so, for the most part, it is. For the most part, we do not regard plants as having any rights—not even those negative passive rights which require no abilities to exercise them on the part of the beings who have them.

More significantly, however, the view that life is at most only of instrumental value explains how the value of human life (that is, the life of a human being) can become morally ambiguous. It is perhaps easiest to see this by considering, first, the simpler case of merely sentient beings.

It is a fact that we often assess the seriousness of an illness or injury by the extent to which it threatens the continuation of life (that is, of independent syntropic capability). The limit of serious illness or injury, in other words, is often thought of as fatal illness or injury.

Now there is nothing wrong with rating threats to the organic integrity of some living being along such a scale, but the practice does contain the seeds of a conceptual confusion. It tempts us to think that a being possesses a (negative, passive) "right to life" which stems from the same moral considerations as its (negative, passive) rights to be protected from willful impositions of illness or injury. It tempts us, that is, to see this scale of "seriousness" as a moral continuum, and to conclude that there should inevitably be moral strictures against the deliberate taking of a being's life—strictures which, indeed, ought always to be stronger than any moral strictures against, for example, the deliberate causing of "less serious" injuries to that being.

Our moral practices, however, reveal this to be a misconception. What we find instead, on the contrary, is that one's obligation not deliberately to injure (torture, maim, mutilate, etc.) an animal is in fact stronger than one's obligation, if any, not to kill it. In the case of merely sentient animals, our practice is not to preserve life at all costs in the face of serious illness or injury, but instead precisely to put the suffering beasts to death—to "finish off" a wounded game animal, to shoot a horse which has broken its leg, and to have our ill and aged pet dogs or cats "put to sleep."

These practices become intelligible, however, once we recognize that it is the intensity of suffering arising from illness or injury, and not the life-threatening "seriousness" of the illness or injury itself, which is, in practice, the morally relevant consideration. If life had the status of a condition of intrinsic worth within our implicit moral theory, such "humane" practices would be morally indefensible (or at least morally problematic). If the condition of life has only instrumental value, however, they become not only intelligible but, indeed, morally justifiable as well.

The condition of life is a causally necessary requisite of sentience in general, but this fact in itself is morally neutral. As our moral practices show, a merely sentient being does not have, on the face of it, an absolute "right to life." In the case of merely sentient beings, what is morally relevant is not the mere presence of life but rather what is sometimes called the "quality of life."

The distinction between intrinsic worth and intrinsic disvalue gives rise to a distinction between two kinds of moral wrongs, that is, two ways in which an act or conduct could in principle be prohibited on moral grounds. An act could be banned, first, on the grounds that it would lead to an ultimate net increase in conditions of intrinsic disvalue, or it could be banned, second, on the grounds that it would lead to an ultimate net decrease in conditions of intrinsic worth. Since conditions of intrinsic worth—exercises of moral autonomy—can be realized only in the actions of rational beings, however, moral censure can attach to our treatment of merely sentient beings only on the former grounds. What we do to a merely sentient, nonrational animal is arguably morally wrong, in other words, only if it can be shown to result in (the likelihood of) an ultimate net increase in conditions of intrinsic disvalue—i.e., in (the likelihood of) an increase in suffering.

When an injury to or an illness of some animal has a certain character, however, it can be the prolongation and preservation of that animal's life, and not the taking of it, which demonstrably has this consequence. In particular, it can happen that an animal becomes organically damaged in ways that result in irredeemable suffering, that is, suffering which (since our medical technology is of only limited effectiveness) we are simply unable to alleviate while, at the same time, preserving that animal's life. In such a case, the prolongation of the animal's life could only result in an ultimate increase of intrinsic disvalue. Preserving that life, it follows, becomes arguably morally wrong. Far from having a duty to keep the suffering beast alive as long as possible, we accept in practice just the opposite moral responsibility—an obligation to "put the poor thing out of its misery," that is, to kill it. Consonant with the overriding moral relevance of suffering, however, any such killing must, of course, be done "humanely," which is to say quickly and painlessly, without intensifying the suffering of the already suffering animal.

In the case of human beings, in contrast, a crucial additional family of moral considerations comes into play. Whereas there was only one kind of morally pertinent fact about merely sentient animals—facts about what is intrinsically of disvalue, about suffering—in the case of human beings, there are two. For we need also to take into consideration facts about what is intrinsically of worth—about the prospects for an individual's realizing in his conduct instances of the exercise of moral autonomy in which (according to the hypothesis which I have defended) such intrinsic worth consists.

It follows that, while there is only one way in which something done to a merely sentient animal could be morally wrong—through its leading to an ultimate net increase in suffering—doing something to a human being could be morally wrong in either of two ways. It could, of course, also lead in the same way to such an ultimate increase in conditions of intrinsic disvalue. Thus we do find that the system of rights embodied in our implicit morality protects human beings against torture, mutilation, willful injury, and the like, just as it protects merely sentient beings. But something done to a human being could also lead to an ultimate net decrease in conditions of intrinsic worth, in the capacity for or the likelihood of exercises of moral autonomy. It is for this reason, I have suggested, that we also find in our implicit morality further ("human") rights protecting human beings from slavery, arbitrary confinement, and the like.

The key point to be made now is that the summary termination of a human being's life—however quick, painless, and free of suffering it might be—would still, on the face of it, be a moral wrong of the second sort. It would cut off the possibility of any further conducts of intrinsic worth on the part of that individual by summarily withdrawing a causally necessary condition of the very possibility of any conducts on the part of that individual at all. In a manner of speaking, death can be thought of as the limit of constraint on an individual's freedom to act, for it cancels the very possibility of that individual's acting, whether morally or immorally, freely or under compulsion.

I have already proposed that it is because a human being—as a rational being—is a (potential) source of intrinsic worth that it has—as a merely sentient being does not—negative passive rights to protection from constraints on its freedom to act. In the light of the observations just made about the consequences of death, however, we can now conclude, further, that a human being has—as an extension of these rights—what a merely sentient being does not have, namely a prima facie, absolute "right to life."

This "right to life" is "absolute" only in the sense that a human being's having it is a direct consequence of its being the kind of being it is and independent of any considerations regarding the quality of life. A human's "right to life," that is, is justified by a moral argument which makes no reference to the intrinsic disvalues of suffering. To call this right prima facie, however, is to emphasize the fact that, although it is supported by moral reasonings which make no reference to intrinsic disvalue, it can be challenged by arguments which turn on the question of increased or decreased suffering—for a rational human being is also sentient and thus also potentially a subject of suffering.

Since there are two ways in which something done to a human being can be morally wrong, in other words, there arises in this instance the possibility of conflicting moral arguments on the question of life. At least in principle, there could exist both a course of moral reasoning which validly led to the conclusion that it would be wrong to terminate some individual's life—and even, perhaps, obligatory (or at least commendable) to do what one can to preserve and prolong it—and another course of moral reasoning, appealing to different matters-of-fact, which led with equal validity to the contrary conclusion that it would be wrong to preserve and prolong that individual's life—and even, perhaps, commendable (or at least permissible) to put it to an end.

And that, of course, is precisely what seems to happen when we turn, as we are about to, to the topic of euthanasia.

CHAPTER 6

"Mercy Killing":
The Question of Taking Life

6.1: THE CASE OF ALRIC

The key insight which we have now gained—the insight which allows us to explain how the deliberate putting to death of a human being can be the object of moral disagreements—is that the prima facie moral wrongness of terminating an individual's life is traceable within our implicit moral theory to a different set of fundamental values from those underlying that individual's prima facie right to be free of imposed suffering. It is this difference in fundamental underlying values which allows a human's prima facie "right to life" to come into conflict with others of his prima facie rights and, at least in principle, to be set aside in favor of stronger moral claims arising from these other rights.

Such conflicts of morally relevant considerations—"moral dilemmas," for short—can, of course, be more or less serious or acute. The seriousness of such a moral dilemma will crucially depend, among other things, upon certain matters of fact—facts about the condition of the human being whose "right to life" is at issue and facts about what it is technologically possible for us to do about that individual's condition.

Consider, for example, a sort of case which is likely to set one such moral dilemma in particularly sharp focus. Let us suppose that, as the result of an inoperable brain tumor, some individual—call him "Alric"—has suffered a complete loss of the functional capacities constitutive of rationality. Alric manifests a total incapacity to speak and to understand what is said to him, he no longer responds differentially to familiar friends or members of his family, and he is also obviously unable to initiate any actions. Alric's sensory capabilities, in contrast, are still generally unimpaired, as is shown by the fact that he reacts to light, loud or sudden sounds, touches, and movements in his vicinity. Alric never indicates that he wishes to be fed, but he will chew and swallow food forced upon him, and while he will not reach for a glass, he drinks from one held to his lips.

In addition, however, Alric appears to be continuously in pain. He periodically cries or cries out; he shudders and winces; and he undergoes spasms or seizures. He sleeps intermittently, but even then fitfully and only for short periods of time. Alric's tumor has responded neither to radiation nor to chemotherapy, and it continues to grow unchecked. The medical consensus is that the organic damage already done by it to his cerebral cortex is permanent and irreversible. Analgesics and even narcotics have proved, at best, only marginally effective—and increasingly less so—in alleviating or moderating the symptoms of Alric's suffering.

Alric, in short, is an example of what is probably the arguably most plausible kind of candidate for humane euthanasia.[1] But there will hardly be any agreement on the matter. There will be some who advocate euthanasia and others, today almost certainly in the majority, who oppose it. What concerns us here are the moral arguments which we are likely to find advanced on both sides of the question.

The opponents of euthanasia are likely to stress the absolute nature of Alric's prima facie "right to life." They will insist that it is simply wrong ever to take the life of an innocent human being. However grievously ill or damaged he may be, Alric remains for all that a human being and, what is more, a human being who has done nothing to deserve being put to death. Every human being, simply by virtue of the fact that it is a human being, and irrespective of the quality of its life, has an innate right to life.

Those opponents of euthanasia who nevertheless view capital punishment (the execution of certain criminals) as sometimes morally defensible may go on to add that an individual can, through his own actions, forfeit or surrender his original right to life.[2] But all opponents of euthanasia—both those who also oppose the death penalty and those who advocate it—will insist that it is simply impossible to revoke or cancel an individual's "right to life." The right to life is a right that a human being has simply because it is a human being. It is therefore, to use a classical turn of phrase, an inalienable right. Since Alric has done nothing himself to forfeit or surrender his right to life, putting him to death now would be a blatant violation of that right, and would thus necessarily be morally wrong.

It is, to be sure, profoundly regrettable that Alric is suffering, and we are, of course, morally obliged to do anything we can to alleviate that suffering—but only if what we propose to do is otherwise morally permissible. Unfortunately, we can in fact do little or nothing here. But that fact certainly does not give us the right to kill Alric—for, as we have seen, in the given circumstances, putting Alric to death would demonstrably be morally wrong. So runs a typical case for the opposition.

The advocates of euthanasia in this instance, on the other hand, will stress the prima facie character of Alric's "absolute right to life." They are likely to argue somewhat as follows: It is just not true that every human being has an innate right to life simply by virtue of the fact that it is a human being. What is true is that every person has an inalienable right to life—but Alric is no longer a person! The right to life which every person possesses derives from the fact that persons are morally autonomous agents (and thereby sources of moral worth). Our granting of an absolute right to life to all persons, our recognition and acknowledgement and respecting of such a right, is justified and justifiable only by an appeal to this moral autonomy. But Alric has completely and irreversibly lost all those rational capacities required for even the possibility of the exercise of moral autonomy in deliberate action. He has become a merely sentient being, and therefore, although he is still of course nominally a member of the biological species *homo sapiens*, that fact has lost all moral relevance. Alric has ceased to be a person.

Of course Alric has not forfeited or surrendered his right to life. But neither are we proposing to revoke or cancel it. One cannot revoke or cancel something which is not there. Alric has simply lost the right to life which he formerly had, for that is a right which only persons have, and Alric has lost all the competences it takes to be a person. The only morally relevant considerations which apply in Alric's instance, then, are those which would apply in the case of any merely sentient being. And here the case is clear. Alric's suffering is irredeemable. There is nothing which in fact can be done to alleviate it. It is, consequently, certainly not morally wrong to put him out of his misery. Indeed, it is arguably even our moral duty to do so (as it would clearly be, for example, if Alric were a dog or a cat). Only a false sentimentality keeps us from regarding Alric as we would any other irredeemably suffering animal and from treating him accordingly. So runs a typical case for the advocacy of euthanasia.

And now for our question. Our question here is not: Who is right? Our question, rather, is: What is it exactly that the two parties to this dispute ultimately are actually disagreeing about?

6.2: FACTS ARE NOT THE PROBLEM

The most important thing to recognize here—the point on which I want to insist and for which I propose vigorously to argue—is that the two parties to this dispute over the morality of euthanasia are not disagreeing about any matter of fact. The facts of the case are these: That Alric is biologically a human being. That Alric has lost all rational functional capabilities. That Alric's tumor is inoperable and responds neither to radiation nor to chemotherapy. That Alric is fairly continuously in pain. And that the measures which could be taken in an effort to alleviate Alric's suffering prove to be by and large ineffective. But none of these facts is in dispute between the opponents of euthanasia and its advocates.

There are, however, no other facts about which our two parties could be disagreeing. In particular, there is no factual matter at issue in the question of whether or not Alric is a person. For "person" is neither a natural nor a functional kind, but rather an ethical kind. For Alric to be a person just is for him to possess the full set of so-called "human" rights—including, of course, an absolute "right to life." But whether or not he does possess the full set of "human" rights is precisely what is in dispute here.

The point is that there are not two steps to be taken here: First, determine whether or not Alric is a person; and, second, conclude on the basis of this determination that he does or does not possess an absolute "right to life." For there is no way to "determine" that Alric is or is not a person other than by settling the disputed questions concerning his rights. There is only one step to be made. We need to resolve the moral question of whether it is permissible to take Alric's life in these circumstances. Resolving that question just is resolving the question of whether or not Alric is a person. If it is morally permissible to put Alric to death, then he must not be a person—for both parties to the dispute would freely agree that it is never morally permissible to take the life of an innocent person.

We do not, in short, discover that some entity is or is not a person. We acknowledge that some entity is a person, or we do not acknowledge it. Personhood, as I have argued, is a bestowed status. We bestow it precisely by acknowledging an individual to possess the full range of "human" rights, and by respecting, enforcing, and protecting those rights. It follows, however, that there can be no way of first finding out that some entity is a person and then using that as a reason for granting that entity all "human" rights, any more than there can be a way of first finding out that some individual is a licensed driver and then using that as a reason for granting that individual the legal right to drive.

We can, of course, discover an entity's natural or functional kind. But neither Alric's natural kind nor his functional kind is in dispute here. Both parties agree that Alric is a human being (that is, a member of the biological species *homo sapiens*), and both parties agree that Alric is, now, a merely sentient animal (that is, that he has irrevocably lost all the functional capacities constitutive of rationality). What they disagree about is the moral relevance of these facts about Alric. In particular, they disagree about whether Alric's ethical kind should, in this instance, be determined by his natural kind or by his functional kind.

Earlier, I pointed out that our moral practice is to count only human beings as persons and to count all human beings as persons. While I argued that there were, in theory, no good reasons for the former practice, we did find some good, if not conclusive, moral reasons supporting the latter. The question of the moral defensibility of these practices, however, was discussed earlier only in a certain context—namely, with a view to the specific moral practice of granting the status of personhood to the offspring of acknowledged persons. Now, however, we see that an additional question which can arise in consideration of the moral justification for these practices was earlier not even mentioned. What I have in mind, obviously, is this question: Given that there are good moral reasons for bestowing personhood on all offspring of human persons, is the ethical status thereby granted these new human beings a permanent and inalienable status, or is membership in the ethical kind "person" a moral standing which an individual can later lose? It appears, indeed, to be about the answer to this question that the opponents of euthanasia and its advocates ultimately disagree.

6.3: THE DISPUTE RECAST

Both parties to the debate over euthanasia agree that, before the onset of his illness, Alric was indisputably a person, and that it would have been morally impermissible then to put him to death. In addition, however, the opponents of euthanasia adopt a further moral principle, which might be phrased "Once a person, always a person." They hold, that is, that the "human" rights which, for good reasons, we bestow on all members of the natural kind "human being" at birth ought to be as inalienable as that natural kind itself. How, then, might this moral principle be justified or defended?

What we are likely to see being appealed to in this instance is a form of "slippery slope" argument. Just as we find a continuum of, for example, skin colors exhibited by human beings—which renders any acknowledgement or withholding of "human" rights on the basis of such structural characteristics morally arbitrary—so, too, it will be pointed out, we find that human beings exhibit a continuum of functional capabilities as well.

The functional capacities constitutive of rationality, in other words, are all matters of degree. Human beings manifest a continuum of degrees of intelligence, planning, understanding, ability to communicate, competence in action, and the like. Any point of division imposed upon this continuum vis-à-vis the acknowledgement or withholding of "human" rights to individuals, it is now claimed, would be equally morally arbitrary. Once we concluded that loss of rational capabilities in any degree can ever be a morally legitimate ground for abrogating an individual's original rights, we would have opened the door to the possibility of such moral atrocities as the extermination of functionally handicapped individuals of lesser degrees—aphasics, agnosics, emotionally disturbed or learning disabled children, or the mentally retarded—in the name of such false goals as "racial purity" or "strengthening the gene pool." The only way absolutely to prevent such moral outrages is to subscribe to and promote a morality which assigns the ethical status of personhood to all human beings unconditionally. Ethical kinds, in other words, should be wholly determined by natural kinds—and they should be as permanent and inalienable as those natural kinds themselves.

The advocate of euthanasia in Alric's case, on the other hand, is likely to be unimpressed by this line of reasoning. The fact that there are borderline cases, he will point out, does not imply that there are no clear cases. There is, for instance, no right answer to the question: How many hairs must an individual lose before he qualifies as bald? But a person who has lost all his hair nevertheless is bald, beyond any possibility of rational disagreement. Alric, the advocate of euthanasia will insist, is such a clear case. The fact of the matter is that Alric has lost all the functional capabilities constitutive of rationality, permanently and irreversibly. And that fact, we will be reminded, is not in dispute between the two parties.

I quite agree, the advocate of euthanasia may continue, that there are good reasons for bestowing the status of personhood initially on all human beings. But we need to remember what those good reasons are: that human beings are normally also rational beings, and that all newborn human infants are potentially rational beings. It is rationality, after all, and the capacity to exercise moral autonomy which rationality conveys—not membership in the biological species *homo sapiens*—which our implicit moral theory conceptually links to the ethical kind "person." While there are good reasons for treating all human beings as persons initially, then, there are no compelling moral reasons for treating this ethical standing as one which an individual cannot lose.

To guard against moral atrocities, concludes the euthanasia advocate, we do not need a blanket and reflexive categorization of all human beings as persons. All that we need are adequate safeguards. In Alric's case, for instance, the unanimous consensus that his loss of rational functional capabilities is total and irreversible on the part of five or six qualified and disinterested psychologists and physicians would surely do.

Keenness of eyesight, for example, is also a matter of degree, and people also form a continuum with regard to their visual abilities. Of course we would not want to issue driving licenses, for instance, to the totally blind, but it is not necessary to deny everyone the legal right to drive in order to prevent this sort of outrage. To be sure, there will be borderline cases. But that does not prevent us from devising rationally defensible tests of visual acuity which totally blind individuals simply cannot pass. The "right to life" is like that, insists the advocate of euthanasia. We do not want to deny it to human beings arbitrarily, but it is not necessary to grant it to every member of the biological species in order to prevent that sort of moral outrage. Here, too, we have the option of devising tests of rational functional capacity which allow us to identify clear cases of the total and irreversible loss of rationality with moral certainty. And doing that, the advocate concludes, is surely morally preferable to continuing to condone the suffering of such profoundly damaged individuals as poor Alric.

6.4: . . . AND THE TRUE QUESTION LOCATED

And now, I think, we are finally in a position to see what sort of a disagreement we are confronting in the debate over the fate of Alric. Our two disputing parties are not in disagreement over any matters of fact. Their disagreement, in other words, is not one which might in principle be resolved by further scientific discoveries. Nor are they in disagreement about ultimate moral values. They both find suffering to be of intrinsic disvalue, and both regard the exercise of moral autonomy as of intrinsic worth. They even agree, indeed, on the full set of "human" rights the possession of which is criterial for membership in the ethical kind "person."

What they obviously do not agree about is the range of beings which fall within the scope of these "human" rights. The reason, I want to suggest, is that, ultimately, our two disputants have been differently impressed by the same facts. They disagree in their sensibilities. Our two dissenting parties have been differently struck by various facts, and, in consequence of this, they assign to those same facts different moral weights.

Surprisingly, perhaps, at least some of the relevant facts turn out to be quite independent of Alric's actual condition and our technological capabilities to ameliorate it. The advocate of euthanasia, of course, is particularly struck by Alric's real suffering. What occupies the center of his moral vision is the continuing increase in conditions of intrinsic disvalue. Euthanasia recommends itself to him in the case of Alric as a way to put an end to this standing evil without in any way immediately diminishing the prospects for realizing moral worth in the world (for Alric has already lost all those functional capabilities of independent rational action on which the exercise of moral autonomy logically depends).

The opponent of euthanasia, however, is much more strongly impressed by the real potential for abuse which lies in any "nonabsolutistic" policy for acknowledging "human" rights. This is not a fact about Alric, but it is a fact nevertheless. A system of moral practices which bases an individual's "right to life" on certain "subjective" judgments made by others (psychologists and physicians, for example)—and which thereby renders the acknowledgement of a "right to life" more or less discretionary—is in fact open to errors and abuses in application in ways that a moral system whose principles link the "right to life" to such "objective" matters as an individual's biological species—and which thus allow no discretionary exceptions—is not.

The opponent of euthanasia, in other words, does not see our agreeing to the moral permissibility of putting Alric to death as an isolated act but rather as our granting acceptability to a system of moral principles which embodies a real risk of engendering widespread future infringements upon the moral autonomy of many persons (and which thereby threatens to diminish the future realization in the world of conditions of intrinsic worth). It is this risk—and the historical record of abuses, outrages, and atrocities which testifies to its being a real risk—which occupies the center of the opponent's moral vision.

The advocate and the opponent of euthanasia, then, look out upon the same factual scene, but they see it in different moral focus. The advocate will accuse the opponent of using a merely theoretical possibility as an excuse for closing his eyes to the fact of Alric's genuine suffering. He will agree, of course, that any policy which accepts euthanasia as morally permissible is open to abuse in principle. But the risk of such abuse, he will continue to insist, is purely theoretical, only slight, and at best remote. It requires of us, to be sure, that any discretionary euthanasia policy be attended by adequate safeguards, but the risk of such abuse pales into moral insignificance in the face of Alric's real and immediate suffering. For Alric's is a case in which any reasonable procedural restriction designed to guard against potential abuse could clearly and obviously be satisfied. The opponent of euthanasia, with his concern over abstract possibilities, concludes the advocate, is simply being insensitive to the realities of Alric's condition.

The opponent of euthanasia, in turn, will accuse its advocate of a kind of moral "tunnel vision." Morality, he will remind us, is not a question of feelings but a matter of principled conduct. Alric's suffering, the opponent will freely agree, is indeed a terrible thing. It is deeply unfortunate that we can do nothing to alleviate it. But, alas, that is just sometimes how the world is. We should not allow ourselves on that account, however, to be moved by momentary impulses of pity or sympathy to abandon our reasoned moral convictions. The advocate of euthanasia, insists its opponent, is underestimating the magnitude of the risk which one would be taking in endorsing any system of principles which morally condones the taking of innocent human life. He is forgetting the lessons of Nero and Hitler. Once a policy is made discretionary, it is all too easy for it to come to be applied expediently and arbitrarily.[3] Morality must always take the long view. It cannot run the risk of sacrificing the only thing which is ultimately of any intrinsic worth—the moral autonomy of persons and its exercise in free and unconstrained human action guided by moral principle. The advocate of euthanasia, blinded by (understandable) humane and sympathetic impulses, concludes the opponent, is simply being short-sighted about the deeper implications of morally condoning the practice which in Alric's case he recommends.

6.5: TWO KINDS OF MORAL DISAGREEMENT

If my diagnosis of the disagreement over euthanasia is correct, then, neither of the two parties to our dispute is being silly or callous, and neither is overlooking or disregarding any matters of fact. Indeed, each is operating with a fully developed set of mature moral sensibilities, and each is able to advance strong and reasoned moral arguments for his own point of view. These arguments draw their strengths, however, from different elements of a single implicit moral theory which both disputants share.

For the advocate of euthanasia, the intrinsic disvalue of Alric's real and present suffering outweighs the merely potential threat to intrinsic worth inherent in a discretionary euthanasia policy. For the opponent of euthanasia, although the facts remain the same, these moral weights are reversed.

The opponent of euthanasia treats the intrinsic worth of moral autonomy and its exercise in free action as of paramount significance. He is consequently prepared to condone a greater degree of suffering in the world than is the euthanasia advocate, rather than assent to policies and practices which carry what he perceives as all too real a risk of encroaching upon such autonomy. The advocate of euthanasia, on the contrary, treats the intrinsic disvalue of Alric's actual suffering as the dominant consideration. He is therefore prepared to accept a certain risk of potential infringements of autonomy as part of the price of morally permitting us to put an end to that suffering.

The advocate of euthanasia, in short, thinks above all of diminishing pointless suffering; the opponent, of protecting the moral integrity of persons and ensuring their continued freedom to exercise their autonomy in principled action. It is these opposed moral sensibilities which the case of

Alric brings sharply into focus. But it is important to see that neither party can legitimately accuse the other of being immoral or uncaring. It is not even that they care about different things. Both of our disputants acknowledge the same moral values. It is only that, in the case of Alric, one of them cares more about the disvalues of (actual) suffering than about (potential threats to) the worth of moral autonomy, and the other has these moral priorities reversed.

This sort of disagreement, however—about which of the disputants' shared moral values should be the dominant consideration in Alric's case—is not a disagreement about any facts and so not one which could be resolved by appealing to any facts. The resolution of such a disagreement, in fact, can come about, if at all, only if one party succeeds in reeducating the sensibilities of the other. As the discussion continues, then, each disputant will attempt to get the other to see the same facts—the facts upon which they agree—in a different perspective.

The opponent of euthanasia may try to convey his sense of the reality of the potential threat to moral autonomy inherent in such judgmental practices by, for instance, emphasizing the continuity of the falling-off of functional capacities and by laying stress on the historical record of actual abuses of discretionary moral policies. The euthanasia advocate, in turn, may attempt to minimize these considerations—by, for example, pointing out the comparative rarity of such extreme cases as Alric's and by suggesting, perhaps, that an individual's having completely lost all rational functional capabilities either is or (with increasing sophistication of techniques of medical and psychological measurement) can come to be as "objective" a fact about him as his membership in this or that biological species (and thus as little open to the abuses of arbitrariness as the ground of moral classification which his opponent himself recommends).

In addition, the advocate of euthanasia will surely continue to emphasize Alric's suffering, attempting to render his opponent forcefully and vividly conscious of it and to evoke from him a sympathetic or empathetic response. And here the euthanasia opponent may well respond by calling attention in turn to various paradigms of "unavoidable evil"—the "bitter medicine" of prima facie morally undesirable means inescapably necessary for achieving an overriding morally desirable end—and by trying to bring the advocate to regard the condoning of Alric's continued suffering in that light, as another such profoundly regrettable, but unfortunately unavoidable, byproduct of the pursuit of moral aims of consummate and overriding importance.

As the discussion over the moral permissibility or impermissibility of putting Alric to death continues, then, the two parties will frequently find occasion to cite various facts. The euthanasia opponent will call attention to the facts of Alric's membership in the human species, facts about the continuous gradations of functional capabilities, and historical facts about abuses of discretionary moral policies and even actual moral atrocities.[4] The euthanasia advocate, in turn, will call attention to facts about the evident intensity of Alric's suffering, the extremity and severity of his functional impairments, the increasing refinement of techniques of biological and psychological measurement, and the limitations of our ability for effective therapeutic interventions.

This frequent citing of facts makes it look like the dispute between the advocate and the opponent of euthanasia in Alric's case were a dispute about facts. It makes it look like each party to the debate were accusing the other of overlooking certain facts, and that the disagreement is one which could be settled if only one of the disputants could get the other to acknowledge the facts which he overlooks.

The main thing which analytic philosophy can teach us here is that the ultimate disagreement between advocates and opponents of euthanasia is not like that at all—even if both parties to the dispute are inclined to think that it is. It is perfectly possible, in other words, for everyone to acknowledge all the same facts and subscribe to all the same values, and to still disagree about whether or not it would be morally permissible to put Alric to death.[5] And, even more importantly, such continued disagreements need not be irrational or morally perverse (although they might be, of course), but can be as well reasoned and morally sophisticated as any disputes one could ever hope to find.

What our investigations here can remind us is that facts may be cited for many reasons. A parent can, to be sure, cite facts to point out to a child some relevant considerations which it has overlooked—and that will be one model. But it is not the only model. An art critic, for example, may direct our attention to certain features of a picture which hangs before our eyes, not in order to get us to notice something which he believes we have overlooked, but in an effort to get us to appreciate, for instance, the special contributions of those features to the picture's excellence which he believes us to have underestimated.

What I have been arguing, in essence, is that—when irrelevant misconceptions have been cleared away and feelings of frustration or outrage set aside—the citing of facts in the rational, sophisticated, debates over what it is morally permissible to do about Alric fits this second model. The disputing parties cite facts, not to point them out, but to point them up—to emphasize the special importance of certain features of a shared moral and factual landscape to the case at hand which each believes the other disputant to have underrated.

6.6: HOW THE BALANCE CAN SHIFT

It should, I suppose, go without saying that such moral debates as the one over the permissibility of euthanasia are not conducted by two theoreticians in some official forum on one occasion but, so to speak, in the public consciousness and across time. The inputs to such debates are as diverse as people themselves. Relevant—and irrelevant—considerations are advanced and argued for by preachers in the pulpit, teachers in the classroom, representatives in the legislature, lawyers and judges in the courtroom, coworkers in the office, and drinking companions in the local tavern. Facts and opinions are disseminated by the public media—newspapers, magazines, radio, and television—not only through their reporting on medical and legal cases and controversies, but also through their editorializing on them, whether formally or casually (as, for example, in the course of television "talk shows").

Moral practices typically do not change suddenly but instead evolve slowly, and often not without difficulty. More than one war has been fought over questions of human rights. Presently, at least in the western world, the moral sensibilities of the majority appear to be inclined against euthanasia. The question, however, is genuinely still open (unlike, for instance, the question of the moral permissibility of incest), and an occasional "mercy killing" does come along to bring it sharply before the public consciousness.

Furthermore, of course, advances in medical technology are being made with gratifying regularity—and being made known. Such medical advances can make a difference to our moral practices by relevantly altering the factual background against which ethical issues are debated and moral sensibilities are formed. They do this, however, not by revealing new facts—that is, by telling us something which we do not already know—but by enabling us to do things which we could not formerly do—to correct, for example, certain formerly incorrectable functional incapacitations or to alleviate certain formerly intractable cases of suffering—or, equally significantly, by raising the level of the confidence we can reasonably have in relevant factual judgments concerning, for instance, the magnitude of some functional impairment, its irreversibility, or the character and intensity of some creature's suffering.

Developments of this kind can, gradually, bring about a shift and realignment of moral sensibilities. Should this happen in the future in the case of euthanasia, its manifestation will not be found, in the first instance, in theoretical legal or moral declarations but in practice. As has recently begun to happen in the cases of, for example, abortion and homosexuality and the use of marijuana, certain individual and social practices can evolve from being largely condemned to being widely condoned (although, as these cases also illustrate, by no means universally condoned). The practices can "come out of the closet," increasing in frequency and in visibility. Ultimately, they can become commonplace.

Legal sanction and "official" religious approvals may well follow, but they are, in an important sense, beside the point.[6] For what it takes to effect a change in the way a practice is morally regarded is nothing formal or theoretical but a change in the moral attitudes by which the practice is actually motivated and shaped. The de facto moral permissibility of euthanasia will have been secured, then, not when people are prepared to say certain things, but when they are prepared to do certain things—e.g., when they are prepared straightforwardly to put such individuals as Alric painlessly to death—and to wonder what all the fuss was all about.

CHAPTER 7

"Letting Die":
The Question of Prolonging Life

7.1: SINS OF COMMISSION
AND SINS OF OMISSION

When we turn from the topic of euthanasia to that of the artificial prolongation of life versus "letting the individual die," some of our earlier observations drop out of the picture and others come into play. There is, in fact, a range of cases which fall under the general heading "letting die." What we need to isolate first, however, is the crucial respect in which the moral question at issue in such cases invariably differs from the question at issue when actual euthanasia or "mercy killing" is under discussion.

To do this, I need to bring to the foreground yet another distinction which is central to our implicit moral theory—the distinction between action and inaction. Our moral deliberations inevitably take place against the background of a certain theoretical understanding of the world. In particular, we think of the world as composed of a multiplicity of interacting physical systems changing in lawful ways across time. Each of these systems is in some sense an integrated unity. It has its own internal dynamic of natural, lawful, (causal) development or evolution, and it will change across time in accordance with this internal dynamic unless something from outside the system actively intervenes.

When moral questions are at stake, what is at issue is deliberate human intervention. A specific action is contemplated against the background of a theoretical understanding which embodies not only beliefs about what will (probably) happen if something is done (the action is taken), but also beliefs about what will (probably) happen unless something is done (if no action is taken).

This background of matter-of-factual beliefs about the world lies behind and is presupposed by the distinction within our moral theory between

148

two further kinds of moral wrong. Earlier, I highlighted the distinction between "wrongs of moral disvalue"—conducts which lead to an ultimate net increase in suffering—and "offenses against moral worth"—conducts which lead to an ultimate net decrease in possibilities for the exercise of moral autonomy. The distinction to which I want now to call attention, however, lies crosswise to that one. It is the traditional distinction between "sins of commission" and "sins of omission."

A "sin of commission" is an action. It is morally wrong by virtue of being a doing of something morally impermissible (forbidden). A "sin of omission," however, is an instance of inaction. It is morally wrong by virtue of being an omitting to do or a refraining from doing something which is morally required of one (mandatory). Someone who sins by commission transgresses a moral boundary. Someone who sins by omission, in contrast, falls short of fulfilling his moral duties or obligations.

What is morally at issue in cases of genuine euthanasia or "mercy killing" is the permissibility or impermissibility of doing something, of taking action. That is, what is morally in question is the permissibility of intervening in the natural evolution of a physical system (a suffering human being) to bring about something (a death) which would otherwise not occur at that time were the system left to develop according to its own internal dynamic.

What is morally at issue in cases of "letting die" versus the artificial prolongation of life, however, is the converse situation. Here the physical system in question (a dying human being) is understood as one which, if left to develop according to its own internal dynamic, will come to lose its physical integrity as a system (for death is precisely the loss of those syntropic capabilities necessary to preserve such systemic integrity). The moral question arises here when techniques of intervention which would prevent or arrest this natural causal systemic evolution are available. What is at issue is whether it is morally obligatory to make use of such interventionist techniques, or, equivalently, whether it is morally permissible to refrain from doing this, that is, not to take the action which is available to us. Thus, whereas in a case of genuine euthanasia we correctly speak of the rightness or wrongness of "putting someone to death," in the cases with which we are now concerned, what is in dispute is the rightness or wrongness of "allowing someone to die."

7.2: PROLONGING LIFE VERSUS SUSTAINING LIFE

What characteristically complicates this tidy picture, however, is the fact that, in actual cases, the step of technological intervention in the process of dying may—for whatever reason—already have been taken. That is, a dying patient—as a matter of administrative policy (automatically applied, without moral deliberation directed to the concrete case), for example—may already have been connected to a respirator for some considerable time before questions of morally permissible alternatives begin to be raised and discussed. The debate which centers around such an actual case, in consequence, will typically have the appearance of a debate concerning the permissibility or impermissibility of an action, for "turning off the respirator"—under that precise description—is, indeed, itself an action, that is, something which someone can do.

Disentangling ourselves from this complication, it will turn out, will require that we first penetrate far and deeply into the thicket of those customary concepts, distinctions, and modes of thinking and speaking about doing and refraining which constitute the only framework in terms of which the whole theme of "human action" can be coherently structured and profitably discussed. It will require, that is, that we undertake a rather extensive excursion through that part of analytic philosophy which nowadays goes by the name "the theory of action."[1] As a first step in that direction, however, it is useful to notice that in adopting "turning off the respirator" as a description of what is morally in question, we have, in an important sense, changed the subject. We have, that is, implicitly restructured our theoretical background understanding of the facts of the case.

The point is that turning off the respirator is not an intervention in the natural lawful development of the integrated physical system which consists of the dying human being *simpliciter*, but rather in the natural lawful development of a complex entity—human being + respirator—which is now itself being conceived of as a (larger) unitary integrated physical system. If we retained our original moral focus on the human being alone, in contrast, the action of turning off the respirator could only be coherently thought of as our discontinuing an ongoing intervention in the natural evolution of that physical system—and that would be a case, not of taking action, but rather of ceasing to take action.[2]

What, in general, does a case of "the artificial prolongation of life" look like? If we take the words at face value, what we are concerned with is a (human) organism, regarded as a more or less closed lawful physical system, which has lost the ability to maintain itself as an integrated system through normal causal transactions with its environment across time. Lacking independent syntropic capacity, this organism, however, can be (or has been) interfaced with an artifact to form an extended complex structure which, again regarded as a more or less closed physical system, is itself capable of preserving its systemic integrity across time through its normal causal transactions with its environment. The extended complex system (organism + artifact), in other words, would possess (or possesses) the sort of independent syntropic capacities which the organism alone, considered as an isolated system, has come to lack. In such a case, we say that the life of the organism would be (or is being) "artificially aided" or "artificially sustained."

But while an individual's life being in this way artificially aided or sustained is a necessary condition of its being artificially prolonged, it is—surprisingly, perhaps—not a sufficient condition. To appreciate this, it is enough to consider such cases as an otherwise normal child afflicted with polio whose breathing is supported by an iron lung, a teenager suffering from renal failure who must undergo regular dialysis treatments, and a

45-year-old businessman whose cardiac functions are sustained by a pacemaker. Each of these individuals lacks independent syntropic capacity. Disconnected from or deprived of such artificial life-support systems, we may suppose, each of them would fairly quickly die. Yet, although each individual's life is clearly being artificially sustained, we would not, I think, customarily describe such cases as examples of "artificially prolonged" life.

Notice that there is nothing morally problematic about such cases. No one would seriously suggest that the iron lung be shut off, the dialysis treatments discontinued, or the pacemaker be removed in order that the child, teenager, or businessman be permitted to "die a natural death." In these instances, on the contrary, we apparently regard the extended system consisting of the organism interfaced with its medical prosthesis as having the same moral standing as a human being devoid of functional impairment. Summarily disconnecting or discontinuing such artificial life-support systems in these cases, in fact, would be counted by most of us as the positive act of killing, rather than the passive refraining of "letting die." Other things being equal, we treat an individual suffering from correctable organic dysfunctions affecting only syntropic capacity as having a prima facie right of access to life-sustaining medical technology, and, other things being equal, we regard the extended system resulting from interfacing the organism with appropriate life-supporting apparatus as itself a person, subject to the full range of moral protections pertaining to persons in general, including a prima facie absolute "right to life."

7.3: IN THE MATTER OF BARTHOLOMEW

What is it, then, which differentiates such morally unproblematic cases of artificially aided or sustained life from morally problematic cases of artificially prolonged life? The phrase "artificially prolonged life" itself suggests life which has been sustained, not merely beyond the point at which, were no interventionist action taken, it would end, but rather beyond the point at which, so to speak, it in some sense should end. The phrase suggests, that is, the picture of a "natural lifespan" or an "allotted term of years," beyond which life could be or is being prolonged. And we do, in fact, have some such picture of the life of a person, for we speak of death in infancy or childhood, for instance, as being "early" or "premature," and of the elderly as dying of "old age."

But although such a picture of the life of a person is, perhaps, inchoately in the background of some of our customary references to the artificial prolongation of life, it would be a mistake, I think, to take these notions as the focus of our moral problematic, for that would quite clearly be to overlook precisely the most morally significant cases. What I have in mind are such crucial and widely debated instances of coma, medically judged to be irreversible, as, for example the case of Karen Ann Quinlan.[3] Rather than risk getting entangled in peripheral historical issues, I shall fictionalize the case a bit. Instead of talking about Karen Ann Quinlan, I shall introduce, analogous to Alric, our candidate for euthanasia, a candidate for "letting die" whom I shall call "Bartholomew."

The facts of Bartholomew's case, let us suppose, are these: As a result of acute but transient viral encephalitis, Bartholomew has been rendered, at age 26, totally comatose. He is completely unresponsive to external stimuli. His cranial cavity is partially filled with fluid, and he registers an essentially flat (isoelectric) EEG. Competent medical personnel judge Bartholomew's coma to be, in all probability, irreversible, and they add that, were he somehow to regain consciousness, in view of the brain damage already undergone, he would in all likelihood be at best profoundly retarded, unable to perform such simple tasks as feeding himself or even, indeed, to initiate voluntary movements. Bartholomew shows no signs of suffering, and deliberately applied, painful stimuli such as pinpricks, in fact, leave him unaffected and unresponsive. Recently, however, portions of his autonomic nervous system have begun to deteriorate, in consequence of which his breathing has become irregular, labored, and at times convulsive. The physicians following the case are unanimously of the opinion that, if they do not intervene, in a matter of days or, at most, weeks, Bartholomew will lose the ability to breathe unaided, will undergo complete respiratory failure, and, in consequence, will die. Now there is available an apparatus—a respirator—which is capable of sustaining Bartholomew's respiratory functions—and thus his life—indefinitely. The question is: Should it be used?

7.4: A CRUCIAL ASYMMETRY

More accurately, to bring the ethical issues here into proper focus, the question here is: Morally speaking, *must* Bartholomew be connected to the respirator? For what is at issue in this case is whether refusing to use (omitting the use of, or, more generally, refraining from using) such artificial life-support systems would be morally permissible. Now it is morally permissible not to do something just in case doing that something is not itself morally obligatory (mandatory or required). The question of whether it is morally permissible to refrain from connecting Bartholomew to the respirator, therefore, is precisely equivalent to the question of whether it is morally obligatory to connect him to it. If the answer to the latter question is "Yes," then the answer to the former is, automatically, "No."

This observation, that rejection of the permissibility thesis is equivalent to the affirmation of a positive obligation to act, sharply separates Bartholomew's case from such questions of potential euthanasia as that which occupied us in Alric's. The equivalence implies, in particular, that the moral principles upon which the opponent of euthanasia based his arguments are simply inadequate to support the views of one who opposes our allowing Bartholomew to die without any outside intervention. To put the point in briefest form: Whereas in cases of possible euthanasia, the "burden of proof" lay with the advocate, in cases where what is at stake is the permissibility or impermissibility of refusing artificially to prolong life, it lies with the opponent.

The reason for this asymmetry is that a person's (prima facie absolute) "right to life" is a negative passive right. In Alric's case, where the moral permissibility of euthanasia was at issue, the opponent of "mercy killing" could rest his case on an appeal to this "absolute right to life," for what was there being proposed was that something be done to Alric which would, on the face of it, have been in violation of that right. The burden therefore lay with the advocate of euthanasia to produce moral considerations in favor of taking action which would be strong enough to override Alric's prima facie absolute right to life.

In the present case, however, the advocate of "letting die" is precisely proposing that nothing at all be done to Bartholomew (or, if something is already being done to him, that we stop doing it). The burden of argument consequently here lies with his opponent, that is, what someone who holds that Bartholomew should be—indeed, must be—connected to the respirator (or remain so connected). It is up to the would-be interventionist to provide sound moral reasons favoring (continued) intervention in Bartholomew's dying. In point of logic, however, Bartholomew's "absolute right to life" cannot be such a reason. As a negative passive right, a person's "right to life" can be appealed to in moral argumentation only to rule out certain conducts as morally impermissible. What it cannot do is serve to support a claim that specific positive actions are morally mandatory. But just that sort of reason is what someone who opposes allowing Bartholomew to die without intervention needs to make his moral case.

And what might such a reason be? If refusing to connect Bartholomew to the respirator is supposed to be morally wrong, what sort of moral wrong is it supposed to be? Within the framework of ultimate values which we have provisionally accepted, there are only two possible answers: Refusing artificially to prolong Bartholomew's life could be held to be wrong either (a) because it implies an ultimate net increase in suffering, or (b) because it implies an infringement of moral integrity, an ultimate net decrease in the possibilities for the exercise of moral autonomy. In the present instance, however, neither of these considerations has much immediate plausibility.

To begin with, Bartholomew himself, ex hypothesi, is not suffering. Someone who opposes allowing Bartholomew to die without intervention, then, cannot argue that he ought to be connected to the respirator in order to alleviate his suffering, for there is no suffering to alleviate. Consideration (a) thus drops out of the picture, and the opponent of "letting die" must therefore rest his moral case solely upon consideration (b), that is, on the claim that allowing Bartholomew to die without intervention offends against moral worth, i.e., implies an ultimate net decrease in occasions for the exercise of moral autonomy.

This, indeed, is how the moral argumentation runs in the cases of the child in the iron lung, the teenager undergoing dialysis, and the businessman with the pacemaker. In those instances, denial of life-supporting or life-sustaining technologies would demonstrably result in an ultimate net decrease in the possibilities for those individuals to exercise their moral autonomy in future choices and thus, given our assumptions concerning moral values, would demonstrably offend against moral worth. Although refusal of dialysis and the like in such cases would not be a violation of anyone's (negative, passive) prima facie "absolute right to life"—for no instance of refraining from acting could, in point of logic, violate any negative right—such a refusal can nevertheless *independently* be argued to be morally impermissible, on the grounds that such inaction would directly offend against the moral integrity and autonomy of persons, that is, would directly offend against those values upon which the derivative "right to life" was itself originally based.[4]

Bartholomew's case, however, is decisively different from these. Ex hypothesi, Bartholomew has aleady lost all capacity to exercise his moral autonomy. In Bartholomew's case, connecting him to the respirator would serve only to preserve and sustain him in his present state of incapacity. It would, however, have no demonstrable—nor even any likely—effect on occasions for the exercise of anyone's moral autonomy in choice at all.

The upshot then is that, insofar as they directly bear on matters of ultimate moral value, both the action of connecting Bartholomew to the respirator and the refusal to intervene in this way artificially to prolong Bartholomew's life appear to be morally neutral. Neither course directly implies either an ultimate net increase in suffering or an ultimate net decrease in the possibilities for the exercise of moral autonomy in choice and action.

Now such neutrality is enough to show that use of the respirator in this case would not itself be prima facie wrong. It imples, that is, that intervention in Bartholomew's dying is not morally forbidden on the face of it. But it certainly does not imply that such medical intervention is itself morally obligatory—and that is the conclusion which the opponent of "letting die" hoped to be able to reach. The moral neutrality of both courses of conduct—acting and refusing to act—when viewed in the light of their implications for matters of ultimate moral value, in fact, is insufficient to supply us with any positive reason at all in favor of using the respirator.

On this showing, then, the moral case goes to the opponent of intervention, to the advocate of "letting die," for his claim is only the weaker one that refusing to connect Bartholomew to the respirator (or refusing to continue so to intervene in Bartholomew's dying) is, in this instance, morally permissible, and that, indeed, is one thing which our arguments to this point may be rightly taken to show. It would not, on the face of it, be morally wrong to refrain from taking interventionist action artificially to prolong Bartholomew's life.

7.5: THE DIM ECHO
OF PRIOR DEBATES

As we saw in the case of opposition to euthanasia, however, relevant moral considerations can have a broader scope than the immediate consequences of action or inaction for the condition of a single individual. We ought therefore also ask whether is anything to be said in this instance about the indirect implications of using or not using the respirator in Bartholomew's case which would tip the moral balance in favor of someone who opposes simply allowing him to die without intervention. What, for example, are the actual and potential consequences of adopting the social practice of refraining from artificially prolonging the life of individuals in cases relevantly like Bartholomew's?

Here we can, I think, uncover something similar to the conflict of moral sensibilities we found underlying debates over the morality of euthanasia—but it will be, at best, only a faint and insubstantial echo of those earlier disagreements in attitude. Here, too, the opponent of "letting die" can point to a risk. He can call our attention, namely, to the risk that we might misidentify some cases as being relevantly like Bartholomew's case and thereby, through our inaction, allow some individuals to die who could have been saved and restored to normal (rational) functioning as moral agents. The last clause is, of course, crucial, for it is only in that case that such a misidentification would result in an ultimate net decrease in occasions for the exercise of moral autonomy. Still, such cases are possible, and, in such a case, to refrain from intervening would be to offend (unknowingly, to be sure) against moral worth and thus would be to behave in a manner which was, prima facie, morally wrong. However slight, then, there is a risk to which adopting the social policy of nonintervention in cases judged to be relevantly like Bartholomew's does subject us.

On the other side, the advocate of "letting die," while he cannot point to Bartholomew's suffering—for, ex hypothesi, Bartholomew is not suffering—can direct our attention to the "mental anguish" of Bartholomew's family and friends. He can point out, that is, that if Bartholomew is (or remains) connected to the respirator, those who care about him will have consciously to endure months, or even years, of agonized waiting for a death which, after all, is inevitable. They will have to live day after day with the reality of their loved one's helplessness and incapacity, to confront repeatedly his insensate and comatose body in its maze of wires and tubes, and, perhaps, to have their hopes for his recovery more than once falsely raised and then cruelly dashed. Here, then, is a kind of "net increase of suffering" which might well result from the artificial prolongation of Bartholomew's life. While this is probably not a sufficiently compelling consideration to allow us to conclude that it would be wrong to connect Bartholomew to the respirator, it does give us a reason for refusing to do so.

In a way, then, we can find here a mirror image of the conflict of moral sensibilities which underlay the dispute over euthanasia. The advocate of "letting die" is impressed by the potential suffering (of family and friends) inherent in Bartholomew's situation; the opponent, by the potential for infringements of moral autonomy implicit in a social policy of refusing artificially to prolong life in such cases.

It is important to appreciate, however, how dim an image of our earlier disagreement in sensibilities we have here. On the one hand, the "suffering" to which the advocate of "letting die" can here appeal is not, as it was in Alric's case, a real and present physical agony (insensitivity to which might suggest a certain callousness or hardness) but a more diffuse and, in a sense, merely theoretical "mental anguish," to be experienced, moreover, by people who will necessarily experience some such emotional disturbance in any event—a protracted "agony of waiting" if Bartholomew is connected to the respirator, but also a sudden and intense "pain of loss" if, instead, he is simply allowed to die.

On the other hand, the "risk" cited by the opponent of "letting die" is nothing like the risk to which the opponents of "mercy killing" could appeal. A social policy of euthanasia is a discretionary policy. Contingent upon a classification of individuals as suffering, "merely sentient" beings, it licenses actions which are violations of prima facie rights. A policy of this sort, it was correctly argued, would carry a real potential for abuse, since such a classification and the discretionary killings justified by appeal to it could be deliberately and perversely extended to violate the rights of, in principle, indefinitely large and wholly arbitrary classes of individuals.

A social policy of refusing to prolong the lives of terminally ill, comatose individuals, however, carries no such potential for abuse. It is, first of all, not itself a discretionary policy but, rather, limited in the scope of its applications to comatose individuals who are judged to be dying and thus not, even in principle, indefinitely and arbitrarily extendable. Secondly, however, the conducts licensed by a policy of nonintervention in such cases are also not violations of anyone's prima facie rights to begin with. A person's "absolute right to life" is a negative passive right which, in point of logic, cannot be violated simply by allowing a dying person actually to die.

A social policy of "mercy killing" proposes to found a class of "justified exceptions"—that is, violations of prima facie rights ostensibly justified by overriding moral considerations—and therefore carries the real risk of being abused by diabolical extensions to unjustified exceptions—that is, cases in which those overriding moral considerations do not in fact apply. A social policy of refusing to prolong the lives of terminally ill, comatose individuals, however, since it does not originally propose that we acknowledge any cases of "justified violations of rights," logically cannot be abused in the same way, for there is no class of "special cases" established by the policy to be extended, diabolically or otherwise. To the extent that we assume any risk here at all, then, it is not a moral risk analogous to that implicit in a discretionary euthanasia policy but only, at worst, the mild "epistemological" risk of occasionally wrongly judging the loss of those rational capacities needed for the exercise of moral autonomy by a comatose individual to be permanent and irreversible, while at the same time correctly judging that individual to be dying—a possibility, to be sure, but one which is only remote, merely theoretical, and not at all morally threatening.

7.6: THE MORALLY RIGHT
AND THE MORALLY BETTER

What the considerations which we have so far developed collectively imply is that the question of the moral permissibility of allowing such irreversibly comatose, terminally ill individuals as Bartholomew (or Karen Ann

Quinlan) to die without medical intervention ought to be significantly less problematic than questions concerning the morality of putting to death such suffering, acutely brain-damaged individuals as Alric. Viewed with regard to their likely consequences for Bartholomew alone, both connecting him to the respirator and refusing to do so appeared, in relation to matters of ultimate moral value, to be morally neutral. Broadening our considerations to encompass the consequences of each alternative course of conduct for other individuals (friends and family) and the implications of adopting one or the other practice as a matter of social policy, we were able to find a pale echo of the real conflict of moral sensibilities and priorities which underlies sophisticated disputes over euthanasia. We did locate, as it were, logical room for divergent conclusions as to whether anything should be done in Bartholomew's case. What we did not find, however, was any cogent (or even plausible) strand of moral argumentation which supported the substantive stand of the opponent of "letting die": that, in such cases as Bartholomew's, something (morally speaking) must be done, that is, that we are morally obligated to make use of the life-sustaining medical technologies at our disposal.

To put the contrast differently, on the question of euthanasia or "mercy killing," what we found was that, even given complete agreement regarding both the facts of the case and matters of ultimate moral value, there could still be a real disagreement, rooted in a difference of moral sensibilities or attitudes, over whether putting to death an individual in Alric's condition was or was not morally permissible. In cases of "letting die" or the refusal artificially to prolong life, however, although participants in the dispute evidently think of themselves as debating the parallel question (whether refusing to intervene in Bartholomew's case would be morally permissible), what our investigations show is that the actual question at issue here must be a different one. For we have discovered that there simply are no cogent, or even plausible, moral arguments in support of the conclusion that refusal to intervene is morally impermissible, that is, in support of the conclusion that intervention is itself mandatory or morally obligatory.

Now it is easy to fall into the trap of supposing that moral considerations are exhausted by determinations of what is obligatory, what is permissible, and what is forbidden. It is important to recognize, however, that the question "What, morally speaking, ought I do?" is not equivalent to the question "What, morally speaking, must I do?" For, in a given situation, there may well be nothing at all which, morally speaking, I must do (or refrain from doing)—nothing at all (among the conducts open to me), that is, which is either morally mandatory or morally forbidden. I might, instead, find myself confronting an array of alternative possible courses of conduct each of which was equally morally permissible and none of which was morally mandatory. That fact, however, would not in itself preclude my sensibly raising the question "What, morally speaking, ought I do?" for I might still be wholly unclear as to which of my various permissible alternatives would be the best one for me to pursue from the moral point of view.

What our investigations of the issue of artificial prolongation of life show us, I want to suggest, is that the real disagreement over whether or not to connect Bartholomew to the respirator must be a disagreement about this sort of question—about whether it would be better, morally speaking, to intervene in his dying or simply to allow him to die. What I propose is actually at issue in (logically coherent) debates over the artificial prolongation of life, in other words, is not whether refusing to intervene in the dying of terminally ill, irreversibly comatose individuals is morally permissible, but the quite different question of whether such refusal to intervene, although permissible, would or would not be morally desirable.

This hypothesis explains quite simply the attenuated character of those moral considerations which, we have seen, do come into play in these disputes. Implications concerning matters of ultimate moral value, and a corresponding divergence of moral sensibilities, are still relevant to the question genuinely at issue here—for it is, after all, a question of moral desirability which is in dispute—but they enter, so to speak, at one remove. Thus, whereas the advocate of euthanasia could argue that Alric's was a case of real and immediate suffering which we were morally obligated to alleviate, the advocate of "letting die" has available only the weaker appeal: "Bartholomew's family and friends must undergo some emotional disturbance in any case. It is (morally) better to get it over with quickly." And, analogously, whereas the opponent of euthanasia could argue that putting Alric to death meant acquiescing in a policy of discretionary violations of prima facie absolute rights, a policy whose real potential for abuse rendered it morally forbidden to us, the opponent of "letting die" again has available only a weaker argument: "If we keep Bartholomew alive, we might find a way of restoring him to autonomous functioning as a rational moral agent. It is even possible that he will spontaneously recover his sentient and rational capacities. This may indeed be highly unlikely, but it is (morally) better not to take any chances."

Here we do again find a disagreement in moral sensibilities. Each party to the debate over artificial prolongation of life again looks out on the same factual scene with a different moral focus—one stressing considerations of suffering and the other emphasizing considerations of moral autonomy. But in this instance the disagreement in sensibilities comes into play at a later stage of moral deliberation—only after primary questions concerning obligatoriness and permissibility have, in principle, been settled. For the moral values which our disputants share do not in this case supply either party with arguments morally excluding or morally compelling either action or inaction, however the weights assigned to considerations of suffering and considerations of moral autonomy may variously be distributed.

7.7: ON WHAT'S WRONG
WITH "RIGHTS"

If what I have been arguing is correct, then, the disagreement over the morality of artificially prolonging the life of a terminally ill, comatose individual or refusing to do so has been almost universally misconceived. A dispute over moral desirability has been regularly mislocated as a dispute over moral permissibility. Now it is not the job of analytic philosophy—in its professional capacity, so to speak—to attempt to settle disputes over moral desirability, any more than it was the job of analytic philosophy to settle the dispute over the moral permissibility or impermissibility of euthanasia. One thing which we can properly and profitably undertake to do here, however, is to offer some hypotheses as to how and why a disagreement of one sort comes to be so widely misperceived as a disagreement of another sort. The quick answer, of course, is that someone is confused about something. But who is it, and what is he or she confused about?

Well, one thing which almost everyone is confused about is the "trap" which I mentioned a short time ago. It is, unfortunately, easy to suppose that moral deliberations terminate once alternative courses of conduct have been sorted according to their "deontic" status, into the obligatory, the permissible, and the forbidden. It is easy to suppose, that is, that once we pass beyond these primary deontic deliberations, we straightaway enter a purely "subjective" territory of individual inclinations and personal preferences. But this is obviously confused, for both within the realm of morally permissible conducts and within the realm of morally forbidden ones, there is clearly still room for distinguishing conducts which are morally better from those which are morally worse. Some right acts are not merely permissible but positively saintly, and some moral offenses are not merely forbidden but qualify as authentic atrocities.

One thing which leads so many people to lose sight of this simple point is a certain limitation which they tend to impose upon their moral vocabularies. Specifically, if one conducts one's moral discussions entirely in the idiom of "rights," it is precisely the distinctions between the morally better and the morally worse which are likely to be overlooked—and talk of rights, we all know, is very much the fashion of the day. The typical upshot of this tendency, however, is a confused idea to the effect that, given two mutually exclusive alternative courses of conduct in some situation, one of them can be morally better than the other only by being morally obligatory, the remaining alternative being ruled out, as morally forbidden, on the grounds that it would infringe upon or violate someone's rights.

Put thus blatantly, the thesis is not one which is likely to seem very plausible to anyone. But, of course, the thesis is typically not formulated at all, but rather tacitly or implicitly taken for granted by the simple expedient of raising only deontic questions about what is obligatory, permissible, or forbidden, and then admitting, as considerations relevant to the limited class of questions thus raised, only arguments to the effect that this or that course of conduct would or would not infringe upon someone's rights.

7.8: SOME KEY POINTS ABOUT RIGHTS ANYWAY

A second source of the mislocation of the dispute over "letting die" can be found in the confusion of artificially prolonged life with artificially aided or sustained life. The coupling of a loss of independent syntropic capabilities with the loss of rational and sentient capacities in the former instance, however, has significant moral consequences. It introduces a moral asymmetry into cases such as Bartholomew's which is missing from such cases as those of the child in the iron lung, the teenager with renal failure, and the business-man who needs a pacemaker, in which the loss of independent syntropic capabilities is unaccompanied by any further functional impairments.

In these latter cases, in fact, one's failure or refusal to intervene artifi-cially to sustain some individual's life is, in an important sense, morally equivalent to a positive act of killing or putting to death. If, for example, only I am in a position to supply a renally dysfunctional teenager—call him "Harold"—with dialysis treatments, and it is easily within my power to do so, then I am, prima facie, morally obliged to do so. My refusing to act or re-fraining from acting here would be as morally wrong as if I were deliber-ately to put to death—say, by stabbing or shooting—some other teenager (call her "Helene") whose kidneys were perfectly in order.

The reason for this moral equivalence of action and inaction here is simply that the consequences of my refusing Harold his dialysis treatments (that is, of my doing nothing) are identical to the consequences of my stabbing or shooting Helene (that is, of my doing something) insofar as those consequences concern matters of ultimate value. In both instances, any further possibility for one specific rational agent ever again to exercise his or her moral autonomy in deliberation, choice, and action is summarily and arbitrarily precluded as a direct result of my choice and conduct (action or inaction).[5]

Now I have argued that our implicit morality in fact acknowledges that every human being possesses a prima facie "right to life." But I have also argued that this "right to life" is not only "absolute" (in that it is a right which human beings have simply by virtue of belonging to the natural kind which they do) and "passive" (in that it is a right to be respected by others, rather than exercised by those who have it), but also "negative" (that is, a right not to have certain things done to one, to be free from certain impositions or limitations). In arbitrarily putting Helene to death by shooting or stabbing her, then, I eo ipso violate her "right to life."

But, one might ask, does not Harold, whom I refuse easily available di-alysis treatments, have an analogous "positive" passive prima facie "abso-lute" right—a right to have certain things done for him—which I eo ipso vio-late by not supplying him with the treatments? I want next to argue that he does not. I want, in fact, to argue that our implicit moral theory does not acknowledge any positive passive "absolute" rights, nor should it.

This is precisely the point at which the present confusion interacts with the former one. If we mistakenly assume that the only way in which a con-duct (whether action or inaction) can be morally wrong is by virtue of being a violation of someone's rights, then we will feel the need to acknowledge a positive passive "absolute" right in this instance precisely to guarantee the moral equivalence of the action of killing Helene and the refusal to act which allows Harold to die. This motivation for acknowledging positive passive "absolute" rights, however, is wholly spurious. Acknowledging such a right here would, in fact, be completely superfluous, for we have just seen that the moral equivalence of action and inaction in this case is already guar-anteed by a direct appeal to the respective implications of action and inac-tion for matters of ultimate moral value. Indeed, it is guaranteed by a direct appeal to the same matters of ultimate moral value to which our implicit moral theory appeals in support of the acknowledgment of negative passive prima facie "absolute" rights (e.g., to life) in the first place.

On the other hand, any moral theory (implicit or explicit) which proposes to acknowledge a class of positive passive "absolute" rights immediately confronts a quite general problem: There doesn't seem to be anybody in particular who is obligated to respect such presumed rights.

Everybody is (individually) morally obligated to respect someone's "absolute" negative passive prima facie rights. That is, everybody is (individually) morally obligated to refrain from doing to someone what he has an "absolute" right not to have done to him. But if we held that an individual has, in addition, some positive passive rights which are also, in the same way, "absolute"—that is, which he has simply by virtue of belonging to the natural kind which he does—and then ask who is obligated to respect these rights—that is, who is obliged to do for him what he supposedly has a right to have done for him—the answer can only be "somebody or other" or, perhaps, "society." The difficulty, here, however, is that neither of these answers picks out a moral agent (or class of individual moral agents) who could subsequently arguably be shown to have violated that supposed right through inaction.

The point is a simple logical one.

(1) I killed Helene

together with

(2) Everybody is (individually) morally obligated not to kill anyone

does entail that

(3) I did something morally forbidden

and, eo ipso, implies that I have violated Helene's negative passive "absolute right to life." But

(4) I refused Harold his dialysis treatments

together with

(5) "Society" is morally obligated to supply everyone with the minimum essentials for life

does not entail that I have done anything morally forbidden, nor, indeed, does it imply that anyone (that is, any person) has violated Harold's supposed positive passive "absolute right to the essentials for life."

Any moral theory which acknowledged positive passive "absolute" rights would inevitably find itself in this inconclusive position. Suppose it were claimed that every human being has a positive passive "absolute" right to have something, X, done for him. But suppose, too, that no one in fact does X for, say, Noreen. Plainly enough, Noreen's right to have X done for her has been violated. The difficulty, however, is that, while such supposed positive passive "absolute" rights would obligate everyone collectively, they would not obligate anyone individually. Thus, although one of Noreen's supposed rights would have been violated, there would be no individual person of whom it could be argued or demonstrated that he or she violated Noreen's right. The information that one of Noreen's ostensible positive passive "absolute" rights was violated, therefore, would remain useless in practice. There would be nothing further that anyone could do with that bit of news.

Now the whole point of having a category of rights within a moral system is to provide individuals with principles—which can be promulgated and enforced—that will serve as moral constraints on conduct and as guides for moral appraisal. But just this is what a supposed positive passive "absolute" right could not do. From the assertion that Noreen has a right to have X done for her (to have someone supply her with X) nothing follows about what I (or any other specific individual) am obliged to do. And from the observation that no one in fact did X for Noreen (supplied her with X), nothing follows about my moral culpability or blameworthiness (nor about that of any other specific individual). As constraints on individuals' conduct and as guides to the moral appraisal of individuals' behavior, in short, positive passive "absolute" rights would be completely useless. There is no reason, then, that a moral theory should acknowledge such rights.

Of course, the matter stands quite differently with regard to "conditional" positive passive rights—rights which someone has, not by virtue of belonging to this or that natural kind, but by virtue of standing in some special relationship to other (specific) individuals. If, for example, I am Harold's father, my refusal to supply him with dialysis treatments is, eo ipso, a violation of one of his positive passive rights. It is not, however, a violation of one of his "absolute" or "human" rights, but rather of a right which he has by reason of the special relationship between us. In particular, it is a violation of one of his "filial" rights. A child does have a positive passive right to have certain things done for it by its parents, and the parents have a correlative moral obligation to do these things for their child (or to see to it that they are done). This is true for the simple reason that, in bringing a child into the world, the parents voluntarily assume such obligations and thereby, automatically, grant the child the corresponding rights.

Unlike our hypothetical "absolute" positive passive rights, then, such "conditional" positive passive rights are not useless or idle. They can and do serve both morally to constrain the conducts of specific individuals and to guide others in the moral appraisal of those individuals' behavior. Along with "conditional" negative passive rights, indeed, such "conditional" positive rights supply the conceptual "fine structure" of our whole moral society. For they are precisely the differentia which subdivide the generic ethical kind "person" into the diverse ethical species "parent," "child," "adviser," "protector," "teacher," "healer," "friend," and the like—which are the categories of thought and action in terms of which we regulate our common expectations and conduct our daily affairs.[6]

7.9: THE MORAL ASYMMETRY OF "MERCY KILLING" AND "LETTING DIE"

The point of this longish excursion through the theory of rights has been to show us how the introduction of sentient and rational functional incapacities into the facts of a case can make a moral difference. I have argued that, although killing Helene and allowing Harold to die are morally equivalent conducts, killing Alric and allowing Bartholomew to die are not. As a result of our trip to the land of rights, we are finally in a position to say precisely why they are not.

The moral wrongness of killing Helene is, so to speak, "overdetermined." We can, of course, argue directly from considerations of ultimate moral value that killing Helene is morally forbidden as an offense against moral worth, for it would terminate the very possibility of her exercising her moral autonomy in deliberation, choice, and action. But we can also argue indirectly for the moral wrongness of killing Helene by appealing to the negative passive prima facie "absolute right to life" which our implicit morality (appealing to the same considerations of ultimate values) acknowledges her to have simply by virtue of the fact that she is a human being, and then noting that putting her to death would, eo ipso, violate that "human" right.

As I have shown, however, the moral wrongness of allowing Harold to die, on the other hand, can be established only by the first, direct, sort of moral reasoning, for there is no positive passive "absolute right to life" to ground an argument of the second, indirect, sort. The crucial point, however, is that the moral wrongness of inaction in Harold's case can be established. In the envisaged situation, it would be as morally wrong for me, through my inaction, to allow Harold to die as it would be for me, through acting, to take Helene's life. In this situation, then, there is moral parity. Acting and refraining are arguably both morally forbidden to me, and so are conducts which are arguably morally equivalent to one another.

In the cases of Alric and Bartholomew, loss of independent syntropic capabilities is accompanied by a complete and irreversible loss of rational functional capacities as well. Ex hypothesi, in other words, both Alric and Bartholomew have already permanently lost any possibility of exercising moral autonomy in rational deliberation and principled action. The immediate consequence of this fact, however, is that the direct way of arguing for the moral wrongness of some conduct vis-à-vis either Alric or Bartholomew is no longer available to us. Neither the action of putting Alric to death nor the refusal to intervene which allows Bartholomew to die has any immediate consequences concerning matters of ultimate moral worth. Neither conduct offends directly against anyone's moral autonomy. Consequently, neither conduct can be argued to be morally wrong on the grounds that it implies an ultimate net decrease in moral worth.

Here, however, the two cases part company. In Alric's case, we still have available to us the indirect way of arguing for the moral impermissibility of putting him to death. For all his functional incapacitation, Alric is still a human being. He therefore still possesses that negative passive "absolute right to life" which all human beings prima facie possess simply because they are human beings. To put Alric to death, then, would still be, eo ipso, to violate that ("human") right.

In the case of Bartholomew, however, there remains no line of moral reasoning which supports the conclusion that allowing him to die by refusing to connect him to the respirator is impermissible or forbidden. Ex hypothesi, the facts of the case preclude our appealing to the direct line of moral argumentation here. But in Bartholomew's case—as in Harold's—there never was any other, indirect line of moral reasoning which led to the conclusion that we were obliged to sustain his life in the first place. Of course, if there were a positive passive prima facie "absolute right to life" which Bartholomew (or Harold) possessed simply by virtue of the fact that he is a human being, then such an indirect line of moral reasoning would have been available. But, as I have attempted to demonstrate, our implicit morality neither acknowledges nor should acknowledge any such "absolute" positive passive rights.

And so we are left without any grounds, direct or indirect, upon which someone opposed to allowing Bartholomew simply to die without intervention could cogently base a charge of moral impermissibility. Despite their many analogies to the cases of Helene and Harold, then, the cases of Alric and Bartholomew are not morally equivalent.[7] We may still raise substantive questions concerning the moral desirability of "letting die," but our implicit moral theory does not render its permissibility problematic in the way in which it does provide scope for genuine and substantive disagreements about the permissibility of euthanasia or "mercy killing."

7.10: IN WHICH WE ENTER THE JUNGLE OF THE THEORY OF ACTION

Finally, we must unravel still a third source of the mislocation of the dispute over "letting die." This source of confusion can be traced to the fact that most of the moral deliberation addressed to cases such as Bartholomew's takes place post facto. Typically, that is, a comatose and dying individual will be connected to a respirator as a matter of course, and only then, if at all, are questions likely to be raised about the morality of some course of conduct. The intricate confusions having their roots in this fact will prove the most difficult of all to untangle.

When moral questions are raised post facto about a case like Bartholomew's, the conduct at issue is likely to be described, for example, as "turning off the respirator." Since turning off a respirator is obviously every bit as much a positive action as, say, administering an overdose of morphine, it is characteristically simply assumed that the question at hand is, morally speaking, no different in principle from the question of whether it would be permissible to take the latter action, for example, in a case such as Alric's. Since the dispute over the morality of euthanasia is a dispute over the moral permissibility of some such positive action as administering an overdose of morphine, it is then a simple matter to take it for granted that any dispute over the morality of "turning off the respirator" must also be a dispute over the moral permissibility or impermissibility of some positive action.

Now I have already pointed out that, although "turning off the respirator" is, indeed, a positive action, the object of this action (that is, the "entity" to whom something is done) is not the human being, Bartholomew, but, at best, the complex system (human being + artifact) consisting of Bartholomew in continuous causal interaction with a respirator. The subject of our moral deliberations post facto, in other words, is apparently different from the subject of analogous deliberations before action was taken to intervene in Bartholomew's dying. So the first point which needs to be made is that, even if the dispute over "turning off the respirator" turned out to be a dispute over the moral permissibility of some course of conduct, it would not follow that a dispute prior to any intervention would also be addressed to questions of moral permissibility. None of our earlier conclusions, in short, is at all affected by our now agreeing that "turning off the respirator" is itself a positive action, for it is a positive action performed upon a different object from that of the positive action "connecting Bartholomew to the respirator"—the action which was contemplated in preintervention deliberations.

But I also noted earlier that we can shift our post facto moral deliberations so that they do address the same subject as analogous deliberations prior to intervention, namely, the human being Bartholomew. When we do so, however, it becomes incumbent upon us to select an alternative description of the positive action which we called "turning off the respirator." What we need to ask ourselves is: "What would we be doing, not to the respirator, but to Bartholomew?" Once the question is focused in this way, it becomes immediately obvious that what we would now be doing (propose to do) to Bartholomew would be an undoing of something which we did to him previously. We would be discontinuing (terminating or ceasing) the (automatically) ongoing intervention in Bartholomew's dying which we initiated by the positive action of connecting him to the respirator in the first place.

Now any positive human action admits of an indefinite number of alternative descriptions.[8] What we might call the "minimum description" of such an action will specify only the bodily movements made by the individual who performs it—for example, "moving my finger." Depending upon other circumstances, however, this "minimum action" of moving my finger might also be the action of pulling a trigger, of firing a gun, of shooting Helene, and even of killing Helene. Here the boundaries of my action are, so to speak, descriptively pushed outward in space and forward in time so as to include, progressively, more and more of the surroundings of the "minimum action" and more and more of its consequences in the description of my positive "total action."

In different circumstances, the same "minimum action" of moving my finger might instead have been the action of flicking a switch, of turning off a light, and of darkening the room. Here we not only push our descriptive boundaries outward in space and forward in time from the "minimum action" to include more and more of its surroundings and consequences, but also backward in time to include, as it were, its preconditions. "Turning off a light" describes something I do by moving my finger and flicking a switch only if, prior to the time of my "minimum action," that light is already on.

For such transitive actions as these—i.e., actions which take an object, actions in which something is done to something—what I do (the verb) is descriptively correlative to whom or what I do it to (the direct object). What I flick, for example, is the switch; what I turn off is the light; and what I darken is the room. Conversely, what I do to the switch is flick it; what I do to the light is turn it off; and what I do to the room is darken it.

There are, in other words, two directions in which the process of selecting a description for some transitive positive action can proceed. It can begin with the specification of an act (that is, with the choice of a verb) and move toward a determination of its object, or it can begin with the specification of an object and move toward a determination of the act. In settling upon an appropriate redescription of "turning off the respirator" in the context of our post facto moral deliberations about what was done, not to the respirator, but to Bartholomew, we have obviously been following the latter procedure. "Turning off the respirator," for example, might also have been correctly redescribable as "moving my finger" or "flicking a switch" had we begun the process of choosing our redescription with specification of an object other than Bartholomew himself.

We have found, however, that by specifying the object of our contemplated positive action as the human being, Bartholomew, we are logically constrained to adopt a description of the act (that is, to select a verb) which is essentially "backward looking in time." To describe some action as a "discontinuing" or "terminating" or "ceasing" of some process or activity logically implies that this process or activity was going on for some time before the action in question. In the specific case of Bartholomew, in fact, this phenomenon of "backward time reference" actually duplicates itself. Let me explain.

The process or activity which the contemplated positive action ceases, terminates, or discontinues in this instance is itself a process of ongoing intervention in another process or activity (Bartholomew's dying). 'Intervention', however, is itself as "backward looking in time" as 'discontinuing'. To describe one process as an "ongoing intervention" in some other process or activity, that is, logically implies that this other process or activity had already begun at some time before it was intervened in, and thus logically implies the prior existence of some event which counts as the "onset" or "initiation" of the subsequently ongoing intervention.

Since the "intervention" in the present instance is a human intervention in a natural process (dying), we can reach, in fact, a more specific conclusion. The event which counts as the onset or initiation of that ongoing intervention must itself have been a human event—that is, something which a human being does or did. It must, in other words, itself have been another positive action.

The upshot of these logical reflections is that our describing what would be done to Bartholomew (in "turning off the respirator") as "discontinuing an ongoing intervention in Bartholomew's dying" logically implies the existence of a prior positive action correctly describable as "initiating an ongoing intervention in Bartholomew's dying." Of course, we know what that prior action was. It was just the action which we could also correctly describe as our "connecting Bartholomew to the respirator."

It will be convenient to have a name for two positive action-descriptions which are logically related in the way that we have found "initiating an ongoing intervention in Bartholomew's dying" and "discontinuing an ongoing intervention in Bartholomew's dying" to be related. Following some customary usages, I shall speak of descriptions of a "doing" and its subsequent "undoing." The logico-linguistic observations which I have just been making, then, can be expressed more compactly by saying that the existence of an undoing logically implies the existence of a prior doing whose outcome it undoes. I shall call the positive action of undoing the outcome of a prior doing "restoring the status quo."

All this complicated business about the multiple descriptions of a positive action is important to us because determining the "deontic status" of such an action—whether it is morally obligatory, permissible, or forbidden—requires that we first settle upon the morally relevant description of that action. It is not moving a finger or pulling a trigger or even firing a gun which is morally forbidden, for example; it is killing Helene.

Now there are just two kinds of morally relevant descriptions of positive actions. The first kind describes an action in terms of its moral consequences; the second, in terms of what I shall call its "moral species." A description in terms of moral consequences specifies the implications of an action for matters of ultimate moral value. If we know of an otherwise unspecified action that it is correctly describable as "causing suffering" or as "diminishing the possibility for exercises of moral autonomy," then we know something about the action which is relevant to assigning it a "deontic status" (although, perhaps, not everything we would need to know about it to settle its deontic status as morally mandatory, morally permissible, or morally forbidden).

A description in terms of moral species, on the other hand, brings the action within the scope of a moral principle. Moral principles specify the prima facie deontic status of kinds of acts—killings, torturings, imprisonings, lyings, promise-breakings, and so on. When we know that an action is correctly describable as belonging to one of these kinds—the kinds mentioned in our moral principles—then we again know something (although again perhaps not everything) relevant to determining the deontic status of that action.

7.11: THE ULTIMATE IRRELEVANCE OF A FAIT ACCOMPLI

We are finally in the position to ask the question which all of this conceptual stage-setting has been leading up to: What are the morally relevant descriptions of the action which we initially identified as "turning off the respirator"? In particular, what we need to know is whether there is any correct, morally relevant description of this action which would assign it to the "deontic status" of being prima facie morally forbidden. If there is not—if no correct description of the action implies, even on the face of it, that it is morally wrong—it will follow that what is genuinely at issue in disputes over the morality of "turning off the respirator" once again cannot be the moral permissibility of that action, whether or not that is what the parties to those disputes (mistakenly) think they are disagreeing about.

The moral permissibility of "turning off the respirator" can be actually problematic only if there is some correct description of that action in the first place which implies, at least prima facie, that it is morally impermissible. Failing the availability of such a correct description of the action, we are forced to conclude that moral disputes over "turning off the respirator," like the disputes over "connecting Bartholomew to the respirator," are actually addressed to questions of moral desirability—the question, for instance, of whether it would be better or worse, morally speaking, to discontinue an on-going intervention in Bartholomew's dying that has already been begun. The deontic status of "turning off the respirator," however, would no longer be in question. Like connecting Bartholomew to the respirator and refusing to do so, both turning off the respirator and refraining from doing so would have the deontic status of acts which were morally permitted.

But now I think that it is a relatively straightforward matter to see that there is, in fact, no correct, morally relevant description of the action of "turning off the respirator" under which it does turn out to be an action which is prima facie morally forbidden. Certainly "turning off the respirator" is not itself such a description, for turning off a respirator is, by itself, no more morally impermissible on the face of it than, for example, firing a gun.

Nor does a consideration of the moral consequences of "turning off the respirator" supply us with any descriptions of a prima facie morally forbidden action. In order to do so, the consequences of turning off the respirator would need to imply either an ultimate net increase in suffering or an ultimate net decrease in the possibilities for the exercise of moral autonomy. In the case of Bartholomew, however, he ex hypothesi neither suffers nor is he capable of exercising his moral autonomy in deliberation, choice, and action—whether or not he is connected to the respirator. When connected to the respirator, Bartholomew is comatose and insentient, and disconnecting him would serve only to restore a status quo in which Bartholomew was also comatose and insentient. Insofar as its implications for matters of ultimate moral value are concerned, in other words, the action of turning off the respirator turns out to be morally indifferent. It follows, therefore, that there is no correct redescription of that action in terms of its moral consequences which is, at the same time, a description of an action which is prima facie morally wrong.

In principle, however, it might still be the case that the action which we have singled out as "turning off the respirator" belongs, under some correct redescription, to a moral species of acts all of which are, at least prima facie, morally forbidden. But this, too, turns out not to be correct. For what moral species could it be? The only remotely plausible candidate is: "killing." Acts of killing are, indeed, morally impermissible on the face of it, and so, if the action of turning off the respirator were correctly redescribable as an act of killing, it would follow that this action, too, would be prima facie morally proscribed. The problem with this line of approach, however, is that the description 'killing' is not a correct redescription of the action which we have identified as "turning off the respirator."

For, if we turn off the respirator, what or whom do we kill? We do not kill the complex system (human being + artifact) consisting of Bartholomew in continuous causal interaction with the respirator, for the simple reason that this system is not alive to begin with—and, in point of logic, one can only kill what is alive. Such a complex system, that is, is not itself a living organism (although it contains one, as a component or constituent), and so it is not even the logically possible object of an act of killing.

Bartholomew, to be sure, is a living organism—at least as long as he remains connected to the respirator—but in turning off the respirator, we do not kill Bartholomew either. For we already know what we do to Bartholomew when we turn off the respirator. We discontinue an ongoing intervention in the process of Bartholomew's dying. That is, we restore a status quo in which Bartholomew was already dying—and then we allow him to die. But allowing someone to die is not killing him.

What is at work here, in fact, is a general feature of undoings: The moral species of an undoing is not determined by its own character as a positive or negative action, but rather by its logical relationship to another action, to the doing whose consequences it undoes. To put the same point in a more useful way, the deontic status of an undoing is logically parasitic on the deontic status of the doing whose consequences it undoes. The deontic status of the undoing of some doing, X, indeed, will be completely determined by the deontic status of X itself.

Suppose, for example, that the doing, X, is "imprisoning Cedric"; its undoing, "freeing Cedric from prison." Now if Cedric is, for instance, a legally sentenced criminal, imprisoning him will presumably have been morally mandatory. Other things being equal, then, freeing Cedric from prison will a fortiori be impermissible. Its moral species will be something like "aiding and abetting a criminal escape." But if, on the other hand, Cedric is unjudged and, in fact, innocent, imprisoning him in the first place will have been a morally forbidden act, a violation of his rights. Freeing Cedric from prison, then, becomes morally permissible—an action in the interests of justice. Of course, if doing X in the first place were itself neither obligatory nor forbidden, then undoing X will also be neither obligatory nor forbidden—both undoing X and refraining from undoing X, that is, will themselves be morally permissible.

The ground of these deontic interdependences is quite straightforward: In restoring the status quo, we restore at the same time its deontic status. It follows, then, that if doing X was, for example, originally morally obligatory, in undoing X we would be restoring a status quo in which it was once again morally obligatory to do X—that is, obligatory, so to speak, to undo our undoing of X. But this is just to say that undoing X in this instance must itself be morally impermissible. It is an action which would take us, as it were, to a place where we have always been morally obligated not to go.

If we now apply these considerations to the particular case of Bartholomew, what we see is that the fact that our moral deliberations take place post facto is completely irrelevant to the correct outcome of those deliberations. The action we have been calling "turning off the respirator" will be prima facie morally forbidden just in case it was prima facie morally obligatory to connect Bartholomew to the respirator in the first place. But that, we have already seen, was not the case. Connecting Bartholomew to the respirator was neither morally obligatory nor morally forbidden to begin with. It follows, therefore, that turning off the respirator (and, parenthetically, refusing to turn it off as well) is itself, on the face of it, morally permissible.

It follows also that there can be no correct, morally relevant redescription of that action on which it turns out to be prima facie impermissible. Not only is the action of turning off the respirator not an act of killing, then, but it is an action which will not be correctly describable as belonging to any moral species of prima facie forbidden acts. The deontic status of turning off the respirator or refraining from doing so, in short, is precisely the same as that of connecting Bartholomew to the respirator in the first place or refusing to do so.

The surprising upshot of all this, then, is that the fact that our deliberations about Bartholomew take place post facto—after he has been connected to the respirator—makes no moral difference at all. It is easy to understand, however, how one might straightaway suppose that it does. After all, the facts of the case have been changed. Bartholomew is now connected to the respirator, his syntropic functioning artificially sustained. Whereas before, if nothing further were done, Bartholomew would have died, now, if nothing further is done, he will live. And surely so great a factual difference must make a difference to the moral status of various possible conducts in the case.

It is precisely this line of thought, however, which I have just shown to be mistaken. Certainly connecting Bartholomew to the respirator does make some difference to the case. In particular, it makes possible certain actions (e.g., disconnecting Bartholomew from the respirator) which were not possible prior to our intervention in Bartholomew's dying. It makes possible, that is, certain new conducts—indeed, even certain new positive actions—whose deontic status as obligatory, forbidden, or permissible we need to take into account. But the deontic status of these newly possible actions turns out to be completely determined by the deontic status of our various alternatives prior to intervening in Bartholomew's dying. While connecting Bartholomew to the respirator does make some difference to the case, in other words, it does not make any moral difference to the case.

Even the fact that turning off the respirator is itself a positive action turns out, surprisingly, to be morally irrelevant. What is morally relevant is that this action, redescribed as something done to Bartholomew, turns out to be the undoing of a doing with which we initiated our intervention in his dying. Its moral species and its deontic status, consequently, are not determined by its own (intrinsic) character as a positive action, but instead are fixed entirely by its logical relationship to the prior doing whose consequences it undoes.

In short, while the facts of the case have indeed been changed, once we connect Bartholomew to the respirator, the morally relevant facts of the case have not been changed. For these morally relevant facts are that Bartholomew is comatose and insentient, that he has irreversibly lost all rational capacity, and that, without artificial life-support, Bartholomew will shortly die—and those are facts which remain facts whether or not Bartholomew has been connected to a respirator.

The tacit supposition that the morally relevant facts of some case must be different post facto is the third source of the mislocation of the dispute over "letting die" as a dispute over the moral permissibility or impermissibility of some conduct. But, however plausible a tacit supposition it may be, we have seen that it, too, rests upon confusions about actions and morally relevant considerations—indeed, upon linguistic confusions about the possible descriptions of some action and the correct morally relevant redescriptions of that action. Ultimately, then, this supposition, too, must be abandoned as a mistake. In the case of Bartholomew, our implicit moral theory delivers a decisive deontic verdict: both intervening in the process of his dying and refusing so to intervene (and both continuing an ongoing intervention already begun and terminating such an intervention) are actions which are prima facie morally permissible. Which of these actions would be morally desirable, however, remains, of course, an open question—and not one for the special interests of analytic philosophy alone to address.

CHAPTER 8

"Rational Suicide": The Question of Abandoning Life

8.1: THE CASE OF DARCY

The questions of euthanasia and refusing artificially to prolong life, "mercy killing" and "letting die," by no means exhaust the topic of the ethics of death. Such cases as Alric's and Bartholomew's, however, are particularly useful for focusing an investigation into moral questions about death, for, involving as they do the complete and irreversible loss of rational capabilities, they put pressure directly on the concept of a (member of the ethical kind) person and thereby bring into sharp relief the family of "human" rights and the duties of respect which are logically bound up with that concept. Such cases are not only striking, then, but, more importantly, they provide relatively clear-cut expository vehicles for structuring a philosophical discussion of the ethics of life and death.

There is another group of cases, in contrast—often discussed under the heading "death with dignity"—which are not so clear-cut. Rather than putting pressure directly on the ethical concept of a person, the cases which I have in mind give rise to moral questions more indirectly, by putting pressure on the functional concept of a (member of the kind) rational being, which our implicit ethical theory intimately links to the concept of a person. What I am referring to, of course, are cases in which an individual deliberately and voluntarily refuses therapy which would be necessary to prolong his or her life. To put a more dramatic edge on it, what I want to discuss next are cases in which a person proposes to commit "rational suicide."

Consider, for example, the case of Darcy, a vigorous and alert woman in her middle sixties, who has just been responsibly diagnosed as suffering from an acute and progressive form of bone cancer. The facts of Darcy's case, as her physicians explain them to her, let us suppose, are approximately these:

The cancer is well established. There are already signs of lymphatic system involvement, strongly suggestive of metastasis. If therapeutic measures are not immediately undertaken, then, what Darcy can reasonably expect is at most three to four months during which she will still be able to carry out the functions of a normal life, although with increasing difficulty. This will be followed by a short period of fairly rapid deterioration, leading to death within a total of perhaps six to nine months from now. During its earlier stages, the principle manifestation of the disease is likely to be steadily increasing weakness, accompanied by a gradual loss of muscular coordination. There will be some pain, although it will probably be largely controllable, becoming severe only in the terminal stages of the illness. By that time, Darcy will have become functionally incapacitated and will require continuous hospitalization in any event.

The alternative is promptly to begin an elaborate course of radiation treatment and chemotherapy. This would require immediate hospitalization, largely for the monitoring and control of side effects which can include pain, debilitation, and nausea, and possibly cosmetic disfigurement as well, in the form of hair loss and rashes or discolorations of the skin. While the likelihood of completely arresting the disease is small—the probability of a total remission being estimated as lying in the neighborhood of 5 to 15 percent—there is a very good chance of slowing the growth and spread of the cancerous cells sufficiently to allow Darcy a life prolonged by anywhere from two to four or five years. Hospitalization would not be continuously needed during this period, but only during the initial phase of treatment—perhaps for one or two months—and during such additional intensive procedures as later developments might make necessary. Maintenance therapy could be handled on an outpatient basis, although, since the weakness and nausea attendant on such therapy would be only partially controllable, Darcy would most probably require help in conducting her day-to-day affairs outside of the hospital. While the envisaged treatment is covered by Medicare and other public programs, they would meet only a part of the total cost of care, and Darcy would therefore need to draw upon her own resources to take care of the remaining expenses.

These, then, are the alternatives which confront Darcy: A short period of relatively tolerable, although by no means pleasant, independent life, followed by a swift and certain, possibly quite painful, death; or a prolonged period, comparatively costly and uncomfortable, although surely endurable, of increasing dependency and helplessness, no less certainly leading up to her eventual death.

And now let us suppose that, confronted with these two alternatives—each obviously in some ways quite undesirable—Darcy declares, after a period of reflection, that she has arrived at the following decisions: First, she wishes to refuse all further therapeutic treatment intended to arrest or retard the development of her disease—including radiation treatments and chemotherapy—although she is willing to accept analgesics and, later, even narcotics to aid in controlling the pain and discomfort of the illness. And, second, when the disease has progressed to a point just short of total incapacitation, the point at which any further independent activity in the world is about to become impossible for her, she intends to take her own life as painlessly as possible—with help, if she can get it, but on her own, if that should be necessary—rather than die helpless and in pain, hooked up to a tangle of tubes and wires in a hospital bed.

Darcy, in short, has considered her situation and has announced her resolve to "die with dignity," to commit a "rational suicide." She has made her decision—and now we (that is, those of us in a position to influence or affect Darcy's subsequent conducts, primarily her family, her friends, and her physicians) must make ours. The question is: What are our moral responsibilities in such a case? What courses of conduct are open to us, and which among those possible courses of conduct are mandatory, permissible, or morally forbidden?

8.2: CHOICES AND ATTITUDES— A PRELIMINARY SURVEY

Darcy's expressed resolve is a complex one, and a variety of responses to it are possible. There is a special danger here, however, that our attitudes or feelings about the act of suicide will interfere with our efforts to think about the moral status of the proposed act and clutter up our efforts to discuss our moral responsibilities with regard to it—a special danger, that is, that our emotional reactions to the very idea of suicide will get in the way of our efforts to reason about it.[1]

In a way, this is only to be expected, for suicide is a dramatic act and, depending upon the kind of case which occurs to one, it is likely to evoke various strong emotions in those who contemplate it. One typical response, for instance, is to react to suicide as to an act of surrender, with repugnance at the cowardice one feels the act to manifest. Precisely the opposite reaction, however, is also not uncommon—that is, admiration at the courage manifested by the person who, in extremis, takes his or her own life. And many more complex emotional responses are possible. The suicide of a prosperous businessman who, let us suppose, has been "wiped out" in the stock market and declares in a final note that life is now "no longer worth living" may well be met with resentment by, for instance, an assembly-line worker. It may, indeed, be felt by such a worker as an insult, a personal affront, for the life of menial labor and limited comfort which the ruined businessman thus rejects as "not worth living" may be precisely the life which the worker has been compelled by circumstances not of his making to live. Again, one's judgment in a case like Darcy's may be colored by one's own ability or inability to identify oneself empathetically with her. One may, in consequence, feel that suicide would be "only natural" in those circumstances—or, conversely, that suicide is incomprehensible in any circumstances.

All of these emotions and attitudes, and many more, are possible here. But none of these attitudes and emotions—neither negative feelings of repugnance, resentment, and incomprehensibility nor positive feelings of admiration, approval, and sympathy—should be mistaken for a reason. None of these attitudes and emotions, however deeply felt, has any logical argumentative bearing on the question of the moral standing of Darcy's proposed act or of our own moral responsibilities with regard to it.

When we turn to these questions and attempt to map out the range of possible answers to them, what we find is a spectrum of deontic moral views which can, in fact, be arranged more or less into a continuum of increasing moral permissiveness. The moral stances open to us in the case of Darcy, in fact, look something like this:

(a) We are morally obligated to compel Darcy to accept treatment for her disease.

(b) While not obligated to do so, we are morally permitted to compel Darcy to accept treatment.

(c) Although we are not permitted to compel Darcy to accept treatment, we are morally obligated to prevent her from taking her own life.

(d) While not obligated to prevent Darcy from committing suicide, we are morally permitted to do so.

(e) Although we are not permitted to interfere with Darcy's decision to end her own life, neither are we permitted to aid her in doing so. We are morally obliged to do nothing at all.

(f) While not obligated to assist Darcy in committing suicide, we are morally permitted to do so.

(g) We are morally obligated to aid and abet Darcy in carrying out her resolve to take her own life.

This, then, is the spectrum of moral choices which confronts those of us whom circumstances enable to affect Darcy's conduct—her family, friends, and physicians. The question for our analytic philosophy now becomes: Which among these are coherently defensible or justifiable moral stands? That is, which among these possibilities can be shown to be coherently and logically grounded in terms of the principles, concepts, and values which collectively constitute what I have been calling "our implicit moral theory"? It is that question, and the confusions and complexities which stand in the way of straightforwardly answering it, which will be the focus of my investigations for the remainder of this chapter.

8.3: THE CASE FOR INTERFERING— AND THE CASE AGAINST IT

At the present time, moral sentiment and moral practice within our culture seem to fall at about the middle of the continuum of deontic stands which we have just sketched, somewhere in the neighborhood of (c) and (d). It is not quite clear whether those who believe that we would be morally obligated to prevent Darcy's suicide constitute an actual majority within our society, but the conviction is obviously a widely held one, and it is reasonably clear that a majority of us would tend toward the view that interference with Darcy's intention to take her own life is, at least, morally permissible.

There is, indeed, a line of moral reasoning which lies behind this point of view. Our typical practice is to urge treatment in such cases—often simply on grounds of hope, or even faith—but usually not to compel it. Part of the reasoning behind this practice is that, in cases such as Darcy's, it is always wise to temporize a bit, in order to be sure that what we're dealing with is at least Darcy's considered judgment and not a rash impulse, and in order to leave the door open for later changes of mind. Now acceptance and refusal of treatment are reversible acts. It may be prudent to begin treatment promptly, in order to maximize the chances for a favorable therapeutic outcome, but, if Darcy remains firm in her refusal at the outset, we can stop short of compelling her to undergo treatment and still retain the possibility of perhaps later persuading her to alter her decision and accept radiation or chemotherapy. By merely refusing treatment, the most that Darcy would be doing would be allowing herself to die, and, as we have seen in the case of Bartholomew, acts of "letting die," while perhaps ultimately undesirable, are arguably permissible within the framework of our implicit moral theory. It would be wrong, then, for us summarily to interfere with Darcy's decision to refuse treatment—for it is wrong, on the face of it, arbitrarily to interfere with any action which is itself prima facie morally permissible.[2]

Suicide, however, is an irreversible act. One cannot "unkill" a person. We've already observed that, within the context of the framework of ultimate values with which we have been operating, the value of life is derivative from the value of the exercise of moral autonomy which it enables. The primary moral characteristic of death, in other words, is that it irreversibly cuts off any further possibilities for the exercise of moral autonomy by the person whose existence it brings to an end. It seems reasonable to conclude, then, that the taking of a human life is always at least prima facie morally forbidden—and that this is so independently of whether the life taken is the life of another or one's own life. Since what Darcy proposes to do is something morally forbidden, continues this line of reasoning, even if we are not actually morally obligated to do what we can to prevent her from ending her own life, we are at least morally permitted to do so—for we are always morally permitted to do what we can to prevent a morally forbidden act from taking place.

This combination of moral considerations would, indeed, appear to land us approximately at (d), the view that we are morally permitted to prevent Darcy from committing suicide, although (probably) not morally obligated to do so. Unfortunately, however, the matter is never that simple.

What works against the reasoning which led us to (d) a moment ago is the peculiarly first-person character of the act of suicide. Darcy's suicide would, indeed, cut off any further possibilities for morally autonomous action on the part of some person—but who is that person? It is only Darcy herself, of course—and she is thus in the unusual position of being able to point out that the intended act of suicide which we claim to be permitted to prevent would be an exercise of precisely that very capacity for morally autonomous action which we are proposing to protect by preventing it.

After all, Darcy may remind us, in any moral decision there are two sorts of considerations to be weighed—considerations of moral worth and considerations of moral disvalue. What needs to be set over against the loss of any further possibilities for Darcy's exercise of moral autonomy which would result from her successful suicide is the actual suffering—Darcy's actual suffering—which would ensue if we were successfully to prevent her suicide. Here, too, a moral balance must be struck—in this instance, in prospect. One must measure the prima facie moral wrongness of Darcy's intended offense against moral worth against the prima facie moral wrongness of her inevitable future suffering in a life which we have compelled her to prolong—and one must attempt to decide which would be the greater, and which the lesser, evil.

Now, as I argued in the instance of Alric, what one decides in such a case, what moral balance one strikes here, will depend upon one's moral sensibilities, upon the weights which one assigns to considerations of moral disvalue and considerations of moral worth. Darcy's case, indeed, is very much like the case of Alric. But there is one crucial difference. Unlike Alric, Darcy can speak for herself. She can point out that it is an envisioned end to her capacity for moral decision and action which is being weighed against the likelihood of her future suffering. And she can therefore insist that, if, in the end, what matters here is a question of moral sensibilities, it must be a question of her moral sensibilities.

But now, Darcy may continue, we must realize that she has already weighed the worth of what she would surrender by committing suicide against the disvalue of what she would endure were she not to do so. Her decision to take her own life is an exercise of her moral autonomy precisely because it is the result of such deliberations. From the perspective of her own moral sensibilities, Darcy has already struck a moral balance. She has rationally weighed the relevant considerations of moral value, and she has arrived at a reasoned moral judgment, which she now proposes to carry out in action. Our moral sensibilities may differ from hers, of course, and so our decision in circumstances similar to hers may well have been a different one. To this Darcy can freely agree. But, as we have just seen, Darcy also acknowledges all the same ultimate values that we do and all the same prima facie moral principles as well. On what moral grounds, then, she may now go on to challenge us, do we claim the right to overrule her? Within the moral framework which we and she share, after all, a mere difference in moral sensibilities conveys no such right—and we cannot deny that it is her life, and hers alone, which is in question here.

So runs the argument—Darcy's own argument—against (d), against the view that we have the moral right to interfere in Darcy's decision to take her own life. And so it appears that we once again have a moral dilemma on our hands. Seemingly cogent moral reasons adduced in support of the deontic viewpoint (d) have apparently encountered equally cogent moral reasons opposed to that viewpoint. In the next section, then, we must see what we can do to break this seeming impasse. Our first step will be to cast the net of our investigations a little wider. What we need to consider, in fact, is how the various alternative deontic standpoints look to us when they are viewed, not in application to a single case, but as matters of social policy.

8.4: IN DEFENSE OF PATERNALISM

Persuasive as Darcy's line of reasoning may be, it is still not the end of the matter. The peculiarly first-person character of the act of suicide which Darcy proposes is indeed significant, we may reply, but so too is its irreversibility. To see this, let us consider another, different, example of an irreversible first-person act, the moral status of which is much clearer.

Imagine an individual, call him Elbert, whom circumstances have left destitute and alone—without family, without friends, without means, and without prospects. The future which he confronts is uncertain, but, to the extent that he can envision it from his present perspective, it is at best bleak and joyless—a life filled with hard toil and meager satisfaction. And so, let us suppose, Elbert conceives a plan. He approaches a wealthy landowner, a woman of high station and great resources whom we shall call Fiona, and he offers to sell himself into perpetual slavery. That is, Elbert proposes permanently to exchange his personal freedom for a level of comfort, care, and security, which Fiona, as her part of the bargain, would guarantee to provide.

Fiona, of course, is initially appalled. What Elbert proposes, she points out, would offend against moral worth. It would imply an irreversible curtailment of any further possibilities for the exercise of his capacities for autonomous judgment and independent action. The act of voluntarily accepting perpetual servitude which Elbert proposes to perform is thus prima facie morally forbidden, and she, Fiona, in consequence, is morally obliged not to accept Elbert's offer.

Elbert, however, is not silenced by Fiona's reply. He proceeds, indeed, to argue in a manner which by now is familiar to us. In any moral decision, he points out, there are two sorts of considerations to be weighed. What needs to be set over against the moral consequences of his irrevocable surrender of individual freedom is the actual suffering—his actual suffering—which will be his lot if Fiona does not accept his offer. Once again, there is a moral balance to be struck—and what one decides would be most desirable from the moral point of view will once again depend upon one's moral sensibilities. But if it is, in the end, a question of moral sensibilities, Elbert insists, then it must be a question of his moral sensibilities—for, he continues, what is at issue here, after all, is his freedom and his suffering. From the perspective of his own moral sensibilities, however, Elbert has already struck a moral balance. He has weighed the worth of what he would be giving up by permanently abrogating his autonomy against the disvalue of what he would in all likelihood endure were he not to do so. And he has, he claims, arrived at a reasoned moral judgment which he now proposes to carry out in action. Fiona's moral sensibilities may, of course, differ from

Elbert's. But within the moral framework which the two of them share, the mere fact of a difference in moral sensibilities does not give Fiona the right to prevent Elbert from exercising the very moral autonomy which both of them agree is the only thing ultimately of intrinsic moral worth.

Now I think that it is pretty obvious in this case that Elbert's arguments are not persuasive. Fiona's moral obligation to decline Elbert's proposal, it seems clear, is simply untouched by the considerations which Elbert adduces. We are convinced, in short, that the act of countenancing someone's voluntary perpetual servitude is as morally forbidden as the act of involuntarily enslaving someone would be. And this suggests that there should be some sound moral reasons why that is so—some sound moral reasons which imply that, whatever Elbert and Fiona might arrange between themselves, no agreement which implied Elbert's permanent surrender of his individual freedom could, in principle, be morally binding. Yet we have already remarked that is Elbert's (proposed) abrogation of moral autonomy and Elbert's (prospective) life of misery and suffering which are at issue here. What, then, could these sound moral reasons be?

Here is where our earlier discussion of the case of Alric will help us. One lesson which we learned there is that it is not enough to consider only the immediate and prospective consequences of some action for the individuals whom it directly affects in order to arrive at a final moral appraisal of that action. It is necessary, too, to consider the risks and benefits, with respect to morally relevant consequences, of a social policy which acknowledges the practice of which the proposed action is an example to be morally permissible in general. When we look at Elbert's proposed voluntary acceptance of perpetual servitude from this perspective, however, we can begin to discern the outlines of a moral argument for overruling his decision in this case.

To put it most compactly, the crucial point is that, although the proposed slavery is permanent and irreversible, its de facto voluntariness most probably is not. The irreversibility of what Elbert now claims to want, in other words, is likely to be in sharp contrast to the transitoriness of his actually wanting it. We understand people well enough to judge that Elbert's notion that voluntary perpetual slavery is an acceptable solution to his current life-problems is almost certainly a counsel of despair, and that the course of action which today appears to him fully appropriate is likely to appear in quite a different light days or weeks or months from now, if he is allowed to carry it out. Imagine now a moral policy which deems it in general permissible for a person confronting a future which, from his current vantage point, he perceives as unendurable voluntarily to contract for his permanent enslavement. What are the moral consequences of such a social policy likely to be?

It is easy enough to see, I think, that they are likely to be disastrous. What is true here of Elbert is equally true of people in general. Temporary unfortunate circumstances can all too easily give rise to attitudes of hopelessness and despair which color and distort judgment. While it may momentarily seem reasonable to abandon one's individual freedom, with the passing of time and changing of circumstances, the feelings of hopelessness which conferred that seeming acceptability upon the action give way to feelings of regret and, ultimately, of resentment. What began as a commitment to voluntary servitude rapidly comes to be thought of as involuntary enslavement. "I know what I said and did," thinks Elbert, "but I was in no condition to exercise my freedom of choice responsibly—and Fiona should have known that. She had no moral right to take advantage of my desperation in that way. No one has the right to do that to another person." In this way, Elbert—and others in his position—would naturally arrive at the conclusion that their agreements, although "voluntarily" undertaken, are not morally binding. For he—and they—would naturally come to see the "voluntariness" of such agreements as a mere sham, a "pseudo-voluntariness" which was only a morally irrelevant byproduct of the unfortunate human tendency in times of trouble to lapse into emotional states which distort reason.

The hypothetical social policy which we are now imagining, however, is precisely one of treating such agreements as morally enforceable. If Fiona and others in her position are morally permitted to accept such offers when they are made, then they acquire the prima facie moral right to see to it that the terms of such agreements are adhered to, just as you have an analogous right to insist that I keep the promises I have freely made. That I have "had second thoughts" or "changed my mind" since making the promise does not, in and of itself, cancel my prima facie moral obligation to carry out its terms, and just the same thing will be true in the cases of Elbert and his like—if, as we are imagining, offers of perpetual servitude may, morally speaking, be freely given and accepted.

Were we to adopt the moral permissibility of such "voluntary" self-enslavements as a universal social policy, then, what we would sooner or later find ourselves with would be a class of slaves and a class of slaveholders in permanent, possibly violent, conflict. What the slaveholders would view as their acceptance of a morally binding agreement, the slaves would see as the exploitation of human weakness and clouded judgment arising from accidental, catastrophic circumstances, and as no more a valid moral ground for abrogating individual freedom than the contingencies of birth or skin color would be. What the slaveholders would see as the legitimate exercise of their moral right to enforce a morally binding commitment, the slaves would view as an illegitimate oppression against which they might rightfully struggle—indeed, against which they were morally obligated to struggle. The inevitable outcome of this sort of moral polarity, however, is familiar to us. It is a state of "standing war," a continuing conflict between two groups of persons of radically opposing convictions, each of which, however, sees its stand as fully vindicated from the moral point of view.

What we can conclude from this imaginative exercise is that the practice of treating irreversible "voluntary" surrenders of individual autonomy as morally permissible—in contrast, for example, to the practice of promise-making—cannot be a morally coherent social policy. Unlike the practice of promise-making, that is, our imagined practice cannot be one the moral validity of which is accepted by all the members of the society who participate in it. Thought of as a social policy, the practice is inherently "unstable." People being what they are, an individual who finds himself on Elbert's side of the fence would inevitably come to regard the actions of a Fiona who accepted the offer of perpetual servitude as "exploiting" or "taking advantage of" another person's difficulties and weaknesses, and thus as morally wrong. But that is just to say that an individual who finds himself in Elbert's position will ultimately come to reject the very moral policy to which he supposedly originally appealed when arguing that a Fiona was morally permitted to accept his offer of "voluntary" enslavement in the first place.[3]

The upshot of this line of reasoning, then, is that the imagined social policy of treating "voluntary" abandonments of individual autonomy as morally permissible turns out to be no different in any relevant respect from treating the involuntary enslavement of persons as morally permissible to begin with. Viewed as social policies, both practices are equally "self-defeating." Neither practice can continue to be accepted as morally legitimate conduct by all the parties whom its exercise would affect.

But we can now see, I think, that the moral values which Elbert and Fiona share in fact do not imply, as Elbert claimed they did, that it would be morally permissible for Fiona to accept Elbert's "voluntary" offer of perpetual servitude. On the contrary, the ultimate intrinsic worth of individual autonomy, together with the fact that people in difficult circumstances tend to lapse into a state of hopelessness or desperation which impairs their ability to think rationally about what is ultimately in their own best interests, implies that Fiona—and everyone else—should, as a matter of policy, be morally forbidden to accept any such offers, that is, morally obligated to decline them.

What the facts about people's irrationality in times of difficulty imply, in other words, is that the moral autonomy of an individual sometimes needs to be protected against the consequences of his own bad judgment. A social policy which views a Fiona's acceptance of some Elbert's offer as morally impermissible exploitation—an illegitimate taking advantage of human weakness and accidental circumstances—has precisely this effect. This is a clear example of a "paternalistic" policy—one which prohibits an individual from performing certain "voluntary" acts "for his own good." But it is also pretty clearly a morally defensible paternalism. For it is based both upon a proper appreciation of moral values—i.e., upon the view that the exercise of moral autonomy is the only thing ultimately of intrinsic moral worth—and upon a factually correct understanding of "human nature"—i.e., upon the observation that reason and feeling are not independent of one another, but that strongly felt emotions can, indeed, have the effect of sabotaging the rational capacities upon which the exercise of moral autonomy in reasoned decision-making logically depends.[4]

8.5: PATERNALISM AND SUICIDE— PRO AND CON

With this sketch of the moral justification of paternalistic practices in hand, we are at last in a position to advance our dialogue with Darcy. Darcy, we recall, proposed to commit "rational suicide." She argued that she had weighed the moral worth of the possibilities for future autonomous action which she would be abandoning in taking her own life against the disvalues of the suffering which she would endure were she not to do so. And she claimed that she had arrived at the reasoned moral judgment that suicide was the morally desirable alternative among the choices in fact open to her. It is her life and her (potential) suffering which are at issue here, she insisted, and consequently we, in turn, have no moral right to interfere with her plans—indeed, we are morally obliged not to do so.

Against this line of reasoning, however, we might now respond that the irreversibility of the action which Darcy proposes to perform "dominates," so to speak, its admitted first-person character. Since the moral autonomy of the individual is the only thing ultimately of intrinsic worth, we might continue, it must be protected. While it would obviously be silly to propose to protect it "at all costs," it is sometimes necessary, as the example of Elbert and Fiona shows, to protect it against an individual's own bad judgment. Darcy's case, we might insist, is one of these times. In Darcy's case, paternalistic interference with her intentions in her own best interests is, morally speaking, fully justified and in order.

Suicide is an act born of hopelessness and desperation, a course of "last resort." While it might now seem to Darcy that it would be reasonable to take her own life, this seeming reasonableness is only the product of her present emotionally disturbed state. In fact, however, she is in no condition responsibly to exercise her freedom of choice—to evaluate her prospects objectively and to deliberate rationally about her options. Our shared moral values are best served in such an instance, then, by allowing cooler heads to prevail as a matter of policy. We are obligated, that is, to attempt, first, to dissuade Darcy from the drastic and irreversible action which she proposes to take. Should persuasion fail, however, we are at least morally permitted, second, to intervene in her plans and to do what we can to prevent her from carrying them out.

The only coherent social policy that is consistent with our moral values is one which renders "voluntary" suicide, like "voluntary" enslavement, a morally forbidden act. If, then, we encounter someone who, like Darcy, is convinced that taking her own life would be morally permissible—indeed, on balance morally desirable—it follows that she must be suffering from a disturbance which has impaired her capacity for moral judgment and, what is more, even her very ability to think rationally about what is in her own best interests. It follows also, then, that we are permitted to overrule her judgment here, that we are morally licensed to do what we can to prevent her from carrying out her proposed suicide.

So runs, in first approximation, the paternalistic case for intervention. Darcy, however, is still not finished with her side of the debate. The case of Elbert and Fiona indeed demonstrates something, she replies, but what it demonstrates is only how very different the question of voluntary suicide is from the question of voluntary perpetual servitude.

We should remember just what line of reasoning led us to the conclusion that "voluntary enslavement" ought, as a matter of social policy, to be regarded as a morally proscribed practice. What we appealed to in that reasoning were certain facts about "human nature," in particular, facts about the transitoriness and changeability of certain attitudes and desires. Feelings of hopelessness, we argued, give way to feelings of regret and, ultimately, to feelings of resentment. With the passage of time and altering circumstances, an individual comes to see the apparent voluntariness of his actions as having been illusory. He will thus, ultimately, abandon his earlier views as to the morality of those actions and arrive, in fact, at a judgment of moral impermissibility which is diametrically opposed to those earlier convictions. It was because these views concerning the moral permissibility of voluntary enslavement are, in this way, "unstable" or "self-defeating," Darcy reminds us, that we could not adopt them as the expression of a coherent social policy.

But a person who has committed suicide ceases to exist! There can be no question, therefore, of her later regrets or her later resentments, and no question of her later abandoning the moral convictions on the basis of which she originally argued for the permissibility of suicide. Someone in Elbert's position may later come to the conclusion that he was in no condition responsibly to exercise his freedom of choice at the time he made his offer to Fiona, but someone who has taken her own life cannot possibly, in point of logic, come to any similar conclusion, for she will no longer exist as the thinking subject of moral deliberations at all. She will have become a corpse—and corpses exercise no moral judgment, good or bad. In the case of suicide, then, the considerations which implied that morally permitting voluntary enslavement could not be adopted as a coherent social policy simply fail to apply. A person who voluntarily commits himself to perpetual servitude must live with the consequences of his act. That is the root of the ultimate "instability" or "self-defeatingness" of the practice. But, while voluntary suicide certainly has consequences, a person who takes her own life precisely does not "have to live with them." And that is the crucial difference.

To this reply, Darcy can add three further points. First, voluntary enslavement is a cooperative affair. An Elbert may make the offer on his own, but nothing of moral consequence happens unless some Fiona takes him up on it. There are, thus, two actions whose moral status comes into question: Elbert's proposal and Fiona's acceptance. The most that our paternalistic arguments from human weakness show, however, is that the second of these actions ought to be morally forbidden. Fiona—and everyone else—ought to be morally obliged to decline such offers. That would render the other action—Elbert's offer—pointless, but it would not automatically imply that making such an offer would itself also be arguably morally wrong. The deontic status of Elbert's first-person action, in other words, is simply not settled by the moral and factual considerations which we have offered in support of paternalistic practices. So, too, Darcy may well insist, the deontic status of her own proposed "first-person" suicide. The most that our paternalistic considerations might show is that we are morally obligated not to aid and abet her in taking her own life. But they do not automatically imply that her committing suicide, alone, would be a morally forbidden act with which we were permitted to interfere.

Second, there is a crucial asymmetry between the cases of Elbert and

Darcy when viewed through the lens of the theory of action. The act of suicide is, logically, a solo. While Elbert cannot "voluntarily" enslave himself unless two positive actions are performed—he must make the offer and Fiona must accept it—Darcy can take her own life without anyone else performing any positive actions. Here, then, there are not two positive actions to be morally appraised, but one positive action—suicide—and one kind of inaction—a refusal to interfere or intervene to prevent the performance of the first act.

And now Darcy can insist that, even if it had been shown that she should regard taking her own life as morally impermissible or undesirable on balance, it would not follow that our refusing to intervene to prevent that action was also morally impermissible. As we have seen in the case of Bartholomew, actions and refrainings are not always equivalent from the moral point of view. Euthanasia or "mercy killing" might be morally forbidden, but allowing Bartholomew to die by doing nothing (or ceasing to do something) turned out to be morally permissible. Similarly, then, although one would hope that killing Darcy is morally prohibited, it does not follow that our allowing Darcy to kill herself, by doing nothing, is also morally prohibited. In fact, no independent moral argument has yet been advanced which bears on the deontic status of such inaction. Our paternalistic reasoning addresses only positive actions, such as Fiona's acceptance, and leaves questions of the moral status of inaction in various instances totally untouched.

And, finally, Darcy can address the charges which we have made in passing concerning her capacity for rational decision-making. We have been speaking of hopelessness and despair, and claiming that her emotional state precludes the exercise of good practical judgment on her part. Now Darcy, I think, can scarcely deny being, in some ways, emotionally disturbed. But she can certainly go on to add that this is only to be expected, for her circumstances are objectively disturbing ones. There is a hopelessness about her situation, but it is not she that is hopeless. Her condition is hopeless. The rational and responsible thing to do in such a situation, however, is not to delude oneself with vain hopes, but to acknowledge that it has become reasonable to treat certain "drastic" courses of action—which are automatically excluded from consideration in "normal" circumstances—as realistic alternatives, and to proceed to weigh them as such.

But that, Darcy can point out, is precisely what she has done. And what is more, she can add, she has done so with full cognizance of the moral implications of suicide. The point, Darcy can insist, is that desperate times may call for desperate steps. She does not propose to act on a transitory impulse, but on the basis of a considered judgment which has measured the shortening of her life against the suffering which continued living, objectively viewed, holds in store. She is not, then, impervious to reason. If we could show her facts which would make a difference, she would change her mind. But no one is disputing any of the facts of the case. We are wrong, therefore, to charge her with irrationality. Without new facts or new arguments, such charges amount to nothing but another expression of our differing sensibilities. But a difference in moral sensibilities, Darcy has already cogently argued, not only conveys no right of interference, but indeed is here without any moral force at all, however deeply it may be felt.

8.6: RATIONALITY—
THE LAST QUESTION

With these last remarks of Darcy's, we reach, I think, a sort of conceptual "rock bottom" to our deliberations over the morality of suicide. The moral considerations on both sides of the question are clear. That is, we understand well enough the moral consequences both of voluntary suicide and of successful intervention to prevent such suicide. The implications of each course of conduct with regard both to the worth of personal moral autonomy and to the disvalues of suffering are clear. As in the case of Alric, however, we reach here a kind of impasse. It is important to appreciate, though, that it is an impasse of a different kind.

The question of euthanasia, we found, was an example of an authentic moral dilemma. Both the advocate of "mercy killing" and its opponent, we discovered, could agree on all the relevant facts and on all the relevant values and could still be at odds in their considered moral judgments by reason of their differing moral sensibilities, the weights which each assigned to the worth of moral autonomy and the disvalue of suffering, and the resulting perspective from which each viewed the same matter-of-factual scene.

Now the dispute between Darcy and someone who believes himself permitted to interfere with her planned suicide—call him an "interventionist"—bears a strong superficial resemblance to this disagreement over the moral permissibility of mercy killing. The interventionist argues paternalistically that the worth of individual moral autonomy is a value which must sometimes be protected against the poor judgment of the person whose capacity for free choice and action is at stake, even if protecting that value implies that the person in question must endure the suffering which her surrender of the power of free action through suicide would avoid. Darcy argues, in contrast, that, in the absence of significant social implications, it is the right of the affected individual to strike a moral balance between the worth of the autonomy which she proposes to surrender and the disvalue of her prospective suffering—and that the act of suicide is unique in that it radically disengages a person from the very possibility of any future actions and interactions (by ending that person's existence) and therefore necessarily lacks all of the social or personal consequences (regret, resentment, ultimate rebellion, and so on) which could morally justify a paternalistic interventionism. It might well appear, then, that the difference between Darcy and an interventionist here is again merely a difference in moral sensibilities. The interventionist assigns greater weight to Darcy's prospective loss of the capacity to choose and act than to her prospective suffering, and Darcy herself strikes the opposite balance between these two moral values. I think, however, that it would be a mistake to understand the disagreement between Darcy and the interventionist in those terms.

As I have reconstructed the debate between them, Darcy and the interventionist do agree on what is ultimately of moral value. But I want to suggest that they do not agree on the facts. Darcy will grant the interventionist's claim that "paternalistic'" policies which permit the overriding of an individual's first-person judgments and decisions are sometimes morally in order.

They are in order, for example, in the case of children, whose capacities for rational deliberation and responsible decision-making are not yet fully developed, and they are in order in the case of such individuals as our hypothetical Elbert, whose capacities for rational deliberation and responsible decision-making are temporarily impaired in accidental circumstances by such transitory emotional states as despair, infatuation, and rage. But, Darcy will insist, the interventionist's paternalistic policies are not morally in order in her case—for her rational deliberative capacities are neither underdeveloped nor irresponsibly distorted.

It is precisely this last assertion, however, that the interventionist will not accept as a statement of fact. Darcy, he will continue to claim, "does not really know what she is doing." She is in no condition to evaluate her situation objectively, deliberate rationally about her options, and responsibly exercise her freedom of choice. And the interventionist will go on to point out that Elbert, too, in the grip of his despair, would insist that he understands very well what he is proposing to do in making his offer to Fiona. But even Darcy must grant that Elbert "does not really know what he is doing." It is only because Darcy herself is in the grip of despair, concludes the interventionist, that she cannot see that exactly the same thing is true of her supposedly "rational" decision.

Now we have already seen Darcy's reply here: We are only justified in concluding that Elbert "doesn't really know what he is doing" because we can contrast his presumed present state with a practically inevitable future state in which he "realizes what he has done," that is, in which he himself regrets having done what he did and he himself rejects the line of reasoning to which he originally appealed. Our confidence in the practical inevitability of such a future reversal of outlook is an empirical confidence. It is warranted, that is, by our collective experiences of the actual attitudes of enslaved persons and others in situations relevantly similar to Elbert's. But such experiences are logically precluded in the case of suicide. We can in principle have no experiences of the thoughts and feelings of persons who have taken their own lives, for such persons have ipso facto ceased to exist as thinking and feeling entities.

We are, of course, acquainted with people who have successfully been prevented from committing suicide, and some of them indeed do later undergo a similar reversal of outlook and realize (and regret) "what they were about to do." But not all of them. For we are also acquainted with individuals rendered helpless by the last stages of an agonizing disease who regret their earlier indecisiveness and who plead for the quick and merciful end which they are unfortunately no longer physically able to arrange for themselves.

It is this latter sort of future which confronts me, adds Darcy, and, in the face of such a prospect, I would be irrational if I were to fail to exercise the option of suicide now open to me by irresponsibly allowing my judgment to be colored by closed-minded denials, empty fantasies, and vain hopes. These are no less emotional states than surrender, hopelessness, and despair, after all, and equally liable to distort reason. But not all emotion is opposed to reason. There are those times when the last objective counsel of reason is simply to "accept the inevitable" and "try to make the best of a hopeless situation." In such sorry times, an attitude of surrender and resignation does not distort rationality but is in full accord with its dictates. For me, continues Darcy, this is such a time. My willingness to consider even so drastic an option as suicide is, in fact, excellent evidence that I am still in full possession of my rational deliberative faculties, for it shows that I am thinking clearly about a situation which is, alas, drastic enough to make even suicide a genuine alternative.

To these last remarks, I think, the would-be interventionist has but one possible reply: Suicide is never a genuine alternative. Suicide is a unique act. Any other action propels a person from one situation into another. The resulting new situation may be better or worse for that person than her old one, and, independently of this, it may bode better or worse for that person than did her old one. Now in our practical deliberations about whether or not to perform some action, we are able to take into account both the actualities and the prospects of the situation into which performing that action would propel us. It is this ability to envision and assess the likely actual and prospective consequences of our considered actions, indeed, which is the special contribution of rational thought to human conduct. This explains why it can sometimes be rational to perform an action which worsens one's immediate situation—for one can weigh such an actual short-term loss against a prospective long-term gain. Thus, it is sometimes completely in order to consider "drastic" alternatives and even to perform "drastic" actions—quitting one's profitable job, abandoning one's secure marriage, amputating a gangrenous limb—and to endure the difficulties and suffering which are the immediate consequences of such an act in the interests of an ultimate long-term betterment of a significant slice of one's life.

Darcy, claims the interventionist, is trying to assimilate suicide to this pattern of rational "drastic" acts. But suicide does not fit this pattern. Suicide alone is not an action which propels a person from one situation into another, but, uniquely, an action which obliterates the person who performs it. Death is not one possible condition of persons which can be weighed against other conditions as more or less desirable. A dead person, we must remember, is not a kind of person at all. When we are considering actions essentially devoid of social implications, first-person practical rationality necessarily consists in the appraisal of alternative courses of conduct in the light of one's self-interests.[5] That is, one attempts to judge which among the possible acts open to one would have consequences which, on balance, best served those interests. The necessary consequence of taking one's own life, however, is that one ceases to exist—and it logically cannot serve one's self-interests to cease to exist. That is, one cannot, in point of logic, be better off vis-à-vis any self-interests, long-term or short-term, if one no longer exists as an interested self. Suicide is therefore excluded in principle from even the class of "drastic" actions which one can rationally perform "in one's own best interests." "Rational suicide," concludes the interventionist, turns out to be a contradiction in terms.

But, if this so, the interventionist continues, it follows that suicidal intentions are eo ipso proof of an impairment of rational deliberative capacity. Our verdict in Darcy's case must therefore be that she has indeed lost the capacity for responsible self-direction and rational decision-making. More dramatically, in popular parlance, Darcy has gone mad. She is insane. Her self-destructive intentions are proof of her madness. It follows, then, that we, in turn, are within our rights to interfere—on moral grounds—and to attempt to prevent her from carrying out what seems to her, in her madness, to be a reasonable thing to do.

I submit, then, that Darcy and the interventionist disagree on the facts. Darcy insists that she is in fact lucid, rational, and sane—and she argues that her willingness to consider even so drastic an alternative as suicide is evidence that she is confronting her desperate and hopeless situation objectively and, a fortiori, evidence of her sanity. The interventionist, in effect, holds her for mad—and he sees her professed suicidal intentions as de facto proof of her madness. And so here we do not have, as we did in the case of Alric, a disagreement which is properly characterized as resting merely on a difference in moral sensibilities.

On the other hand, however, this is no ordinary disagreement "about the facts." It does not appear, that is, to be the sort of disagreement which could be settled by further empirical investigations. Both Darcy's medical condition and her psychological state are clear enough. It is clear enough, that is, that Darcy's bone cancer is in an irreversibly advanced state, and clear enough what the consequences of that fact are. And it is clear enough that Darcy has indeed formed the settled intention to commit what she calls "rational suicide" and is able to converse coherently, intelligibly, and connectedly—in fact, with considerable subtlety and sophistication—about her condition and her intentions. In all likelihood, then, additional medical and psychological testing would only serve further to confirm what we already know about such facts.

What is not clear, then, is what one can legitimately conclude about Darcy from the fact that she has that intention in those circumstances. In order to arrive at a final judgment about the morality of intervention in Darcy's plans, in other words, what we would need to determine is whether her having precisely that intention in precisely those circumstances counts for her being in full possession of her rational deliberative faculties (as Darcy herself claims) or against it (as the interventionist insists). We would need to determine, that is, whether there is such a thing as a rational first-person attitude toward death—toward one's own death. What can one intelligibly and coherently think and know about one's own death, and what attitudes can one rationally adopt toward the inevitability of one's own mortality? And with this we arrive at the next, and final, topic of our investigations: "death in the first-person." It is to these, and related, questions, in other words, that I intend now, and finally, to turn.

CHAPTER 9

"Death in the First Person": Expectations and Attitudes

9.1: "ONE'S OWN DEATH"

The issue which confronts us now is the question of rational attitudes toward one's own mortality. It is typically held, I suppose, without much reflection on the matter, that death is a bad thing, an evil. The Biblical creation myth recounted in Genesis in fact assigns to death the status of a punishment—the first and greatest of God's punishments for the first and greatest of our sins of disobedience. Although the moral principles suggested by this story are dubious at best, the valuational status which it mythopoetically assigns to death is clear enough. Death is an evil which we have brought upon ourselves. The world would be (and, according to the story, once was) a better place without it. And in our own times, too, we find the poet's counsel not to "go gently into that good night." Death, in other words, is something to be feared, to be shunned, to be avoided, to be postponed as long as possible, and to be fought against with all our force and being when at last it looms imminent upon our personal horizons.

Played contrapuntally to this dominant theme throughout our history, however, has been a quieter melody to the effect that, as Lucretius put it, "death is nothing to us, and does not matter at all." According to this view—most intimately associated, perhaps, with the Stoic philosopher Epicurus—death is simply one natural phenomenon among others and totally devoid of any evaluative status, either as an evil or as a good. From this Stoic viewpoint, in fact, death is not the sort of thing which, in point of logic, can be feared, for it is not something which can be experienced. A person's death is simply that person's annihilation. "When death is there, we are not; and when we are there, death is not."[1]

And, as we shall see, there are even a few faint strains of a third tune—one which holds it to be a good thing that people ultimately die. Immortality, according to this view, would be nothing short of an unrelieved and unbearable tedium, and freedom from death is consequently not a state to be desired and sought but would itself be an evil to be shunned and avoided. The classic literary embodiment of this outlook is probably Jonathan Swift's cautionary tale of Gulliver's encounter with the "Struldbruggs" of the land of Luggnagg, that small minority of the population of Luggnagg who have the misfortune, as Swift penetratingly illustrates, to be born gifted with eternal life but not with eternal youth, health, and vigor.[2]

When one impending phenomenon—a person's death—can give rise to three such mutually exclusive valuations and attitudes, we are certainly within our rights to suspect that some terminological ambiguities and conceptual confusions are probably lurking in the surrounding discussions. In the present case, I think, these suspicions are well founded. Before turning to the question of which, if any, of these attitudes are reasonable ones and which, if any, grow out of muddles, mistakes, and illusions, then, there is a good bit of preliminary spadework which needs to be done to unearth those confusions and those ambiguities.

The question of what evaluational attitudes one might rationally adopt with regard to one's own death depends, of course, upon the question of what expectations one can rationally have about the inevitability and about the nature of one's own death. We need to inquire first, in other words, into what one can, in point of logic and in point of fact, know about one's own death, into what one can reasonably believe about one's own death, and even into what one can intelligibly and sensibly imagine in connection with one's own death.

But prior to all of these questions, we need to ask another—the question for which analytic philosophy is, by now, notorious: What are we talking about? For there are some significant distinctions that we made earlier which need to be respected in our present investigations as well. In particular, I argued earlier that the term 'death' was importantly ambiguous, especially with regard to its implicit temporal structure. What is true of the word 'death', however, is equally true of the phrase "one's own death." "One's own death," too, is importantly ambiguous—and it is precisely these ambiguities that are at work in the competing attitudes and evaluations which we have just finished surveying. We need to inquire, therefore, into the question of what, in each case, is supposed to be being picked out or designated by the expression "one's own death." Is the phrase, for example, intended to designate a process or an event? And, if it is meant to pick out an event, then what sort of event—an instantaneous event or the sort of event which is contextually correlative to some process?

What we will find, of course, is that the phrase "one's own death" is sometimes used in each of these ways. But the first thing we need to notice is that this expression is also sometimes used in quite a different way. The first thing we need to notice is that the phrase "one's own death" is sometimes used as if it were supposed to pick out a state or a condition of a person. Once we are clear that this ostensible use is, in fact, an incoherent one, we will be well on the way to unraveling the confusions which stand in the way of a sensible determination of arguably rational attitudes toward the fact and phenomenon of one's own death. It is to this, deeply mistaken, use of the expression "one's own death," then, that I want next to turn.

9.2: THE "DARK KINGDOM" OF DEATH

The metaphor recalled in the title of this section is deeply embedded in our customary ways of thinking and talking about death. Death is pictured as terra incognita, a mysterious and unknown territory into which all men must journey but from which no man ever comes again—"The undiscover'd country from whose bourn no traveller returns".[3] It is celebrated as an obscure, blank region on the map of human possibilities, akin to those long stretches of uncharted land over which early cartographers would draw fanciful pictures of monsters or write only that "Here there be tygers."

Or, again, death is often poetically limned as "endless sleep"—but, alas, no common sleep. "Ay, there's the rub; For in that sleep of death what dreams may come . . . must give us pause."[4] Or, again, death is not this endless sleep itself but its predestined home, an "eternal night"—"darkness everlasting"—through which may walk dim spectres and terrifying apparitions undreamt of in even the blackest nightmares of our earthly sleeps.

These metaphors and others like them are the common currency of an everyday idiom in which people "depart this earthly life"—"shuffle off this mortal coil"—and "pass on" or "pass over" to their "eternal rewards." Viewed simply as poetic coinages, such expressions are, of course, logically guiltless. But the underlying idea to which they give expression is far less innocent. For all of these idioms and metaphors suggest that there is something important about death of which we are unavoidably ignorant, something important which is unknown—and which must necessarily and forever remain so. And when we try to put our finger on precisely what it is about death which is and will inevitably remain unknown to us, what emerges is something like this: No living person knows, nor can he know, what it is like to be dead.[5]

This, however, is the expression of a conceptual muddle of the first order. To see this, we need only ask: What it is like for whom to be dead? The point is that not only does "knowing what something is like" require a subject, but "something's being like something" requires a subject as well. When we say, for instance, that no bachelor can know what it is like to be married, what we mean is that no bachelor can know what a married person knows about being married, that is, can know what being married is like for a married person. To put the point even more revealingly, when we say that no bachelor can know what it is like to be married, what we mean is that no bachelor can know what married life is like for the person who is living it, can know the "experiential inside" of married life.

When we attempt in the same manner to paraphrase the claim that no living person can know what it is like to be dead, however, the results are the purest nonsense. We certainly cannot mean that no living person can know what "dead life" is like for the person who is living it. Nor do we mean that no living person can know what it is that a dead person knows about being dead. For death, as we have already seen, is not a state or condition of persons. A dead person is not a kind of person, as a married person is a kind of person. A dead person is a person who has died—or it is a corpse, a cadaver. In neither case, however, is a dead person a possible subject of experiences. A person who has died no longer exists, and a corpse or cadaver, although it most certainly exists, is not an experiencer but a "mere object," lacking life and, therefore, lacking sentience as well.

All of those common metaphors in which death is cast as an "endless journey"—waking or sleeping—through a "dark kingdom" of "eternal night" covertly presuppose just this conceptual confusion. Death, however, is not a condition of persons, coordinate with sleep, or an activity of persons, coordinate with travel. There is nothing that it is "like" to be dead, as there is something that it is like to be on a journey or even to be asleep.[6] In point of logic, there couldn't be. In point of logic, that is, death can have no "experiential inside." For death is not a state or condition or activity of an existing experiencer. To frame a metaphor of our own, death is "subjectless."

The real point, of course, is linguistic or grammatical. We are misled by the noun 'death'. We succumb all too readily to the tendency to think that, since 'death' is a noun, it must be the name of something. But the noun 'death' is a nominalization of the verb 'to die', just as the noun 'smile' is a nominalization of the verb 'to smile'. In the logical or conceptual order, however, it is the verbs which come first. Deaths are no more a part of the "furniture of the world" than are smiles. They are not "in the world" as part of its contents. Rather, things happen in the world. People smile, and people die. But whereas smiling can be an ongoing activity of a person who continues to exist, dying, as we have already seen, is one way (although not the only way) in which a living being ceases to exist. It ceases to exist by becoming something else—a corpse or a cadaver, its remains. A smiling person is a person who is smiling, but a dead person is not a person who is dead, for, as we have already noted, the phrase "is dead" is not a genuinely present tense predicate of persons. A person who is dead is a person who has died, and who, therefore, no longer exists, having become or changed into a corpse—or a dead person is the remains of a person who has died, that is, the very corpse which that person has changed into or become.

It was, of course, primarily on this conceptual point that the Stoic philosophers were insisting when they concluded that "death is nothing to us, and does not matter at all." The way in which death does not matter is the way in which a state or a condition or an activity of a person can matter—by virtue of its attendant experiences. An actual journey through distant and unknown territories or an actual night's sleep is something to be lived through. For better or for worse, it has an "experiential inside" which must be enjoyed or which must be endured by the person who lives through it. What the Stoics saw clearly, however, is that death is not at all like that. Death logically cannot have an "experiential inside" to be enjoyed or to be endured, for "when death is there, we are not." A person who dies ipso facto ceases to exist. Dying is not, even in principle, something which a person lives through, and being dead, therefore, is not, even in principle, a state or a condition or an activity the experiential character or consequences of which a person must live with. The phrase "being dead" does not pick out a state or condition or activity of persons at all. A fortiori, then, it does not pick out a mysterious and unknown state or condition or activity, a state or condition or activity of whose "inner nature" we are condemned to remain forever ignorant.

Parenthetically, it is perhaps instructive to play—in a science fiction sort of way—with the question of what sort of "life" a "dead person" or "disembodied soul," per impossible, could have, for I do not think that the matter is as unknown or as unknowable as our poets would have us believe.[7] On the face of it, it would not be a very desirable "life"—for a "disembodied soul" would be, to begin with, completely insensate. Lacking eyes, it would be blind; lacking ears, it would be deaf; lacking nose, tongue, and skin, it would know neither smell nor taste nor touch. The myths about "the soul" are many and varied, of course, but in none of them does a soul create the very world which it knows. In all of them, it builds its picture of the world in which it moves and has its being from data which is ontologically alien to it, from sensory input—and sensory input, whatever it may be transformed into in the end, begins its existence as stimulations of the sense organs, as stimulations, that is, not of "the soul" but of parts of the body.

It follows, of course, that a "disembodied soul" would also, and necessarily, be irrevocably and forever alone. For let it be aswim in an ethereal sea of however many multitudes of its kindred, a "disembodied soul" could never reach them. A "disembodied soul" lacks voice, and it lacks gesture—and thus it lacks all human means of outreach and communication. However "mentally" it may begin—with a thought or with a volition—communication, too, in the end is not a matter of "the soul" but of the body. For a thought is not communicated until it is expressed in a manner accessible to others, and a "disembodied soul" necessarily lacks any such means of open and public expression.

The best model for the "life" of a "disembodied soul," then, is the life of a person in a "sensory deprivation" tank, afloat in a pool of body-temperature water designed to minimize all tactile sensation and cut off from light and sound and taste and smell. But we do know what happens to people in such circumstances. First, they remember and they fantasize. Later, they hallucinate. And, after a long enough time, they go stark raving mad.

The picture of death as a dark and mysterious kingdom is doubly muddled, then. The deep confusion, of course, is that death is not a "kingdom" at all—that is, death is not a state or condition or activity of persons, coordinate with marriage or travel or sleep, which has an "experiential inside" of which people could be ignorant. But, second, even if death, per impossible, were a "kingdom," it would not be one mysterious and unknown to us, but one which we could easily conceptualize and readily imaginatively reconstruct—one which would be "dark" only in its unpleasantness and ultimate undesirability. Let us therefore now leave this logically misbegotten territory of idiom and poetic metaphor behind us. I want next to turn to some rather different uses of the expression "one's own death"—uses which, although suffering from temporal ambiguities, at least have the virtue of being conceptually coherent.

9.3: ON IMAGINING ONE'S OWN DEATH

One perfectly legitimate use of the phrase "one's own death," obviously, is to pick out an event, the event of one's dying. We should remind ourselves, however, that such event-talk is also subject to certain crucial ambiguities. Used in this way, the expression "one's own death" may be intended to pick out an instantaneous event, or it may be intended to pick out an event which is contextually correlative to some process—what I shall call an "historical event." It is only the second of these uses which is potentially of interest when what concerns us is the question of rational, first-person attitudes toward death, toward one's own death.

The reason, of course, is that "instantaneous events" are nothing real. An "instantaneous event," we can recall, is only the "ideal limit" of some process, a boundary marker which we erect in our speaking and thinking. It answers to nothing in experience. The notion of an instantaneous event instead encodes the idea that we could theoretically "bracket" some experienceable change of state, condition, number, or kind by a nested series of ever shorter intervals, each of which contained subintervals in which both the prechange state, condition, number, or kind and the postchange state, condition, number, or kind were experientially manifested.

Thought of as an instantaneous event, then, one's own death—indeed, any death—is not the sort of thing toward which one might coherently have attitudes at all, rational or irrational. It is not something with which anyone needs to "come to terms," an experience which one must emotionally or valuationally assimilate, but a mere "theoretical construct"—a way of thinking and speaking about those experienceable, historical events which are the logically possible objects of evaluations and emotional responses. The "instantaneous event" of death, too, then, "is nothing to us, and does not matter at all," not because there is something special about death, but because all "instantaneous events" are nothing to us, and do not matter at all.

The historical event of one's own death, however—the last event in the process of one's life, in one's history—is another matter. That is, indeed, an experienceable occurrence with which at least some people must come to emotional and valuational terms. The point which needs to be stressed here, however, is that one's own death, thought of as an historical event, is not an occurrence with which one must oneself in this way come to terms, for it is not an event which one oneself experiences.

This, to be sure, is not a new point. Any death, including one's own, is not a change of state or condition, but a change of kind. A living being changes into or becomes a corpse or cadaver, its remains. When one dies, then, one ceases to exist, and, a fortiori, one ceases to exist as the experiencing subject of any attitudes or evaluations. If "coming to terms with an occurrence" means dealing with the emotions and with the life-problems precipitated by an historical event which one lives through, then, one is logically precluded from coming to terms with one's own death.

But there is, of course, another way in which one can come to terms with an event. One can come to terms with an impending event, for one can come to terms with it in prospect. Here it is not necessary that one be able actually to experience the historical occurrence in question. All that is required is that one be able to envision it, to imagine experiencing it. But can one imagine one's own death, even when that death is thought of as an historical event? It is, in fact, frequently claimed that one cannot. That, I think, is a mistake—but we need to be very, very careful.

Thought of as an historical event, one's own death is perfectly imaginable. That is, we know perfectly well what our own deaths will entail—the loss to our families and our friends, their grief and mourning, various rites and ceremonies, complex legal proceedings, and so on—and all of this is perfectly imaginable and easily visualized. Indeed, we can not only picture our own deaths in this sense, we can even plan for them. We can prepare our acquaintances to carry on without us, remind them of good times and bad times, and attempt to counsel and console them in anticipation of the anticipated realities of the event. We can design our own funerals—even write our own epitaphs and eulogies, if we are so inclined. And we can draw up wills and testaments to facilitate the disposal of our properties and the unraveling of our legal affairs. All of this can be done in advance and in prospect, and the effects of all this prior planning and arrangement can equally be pictured or imagined in advance and in prospect. There is nothing in point of logic, in other words, to prevent one from claiming, quite correctly, that he knows just what his death will be like: "I've arranged for everything in advance. I can visualize it perfectly, down to the smallest detail."

At this point, we may encounter an objection. It runs something like this: "Perhaps you can, in this way, visualize or picture your own death. But that is not what is meant when it is claimed that no one can imagine his own death. What is meant is that no one can imagine *experiencing* his own death. The most that you have shown is that one can imagine some event. What you have not shown, however, is that one can imagine experiencing that event. And when the event in question is one's own death, this last feat of imagination is simply impossible."

Now there is, of course, a difference between imagining something and imagining experiencing something—if for no other reason, then at least for the reason that one can imagine something's not being experienced (e.g., the proverbial tree falling in the empty forest).[8] But I think it is reasonably clear that one can, indeed, imagine not only one's own death but even experiencing one's own death. One can imagine, for example, that one is a doctor in attendance at that event—that one is bending over the fading patient, touching him, listening to his heartbeat, trying to revive him but failing, pronouncing him dead, informing the weeping relatives, filling out the death certificate, and so on. Or one can imagine being a witness at one's own funeral—smelling the flowers, hearing the organ music and the eulogy, seeing the procession, comforting the family, and so on.

In other words, one can not only imagine these events themselves, one can also visualize them from a participant's perspective.[9] One can not only imagine one's own death, for example, but one can also imagine observing that death. One can not only picture one's own funeral, one can also imagine witnessing that funeral. One can visualize, that is, being present at that funeral—seeing its sights, hearing its sounds, and smelling its smells. If that is what is meant by "imagining experiencing one's own death," then, once again, there is no logical obstacle to accomplishing the task. If we can imagine the event itself, as I have argued we can, then we can equally imagine experiencing the event—seeing it, hearing it, smelling and tasting and feeling it—as well.

What one cannot imagine—and this is perhaps the point which our hypothetical objector had in mind—is *oneself* experiencing one's own death. I can easily imagine myself witnessing a funeral—that is, picture myself witnessing someone's funeral—and I can easily imagine witnessing my own funeral—that is, being someone who is witnessing a funeral which is, in fact, my own. What I cannot do, however, is imagine myself witnessing my own funeral—that is, picture myself observing a funeral which is, in fact, my own—for that is a contradictory, and thus incoherent, description of whatever it is that I do succeed in visualizing.

This is a lesson which we learned earlier during our reflections on the strange case of John and Emma. The relevant question is never whether or not one can picture, imagine, or visualize something. One can always picture, imagine, or visualize something or other. The relevant question is linguistic—how one can coherently and correctly describe whatever it is that one has succeeded in visualizing, picturing, or imagining.

In the present case, two descriptions of an imaginative accomplishment are logically completely in order, but a third description, which combines features from those two, turns out not to be. "Myself witnessing a funeral," for example, is a fine and coherent description of something which I could more or less easily (depending only upon my powers of visualization) picture or imagine. "Witnessing my own funeral" is another. But put them together and the result is logical hash. "Myself witnessing my own funeral" is not a coherent description of something which I could picture or imagine, for it is not a logically coherent description at all. That I am witnessing something implies that I exist at that time as an experiencing subject. That what is being witnessed is my own funeral, however, implies that I am dead at that time, and, a fortiori, that I have ceased to exist as an experiencing subject. But these two implications straightforwardly contradict one another, and no description which logically implies a contradiction can itself be a logically coherent description. It follows that "myself witnessing my own funeral" is not a coherent description of something which I could picture or imagine, quite independent of the strength or paucity of my powers of visualization.

The same point holds, of course, for the ostensible description "myself experiencing my own death." I can imagine myself experiencing a death (that is, the historical event of someone's dying), and I can imagine (being someone who is) experiencing a death which is, in fact, my own. But I cannot, in point of logic, imagine myself experiencing my own death—and this conclusion, too, is quite independent of the strength or paucity of my powers of visualization. "Myself experiencing my own death" is not a logically coherent description of anything, and, a fortiori, not a logically coherent description of anything imaginable.

There is, by the way, another way in which our hypothetical objector might intend his assertion "No one can imagine experiencing his own death." He might be trying to claim that no one can imagine being dead. But if that is what he is trying to say, then we already know how to reply, for we already know that "being dead" does not pick out a state or a condition or an activity of a person at all, and, therefore, that "being dead" is also not a logically coherent description of something which one might imagine or fail to imagine. To say that no one can imagine being dead, in short, is to lapse back into the metaphor of the "dark kingdom"—to say that no one can imagine what it is like to be dead—and that is a metaphor whose logical and conceptual shortcomings we already well and fully understand.

In any way in which coming to attitudinal, emotional, or evaluational terms with one's own death requires that the phrase "one's own death" pick out an historical event which one can imagine or imagine experiencing, then, there is no logical obstacle to one's in fact coming to such terms with one's death. The historical event of one's own death is something which one can rationally anticipate, plan, and provide for in prospect, and visualize or imagine in as much detail as anyone might desire. In this sense, there are such things as rational attitudes toward one's own death, considered as an historical event.

What does not make sense, however, is the proposal that one's own death, considered as an historical event, is something to be, for example, feared or dreaded. For such attitudes are logically appropriate only to historical events which one could, in principle, live through—and one's own death is necessarily not such an historical event. One's own death, viewed as an historical occurrence, while it is indeed an event which someone else could experience, is not, in point of logic, an event which one can oneself experience, nor even, as we have just seen, an event which one can imagine oneself experiencing. Those attitudinal responses and emotional reactions which are logically appropriate to experienceable events, therefore—fear and dread and terror, and, for that matter, eager and joyful anticipation—are not logically coherent, first-person attitudes toward the historical event of one's own death—although someone else, a relative, a friend, or an enemy, might perfectly well and quite rationally react to precisely the same historical occurrence with fear or dread or terror or eager anticipation.

The historical event of one's own death, then, does not have the logical status either of an evil which is to be dreaded and avoided or of a good which is to be sought and welcomed in the first person (although the very same occurrence can be either of these things "from outside," that is, to someone else). Perhaps, then, it is not this historical event which is supposed inevitably to evoke one's thanatophobia or thanatophilia (fear of or fondness for death), but rather "one's own death" in one of the other meanings of that slippery and ambiguous phrase. And, indeed, there is still one sense of the expression "one's own death" which we have not yet investigated. We have examined it as intended to pick out a state, a condition, or an activity, as intended to pick out an instantaneous event, and as intended to pick out an historical event—but we have not yet examined the phrase "one's own death" as it is used to denote a process. Let us make that, then, our next order of business.

9.4: FEAR OF DEATH
AND FEAR OF DYING

When the expression "one's own death" is used to pick out a process, the process in question is one which terminates in the "instantaneous event" of death. It is, in other words, a process of dying. This ambiguity, too, we have seen before. The process of falling asleep, for example, is a process which terminates in the "instantaneous event" of falling asleep. As we phrased it earlier to remove the ambiguity, it is a process of "dropping off to sleep." When it is asserted, then, that thanatophobia or "fear of death" is a natural, universal, and unavoidable human emotion, perhaps what is meant is that all persons have a natural and inevitable dread, not of the event of death, but of the process which culminates in that event, of the process of dying.

Now it is not at all obvious why anyone would believe that such thanatophobia is a universal and necessary characteristic of human consciousness.[10] We are all acquainted, if only at second hand, with persons who at least gave no evidence of fear or dread or terror as they confronted their imminent deaths. According to Plato's recounting of his last days (in the *Phaedo*), indeed, Socrates faced his impending execution not with fear but with welcoming anticipation—arguing, in fact, that this was the attitude appropriate to a philosopher, to a "lover of wisdom." And history is filled with accounts of such persons who have gone to their deaths quietly—if not with enthusiasm, then at least with a calm resignation and with no signs of terror or of dread. The Stoic outlook that "death is nothing to us, and does not matter at all," in other words, has certainly not been without its historical adherents—adherents whose lives and conducts in fact reflected the unconcern and lack of fear which their espoused philosophies theoretically professed.

It is, of course, possible to argue—Freudianly, so to speak—that what we see in such cases is only the enormous power of self-deception, the extent to which unpleasant emotions can be repressed and kept from actual consciousness. But without some independent reason for supposing that a fear of death is genuinely natural and universal in humans, such psychoanalytic arguments always ring rather hollow. It is one thing to diagnose repression when the emotion which a person consciously denies feeling manifests itself elsewhere in his behavior, through obsessive neatness, compulsive handwashing, or what have you. It is quite another thing, however, to continue to insist that some unpleasant emotion is being repressed when an individual's conscious denials remain uncontradicted by any other such behavioral evidences. Such continued insistence then takes on the character of a baseless dogmatism, which, in the absence of any independent grounds for believing in the existence of the supposedly repressed emotion in the first place, we are within our logical rights to dismiss.

I think, in fact, that the common conviction that all persons do fear death is not characteristically advanced as an empirical claim, a generalization based on inquiry and observation, but as a logical implication of the a priori conviction that all persons must fear death, since death is itself something intrinsically dreadful. It is just this supposed intrinsic dreadfulness of death, however, and especially of one's own death, which we have so far been unable to locate. Yet our search is not quite finished. Before embarking on this short digression, we were considering the hypothesis that the proper object of our ostensibly natural and universal thanatophobia was the process which culminates in death, the process of dying. Let us therefore return to that hypothesis and see if we can arrive at a verdict concerning its logical cogency and plausibility.

Here, at least, we are in the right logical and conceptual territory for such attitudes as fear and dread and terror, and even eager or joyful anticipation. These attitudes, we should recall, are logically appropriate only to what could in principle be experienced, be lived through. Now one's own dying, of course, is necessarily not something which one will live through. But it is, so to speak, something which, for a time at least, one will be compelled to live with. The process of dying, that is, has an "experiential inside." It has a duration, and it has an intrinsic character. One may die quickly or slowly, suddenly or gradually, and one's dying may be agonizing and painful or pleasant and easy. One's dying, in short, is a part of one's life. It belongs to one's history, to the collection of one's experiences. While it is going on, while a person is "on his deathbed," that person continues to live, to exist as an experiencing subject. And thus what is occurring—what is happening to him and what he is experiencing—is a suitable object of emotional reactions and attitudinal responses. It is an experiential process which logically can be savored and enjoyed, shunned and struggled against, or merely endured.

What is true contemporaneously of the process of dying, however, is equally true in prospect. Unlike the historical event of one's death, the process of one's dying is the sort of thing which can coherently be the object of such future-directed attitudes as terror, dread, and anticipation. It is an experiential process which, for a time at least, one will be constrained to live with, and consequently it is something that one can, in point of logic, consistently consider with full emotion in prospect—with fear or with hope, with eagerness or with reluctance.

But having said this, it immediately becomes clear that the process of one's dying also cannot be the logical object of a thanatophobia which is supposed to be natural, universal, and unavoidable. The reason, to put it crisply, is that it is only very rarely that anyone in fact knows in advance what his or her dying is going to be like.

Some dyings are indeed dreadful. If I had solid and incontrovertible reasons to believe, for instance, that I was going to die by being torn to pieces by wolves, it would indeed be only rational for me to confront that prospect with fear and with terror, to do everything within my power to avoid it, and, failing that, to try at least to postpone the occurrence as long as was humanly possible. But if, on the other hand, I had equally good reasons to believe that I was going to die comfortably and painlessly, at an advanced age and after a life rich with love and friends and achievements, then it would, I suggest, be positively irrational for me to regard that prospect with precisely the same attitudes of rejection and dread. Instead, a happy "How very nice! I'm certainly glad to know that." is what would be rationally appropriate and logically to the point.

Someone who proposes that fear of death is a natural and universal human emotion—one which may sometimes be successfully repressed but which cannot be completely expunged or totally avoided—thus encounters inescapable logical difficulties. If he advances his proposal as an empirical, matter-of-factual claim, supposedly based upon inquiry and observation, then it appears to be, in point of fact, simply false. But if he advances his proposal as the logical consequence of an a priori conviction that death must be naturally and universally feared, since death is intrinsically dreadful and terrible, then he will in fact be unable to locate, under the rubric "death," any object of experiential attitudes and emotional responses which both actually is a universal and natural aspect of human reality and also, at the same time, actually is fearsome and dreadful in its intrinsic character. For although both an historical event of death and a process of dying do unavoidably belong to the history of every person—as its last event and the process which culminates in that event—the former (the historical event of death), as we have seen, is not a logically possible object for any first-person attitudinal or emotional states appropriate to experiences, and the latter (the process of dying) is at best only sometimes intrinsically fearsome and dreadful, but not universally so.

It follows, we may conclude, that the common and unreflective convictions that death is a fearsome and dreadful evil and that an emotional acknowledgment of this fact is somehow an intrinsic part of every person's inherent psychological makeup are merely elements of a popular myth. What our investigations have rather revealed is that both of these common convictions are, in fact, logically and evidentially groundless. I suspect, indeed, that what lies at the basis of this myth is, once again, only the incoherent metaphor of the "dark kingdom." If death were, in fact, something mysterious and unknowable, then it would be plausible to conclude that fear of death is, or at least ought to be, as universal and as reasonable as fear of the unknown. Once the conceptual muddle which underlies this picture of "the dark kingdom of death" has been cleared away, however, it turns out that nothing which both logically can be feared and universally ought to be feared remains to be found under the heading "death." And so it is time for us to pass beyond the myth of universal thanatophobia.

There remains, inevitably, the fact of death—the fact, that is, that "all men are mortal"; that each of us will, indeed, some day die. It is an equally common conviction, I think, that this fact, too, is a "bad thing." It is, in other words, generally and unreflectively supposed that it is regrettable that each of us will, indeed, some day die; that this is, all things considered, a sorry state of affairs and not, for example, one about which we can or should remain complacent and untroubled nor one in which we may take comfort. But perhaps this conviction, too, is nothing more than another groundless element of the same popular myth. And that brings us to the next stage of our investigations. Whether this common conviction is defensible and correct, in fact, is the topic of my next section.

9.5: THE PERILS OF IMMORTALITY

In his short story "The Immortal," Jorge Luis Borges recounts the life of one Joseph Cartaphilus, nee Marcus Flaminius Rufus, who, during the reign of the Roman emperor Diocletian, sought, found, and drank from "the secret river which cleanses men of death."[11] Cartaphilus, so Borges' story runs, finally achieved his death more than 1600 years later, in October of 1929, but not without first having stumbled upon and drunk from the inevitable second river, the river whose waters remove the immortality which the waters of the first bestow.

The picture of immortality which Borges sketches between his telling of these events is not a pleasant one. The immortals who inhabit the region of the secret river have been eroded by time, reduced to a pitiless and uncaring weary bestiality. They have built a mad labyrinthine parody of the once-glorious city which, aeons earlier, they inhabited, and they live now in caves as uncommunicating and primitive troglodytes, empty and purposeless, drinking from fetid pools of rainwater and eating the flesh of serpents. And when at last they do conceive of one goal worth pursuing, it is only that they go in search of that second river, the river whose waters cancel immortality, which their faith in cosmic symmetries convinces them must somewhere exist.

That "everlasting life" would inevitably become an intolerably burdensome tedium, from which even the strongest and most creative of persons would finally seek to be released, is in fact not uncommon as a literary theme. We find it, too, as I have already noted, in Swift's tale of Gulliver's encounter with the Struldbruggs, and we find it again in Karel Capek's play "The Makropulos Case," whose protagonist, a woman who by virtue of an "elixir of life" has attained the age of 342 years, deliberately refuses to prolong her joyless and indifferent life by even one day more, arguing that "in the end it is the same, singing and silence."[12]

These bleak portraits naturally suggest the view that it is a good thing that "all men are mortal," that people die. They suggest that a complete freedom from death, a life indefinitely prolonged, is not a state to be wanted and sought after at all but rather is itself an undesirable evil—or would, in any case, inevitably come to be thought of as such an evil by anyone unfortunate enough actually to possess it.

It seems reasonable to ask, then, whether this view is indeed correct, whether we can in fact say anything useful from our present "analytic" perspectives about this notion of corporeal immortality, of indefinitely prolonged life, and about what attitudes toward it might be coherently and rationally defensible. It is not at all obvious that we can.

Corporeal immortality, the complete freedom from death, would be a rather peculiar condition. It is not clear that a person who happened to possess it could ever know that he possessed it. He could, of course, know that perhaps hundreds, or even thousands, of years had elapsed and that he hadn't died yet. What is not clear is whether he could know, not just that he hadn't died, but that he couldn't die, for it is not obvious what might empirically differentiate such actual immortality from, for example, an extraordinary (but still bounded and finite) lifespan of, say, one or two million years.

These remarks suggest, however, that we may not yet have formulated our question properly, for there is surely something incoherent about inquiring into the a priori desirability of a goal which one could never in fact know whether or not one had attained. As a literary device, authentic corporeal immortality can simply be stipulated, but as an evidentially well-grounded description of the state or condition of some actual person, the concept appears to suffer from emptiness. It apparently lacks any specifiable conditions of application. And if the concept of corporeal immortality cannot coherently figure into our theoretical reasonings about the actual states of persons, it would be at least peculiar to try nevertheless to factor it into our present practical reasonings about the rational attitudes of such actual persons.

But if the question we should be asking is not "Is genuine corporeal immortality a condition rationally to be desired or to be shunned?" then what is it? I suggest that the question which is in fact typically at issue in discussions framed in terms of "immortality" is rather something more like this: "Is the condition of life itself a good which it is always rational and reasonable for a person to want to have more of?" To this question, however, I think we can give a definite and arguably defensible answer. The answer is "No."

The condition of life itself, in fact, is arguably value-neutral. It is neither a good nor an evil, but rather a necessary condition of everything which is either a good or an evil for us. This valuational status is borne out by the fact that we can and do speak sensibly of "the quality of life." One can live a happy life or a miserable one—that is, one can be alive and happy or alive and miserable. But simply being alive, in and of itself, is neither being happy nor being miserable. It is reasonable to suppose that happiness is itself a good (or, at least, the state of having on balance more goods than evils)[13] and misery itself an evil. In the case of such states or conditions which are themselves goods or evils, however, we do not speak of their "quality" but of their magnitude—the intensity of a person's happiness, for example, or the depth of his misery. The quality of a person's life, in contrast, is completely independent of its magnitude, that is, of its length. One can live a long and miserable life or a short and happy one.

We can see now that the authors of our various bleak tales of immortality are in fact making a sort of prediction. What they are claiming, roughly, is that, however happily a person's life might have begun, extend it long enough and it will inevitably become miserable. Since, to the best of our knowledge, no one has ever in fact succeeded in living for more than one hundred and some odd years, whatever conclusions we might reach about this prediction will necessarily have to remain somewhat speculative and hypothetical. But I would like to suggest that, although it would almost certainly be the case that some originally happy persons would, in time, become bored, cold, indifferent, withdrawn, and miserable were their lives sufficiently prolonged, I do not see any particular reason why that would necessarily need to be true in the case of everyone who was granted a greatly prolonged lifespan.

Of course, if a prolonged lifespan implied only a prolonged period of weakening, loss of competences, and dependency—a prolonged senility, so to speak—then the prediction becomes an eminently plausible one. While being alive is a necessary condition of our possessing those goods which are or contribute to our happiness, it is certainly not a sufficient condition. Strength, health, vigor, and unimpaired mental alertness, at least, are equally necessary conditions of a "good life."

But if the hypothetical prolongation of life which we are envisioning were instead accomplished by an effective retardation of the processes of aging, so that a person could remain indefinitely in full possession of his physical capabilities and rational faculties, then it is no longer obvious that the quality of every person's life would unavoidably deteriorate into the weary state of ineradicable boredom and indifference. The world, after all, contains an indefinite number of potentially interesting things to do or learn or be, and it contains a steadily increasing number of potentially interesting people to get to know. Nor, in this age of space shuttles and Mars missions, is there any a priori reason why the scope of an "immortal's" activities need to be limited to but a single world. With time enough to get there, even the stars are within reach.[14]

What I want, somewhat tentatively, to conclude, then, is that the dramatic literary accounts of bleak and burdensome immortality which we have been considering are not reflections of a point of view which can be argumentatively well grounded in a priori considerations about the intrinsic character of what makes a life desirable or undesirable but rather are fictional embodiments of a certain pessimism about human potentialities. Such stories do have their logical virtues—as cautionary tales—for they serve to remind us that immortality would not be without its perils. They remind us, that is, that life itself is neither a good to be sought for its own sake nor an evil to be shunned in its own right but only, so to speak, the essential background against which any human drama of happiness or misery, joy or sorrow, must necessarily be played out—and that therefore more life, were it somehow to be granted us, would finally be neither more nor less than what we ourselves in the end would make of it.

Both the common conviction that it is a "bad thing" that each of us will indeed some day die and the literary proposal that it is a "good thing" that we humans are all indeed mortal, in other words, appear to belong to competing myths. The fact that we persons are dying beings—beings who, after a hundred or so years, cease to exist—is neither something invariably to be regretted nor something universally to be celebrated. It is only a fact, one more among the many facts which collectively define who and what we persons actually are. The attitudes which it is reasonable and rational for some individual person to assume toward that fact, however, are not universally determinable a priori but rather depend upon the contingencies of that individual's existence, upon the quality of his or her life. For, if one's life is a happy one, then it is surely not unreasonable to regret that it must, indeed, some day come to an end, and if one's life is a miserable one, then it may very well be equally rational to take comfort in the thought that, sooner or later, one will be quit of it.

What is perhaps of more universal significance is the fact that we know our mortality to be a fact, that we are aware of the fact that each of us will indeed some day die. This, too, is one among the many facts which collectively define who and what we persons actually are—but it is frequently taken to be a particularly important one among them, for we humans are evidently unique in this consciousness of our own mortality. Dogs and fish and apes will all someday die, but only we humans know that what is true of them is equally true of us, that each of us, too, will also someday die. Unlike apes and fish and dogs, it is said, we humans live "toward" our deaths.

Our search for rational attitudes toward one's own death has led us to range widely over a broad territory. We have looked at the supposed state or condition of being dead (the mythical "dark kingdom" of death), the "instantaneous event" of death and the historical event of death, the process of dying, and, most recently, at the fact of death, the fact that each of us will someday die. Nowhere in this territory, however, have we discovered any grounds for a universal rejoicing or a universal regret. Nowhere did we find any coherent object for a universal fear or a universal anticipation. The attitudes and evaluations and emotions which were logically suited and rationally appropriate to one's own death have remained particularized, different attitudes and evaluations and emotions being both possible and fitting for different persons in differing circumstances.

One corner of the territory marked out by the expression "one's own death" remains now to be explored—the region picked out by the evidently unique and universal human awareness of mortality, the region labelled "consciousness of one's own death." It is to that exploration, therefore, that I next—and finally—turn.

9.6: "LIFE TOWARD DEATH"

We humans are conscious of or aware of our own mortality. Each of us knows, that is, that he or she is someday going to die. A plausible first question to ask, then, is how each of us knows this. How, for example, do I know that I will someday die, and how do you know that you will someday die?

Here we need to be wary of a certain suggestion, the suggestion that none of us in fact knows any such thing. At best, continues this line of thought, each of us believes that he or she is destined someday to die. Although we may be right in these beliefs—indeed, although we are probably right in these beliefs—the mere likelihood of being right is not enough to convey knowledge. For there always remains the possibility, however remote, that one of us in fact is wrong, that one of us in fact will not die, and as long as this possibility remains logically open, it is incorrect to claim that each of us genuinely knows that he or she is mortal.

Now this line of thought is actually a particular instance of a much broader skepticism about matter-of-factual knowledge in general, and it would lead us too far afield to attempt here to come to terms with radical epistemological skepticism in all its variants and ramifications.[15] We can point out, however, that if one could indeed correctly claim knowledge only in those cases in which any possibility of error was excluded on logical grounds, as the current suggestion evidently presupposes, then it would follow that no one could ever correctly claim to know any contingent empirical fact. For, in the case of any assertion which is based directly or indirectly, on observation, experiment, and matter-of-factual empirical inquiry, it will always be logically possible—that is, it will not be self-contradictory—to suppose that an error has somewhere crept into our investigations.

What this observation should be taken to show, however, is not that no one actually ever does know any matter of empirical fact. Rather, what this observation shows is that the concept of matter-of-factual knowledge does not at all resemble the concept of logical certainty or incorrigibility. In order correctly to claim that one knows some matter of fact, in other words, it is not necessary that one somehow, per impossible, be logically insured against the very possibility of error. It is only necessary that one's grounds or reasons or evidence for whatever it is that one claims to know be good enough to warrant or justify or legitimize one's claim to know it.

What sort of grounds or reasons or evidence are good enough, in turn, will depend upon the particular claim which is being made, upon the character of the particular assertion which one is claiming to know to be true. If what one is claiming to know, for example, is that some complicated equation is a theorem of some mathematical system, then what is needed to validate or warrant one's claim to know is a demonstrative proof of that equation from the axioms which define that mathematical system. But if what one is claiming to know, in contrast, is that one's car is parked on Main Street, then proofs and axioms are simply beside the point. What needs to be the case here if one's claim to know is going to be legitimate, for instance, is that one in fact parked the car on Main Street, that one remembers having done so, and that one has no special reasons to doubt that the car is still where one remembers having left it.

It always remains, of course, logically possible that one is mistaken. We do, after all, sometimes misremember, and cars are sometimes stolen or towed away. But even if one later discovers that one was indeed mistaken—that one's car was not, in fact, parked on Main Street at the time that one claimed to know it to be parked there—it does not follow that one's claim to know was unjustified or unwarranted at the time at which it was made. What follows is only that one's claim to know some empirical matter of fact is itself just another empirical, matter-of-factual, assertion which, like any such assertion, can turn out to be true or false. That is, one can not only, in point of logic, be wrong about whether or not one's car is parked on Main

Street, one can also, in point of logic, be wrong about whether or not one in fact knows that it is parked there. But these mere possibilities do not show that the concept of empirical knowledge has no application. Rather, they show that the correct application of the concept of empirical knowledge does not require, per impossible, that such possibilities be first logically excluded a priori. For sometimes one's car is parked on Main Street—and sometimes one does know that it is parked there.

That I am going someday to die is something that I know in much the same way that I know any matter of fact. I know that I am mortal, to begin with, because I know what sort of creature I am. I know, that is, that I am a particular kind of animal—a human being, that is, an animal of the species *homo sapiens*—and I know that all members of that species are mortal. I know this, in turn, in the same way that I know anything in general about the members of a particular species—as the result of experience, observations, and experiments. In this way, I know—in this way, indeed, we all know—that all human beings are vertebrates, that all human beings are mammals, that all human beings require Vitamin C . . . and that all human beings will someday die.

There is, in other words, nothing special or mysterious or private about one's knowledge of one's own mortality. It is not something which one knows in any "privileged" way, "from inside," so to speak. That everyone will someday die is just another fact, and one knows it in precisely the way that one knows any matter of fact—not beyond the logical possibility of being mistaken, but on the basis of good and sufficient grounds, reasons, or evidence for believing that it is true. One knows that human beings are mortal in the same way that one knows that cats are carnivorous or that sea water is salty. And thus one can know that one oneself is mortal in the same way that one can know that the neighbor's cat is carnivorous or that the sea water behind the mayor's beach cottage is salty—not because one has made special observations of the neighbor's cat or experimented privately with the sea water behind the mayor's cottage, but simply as one more instance of a general fact about things of that kind.

The "philosophical" assertion that we human beings live "toward" our deaths suggests, however, a different picture.[16] It suggests that, for each of us, his or her own death is somehow "already present" as a "special" datum of consciousness. It suggests, that is, that one knows that one will oneself someday die in a different way from the way in which one knows that one's friends and acquaintances will someday die. One can only "surmise" that others will die. One's own eventual death, however, is something which one knows about "from inside." It is somehow "prefigured" in one's consciousness, silhouetted against the "horizon" of one's inner awareness as a goal or terminus toward which one can "perceive" oneself to be moving.

Now there can be no doubt that this is in some ways a dramatic and compelling picture. But it is unfortunately not clear that there is any literal sense to be made of it at all. For what is it supposed to be a picture of ? In what way is my own death supposed to be consciously accessible to me here and now in which the death of, say, my brother is not equally here and now consciously accessible to me? Neither of us, in fact, has yet died. Both of us, in fact, will someday die—and both of us know that. But just how is my knowledge of my own mortality supposed to be different from my knowledge of my brother's mortality?

It is obvious, I think, that these questions have no coherent answers. Such dramatic and metaphorical talk about "life toward death," in fact, is only an attempt to assimilate one's knowledge of one's own mortality to a confused epistemological model which, in any case, it will not actually fit. There are facts about myself which, speaking informally, I might perhaps intelligibly be said to "know" in some "special," "privileged," or "private" way. It could, for example, be a fact that I now have a headache. If that were indeed a fact, it is tempting to say that it is a fact of which I would have a "special" or "privileged" or "private" first-person knowledge. I would know whether or not I now had a headache; others could only "surmise" it. I am "acquainted" with my own headaches—"at first hand," so to speak—but others can know about my headaches only on the basis of "external signs"—"by hearsay," so to speak.[17]

What we should recognize, however, is that all this talk about "knowing" is here really not to the point. For what actually are the relevant differences here? When I have a headache, it is, of course, my head which aches—not yours and not my brother's. My headaches are mine in the same way that my smiles are mine. But just as a smile is not a mysterious and elusive "outer object" which belongs to just one person in some "special" or "privileged" way, so, too, a headache is not a mysterious and elusive "inner object" with which just one person is "acquainted" in some "special" or "privileged" way. When I have a headache, there is something which is true of me that is not also ipso facto true of, say, my brother. But it is not that I know something which he cannot know. It is only that I feel something which he does not feel. Even less misleadingly, it is only that my head aches, and his (let us hope) does not. That is, to be sure, a difference between us. But it is not a difference which is correctly describable as a difference in what we know or in how we know it, for having a headache is no more a special way of knowing something than is smiling.

The epistemological model of "privileged" knowledge of "inner objects," then, is misconceived and misguided to begin with. Such "inner objects" as headaches are, like smiles, merely nominal objects, and thus having a headache is not a special kind of "observing" or "perceiving" or "being acquainted with" something any more than wearing a smile is a special kind of "dressing up." Wearing a smile is simply doing something, smiling, and having a headache is simply undergoing something, one's head's aching—but neither this doing nor this undergoing is a form of knowing anything, and, a fortiori, neither is a "special" or "privileged" or "private" form of knowing anything.

But even if this epistemological model of "special" knowledge were itself a coherent one, there would be no way to extend it to encompass a "special" knowledge of one's own death. For, as we have seen, except in the sense of "one's own death" in which that expression picks out the process of one's dying, the phrase "one's own death"—unlike the phrase "one's own headaches"—does not designate anything which one could, in the first person, experience or even imagine experiencing. And, of course, what the process of one's own dying will be like is almost always something of which one has in advance, not only no "privileged" knowledge, but no knowledge at all. None of the nominal objects ostensibly denoted by the expression "one's own death," in other words, is even to begin with an experiential reality of the sort which—like such nominal objects as headaches—might, however mistakenly, be thought to be the target of a special "private acquaintance" or "inner observation." The extension of the model of "special first-person knowledge" to the case of one's own death, then, is doubly confused—first, because the model itself is inherently a conceptual muddle, but, second, because one's own death turns not to be the sort of thing to which that model, even in its muddled form, can coherently and intelligibly be applied.[18]

In spite of all this, however, I want finally to suggest that there is a sense in which we human beings do live "toward" our deaths, and in which the fact that each of us will someday die does form a part of the present reality of our lives. What I have in mind is this: The events of birth and death form a sort of frame into which each person must necessarily fit his conception of his own life and of the lives of others. The fact that every person's life is of finite duration and bounded at both ends gives one's own life of actions and experiences—and the lives of others with whom one perforce interacts as well—a distinctive shape which structures and colors those experiences and actions and interactions. The notion of an "allotted term of years," of a "normal lifespan," functions to allow one to place oneself and others relative to the envisioned totality of a typical individual history, to think of such a life history as a whole which is characteristically divided into stages, and to think of oneself and of others as occupying some definite one of these stages or as in transition between them.

The Biblical "three score and ten" years—now perhaps extended by medical technology to a full four score—is still the appropriate framework within which to delineate "the ages of man." The seventy to eighty or more years comprising the life expectancy of an "average" person are patterned years: childhood and youth for growth and learning, physical maturation, and the acquisition of life skills; young adulthood for assuming responsibilities, building a family, and settling life plans and life projects; mature adulthood for bringing one's plans and projects to fruition, seeing one's children enter into the independence of their adult years, and coming to terms with the deaths of one's own parents; and old age, for bringing one's plans to completion or relinquishing the responsibility for uncompleted projects to others younger than oneself, for reflection and summing up, and for preparation for one's own death.

In these ways, and in many others, the fact of universal human mortality structures the very concepts in terms of which we experience the living out of our lives. In these ways, the fact that each of us will someday die shapes and colors our consciousness. Our deaths are then indeed, in a sense, present to us here and now—not as the private objects of a special, privileged, first-person acquaintance, but as inherent structural aspects of those concepts in terms of which we humans uniquely, as rational beings, experience ourselves and our world. And that, I suggest, is one truth which does lie hidden in the dramatic "philosophical" claim that we persons, we thinking beings—unlike the unreasoning beasts of the field and the forest—do live "toward" our deaths.

9.7: LOOSE ENDS—
AND SOME SUMMING UP

Is there then, all things considered, anything which can properly be termed a "rational attitude" toward death—and, in particular, toward one's own death? In the sense in which the question was originally meant, I think, we can now conclude that the answer is "No." We have found the phrase "one's own death" to be rich in ambiguities, but we have also found that in none of its many senses does the expression designate anything which it is always and necessarily appropriate to welcome or to fear, to seek or to shun, to celebrate or to deplore. In none of its many senses, that is, does the phrase "one's own death" universally pick out anything intrinsically good or anything inherently evil. Considered simply in and of itself, in other words, death is value-neutral. Considered simply in and of itself, that is, death is indeed "nothing to us, and does not matter at all."

And now I believe that we are also finally in a position to say something more about the unresolved debate between Darcy and the interventionist. The interventionist, we recall, asserted that Darcy's judgment had manifestly been distorted by emotions of hopelessness and despair, and he cited Darcy's suicidal intentions as de facto evidence of this impairment of her rational competences. Darcy herself, in contrast, argued that she was perfectly lucid and sane, and she in fact offered those same suicidal intentions as de facto evidence of her unimpaired rationality. The question which we left unresolved was which of these competing outlooks, if either, was actually correct. And it appeared that what we needed to know before we could arrive at a verdict in this case was whether there was such a thing as a "rational first-person attitude toward death."

In light of the investigations which we have recently concluded, I would propose that we can now award the case to Darcy. I suggest, in fact, that the interventionist's notion that a person's intention to take her own life is always and automatically evidence of impaired rationality is really only another chapter in the popular myth of universal thanatophobia. If death were actually something intrinsically fearsome and terrible, and if an emotional acknowledgment of this fact were actually an essential part of the inborn psychological makeup of every normal person, then the absence of this supposedly natural dread of death, to which suicidal intentions would testify, would be prima facie proof of psychological abnormality.

As we have seen, however, neither the conviction that death is naturally and universally feared nor the conviction that death is naturally and inherently fearsome is either demonstrably true a priori or empirically supportable by any available evidential matters of fact. And this being so, it follows that a person's expressed intention to commit suicide is not, in and of itself—by virtue of its testifying to a lack of thanataphobia—automatically evidence of distorted judgment or impaired sanity.

Our earlier reflections on "the perils of immortality" imply instead that what needs to be taken into consideration when the appropriateness of attitudes and evaluations is at issue is not the mere condition of being alive but rather the quality of a person's life. I suggested there that a miserable enough life could, in fact, become a burden which a person might well reasonably desire to be quit of. Now our interventionist, we may recall, rejected this suggestion. He argued that, since one can never, in point of logic, be better off vis-à-vis any self-interests if one has ceased to exist, the suicidal act of self-annihilation is necessarily excluded from the class of possible self-interestedly rational actions. At the time, this argument was left unanswered, but I want now to propose that it contains a subtle flaw.

To put a sharper edge on it, the interventionist's argument proceeds from the undeniable premiss that one can be better off at some later time than one is at present only if one still exists at that later time to the conclusion that it cannot in principle serve one's interests (be in one's best interest) to cease to exist. Once the argument is so formulated, however, it becomes obvious that an additional premiss has been left unstated. For the interventionist's conclusion follows from his explicit premiss only if it is also granted that no action can serve one's interests or be in one's best interest unless one would sooner or later be better off as a result of having performed it than one is at present.

It is this additional tacit premiss, however, which Darcy will surely deny. Instead, she will respond that she is not proposing to commit the "drastic" act of suicide in order sooner or later to be better off than she is then and there. Rather, she is proposing to take her own life in order to avoid becoming unbearably worse off than she is then and there. The interventionist, Darcy can argue, has assimilated her intended suicide to the wrong class of "drastic" actions. He has tried to categorize it as an extreme example of risk-taking, as a "desperate gamble," analogous to quitting one's profitable job or abandoning one's secure marriage with the expectation, or at least the hope, of ultimately finding something better. But there is another class of situations in which "drastic" actions may be rationally defensible and to the point—those situations in which nothing short of a "drastic" action can avert an impending catastrophe—and Darcy's present situation, she can argue, properly belongs to this class of cases.

Of course, Darcy can continue, she does not have the logically incoherent expectation of being better off as the result of taking her own life. But that is not the only expectation in terms of which a "drastic" act of suicide could be shown to be rational. For Darcy is now confronting a personal catastrophe which only that drastic action can forestall. Her circumstances have become objectively hopeless—and that fact is not in dispute. Her choice, then, is not one between an undesirable present situation and an uncertain, but possibly better, future—as is the choice in any "normal" situation of risk-taking or "taking a desperate gamble." Her choice is between a dreadful future, where intolerability is not problematic but certain, and no future at all.

In such rare and wretched circumstances, then, concludes Darcy, it can be in one's best interest to cease to exist, not for the absurd reason that one will be better off not existing than existing, but for the reason that one has, then and there, a paramount and overriding interest in averting a catastrophe which looms ineluctably before one, and that nothing short of a drastic act of self-annihilation can in fact serve that dominant interest. Nothing short of suicide, that is, can in fact prevent the awful prospect from becoming an unendurable reality.

To this last line of argument, I think, the interventionist has no further cogent rebuttal. He could, to be sure, attempt to deny that the future which Darcy would confront were she to reject suicide and accept therapy actually is as horrible as Darcy judges it to be. But, since both he and Darcy are in agreement about what that future would be like in point of fact, such a denial would amount only to a further expression of a difference in sensibilities which, as we have seen, is not adequate to convey a moral right of interference with Darcy's plans. And if the interventionist attempted instead to argue, not that Darcy's prospective future was not in point of fact as terrible as she judged it to be, but that no prospective future could, in principle, be as terrible as death itself, we could rightly conclude that he had thereby abandoned the project of reasoned debate and retreated instead to a position of ungrounded dogmatism which we have ourselves found good reasons to believe reflects nothing logically or evidentially defensible but only a widespread and popular myth.

To the extent that one can usefully speak about a "rational attitude toward death," then, what is in question is not an attitude toward an experiential reality but an attitude toward a fact. It is a fact that each of us human beings is mortal, and so, too, it is a fact that one will oneself someday die. The "rational attitude" toward these facts, however, is the same as the rational attitude toward any others: One should face them. That is, one should acknowledge them as facts, and one should take them into account in one's planning and in one's practical deliberations.

As we have now seen in the case of Darcy, in extreme circumstances "taking the fact of one's own mortality into account in one's practical deliberations" can even mean entering the act of suicide on the list of options open to one which it is reasonable to consider. One's situation can, indeed, objectively warrant the entertaining of even so "drastic" an alternative as taking one's own life, and, when it does, making the act of suicide one among the possible courses of action about which one must arrive at a decision is not de facto proof of irrationality but itself a logically defensible rational act.

What is, I want to suggest, always prima facie irrational is the refusal to face the fact of one's own mortality. It is not the contemplation of suicide in extremis which testifies to an abnegation of reason and a retreat into empty fantasies but rather baseless denials, vain wishes, and self-deceptive pretence. One mark of a rational individual, in other words, is that he lives a life appropriate to a dying being—that he acknowledges without denial and without complaint the unavoidable transitoriness of his own existence, accepts with dignity and with grace the inevitable passage from youth to old age which is the outward sign of that transitoriness, and prudently plans and provides for his own death and, to the extent that he can, for the well-being and betterment of those whose lives will continue after his life, and thus his very being, has come to an end. The "rational attitude toward death," in short, is neither fear nor dread, neither joy nor anticipation. The "rational attitude toward death," if it is anything, is realism.

EPILOGUE

The Limits of
Philosophical Understanding

I began this study, many pages ago, with a brief sketch of the history of death as a problem for philosophy. For the occasional reader whose prior expectations had been shaped by the high drama of Plato's dialogues or by the dark obscurities of Heidegger's phenomenological ruminations, what I then proceeded to do for those many ensuing pages has probably been something of a disappointment. For the more typical reader, who came to this book without any prior expectations at all, it has probably been even more of a disappointment.

In the end, I have offered no dramatic eyewitness reports of dark tunnels, bright lights, and ethereal music, no profound psychological insights into the dynamics of grief or denial or reconciliation, and no deep and suggestive "philosophical" accounts of "spiritual realities" or "ineffable truths" beyond the reach of the human mind. In the end, I have offered only page after page of language lessons and logical gymnastics. Like Plato, I have evidently banished the poets from my small Republic, but unlike Plato, alas, I am not genius enough to have made that very banishment itself a work of magnificent poetry—and so, when I have mentioned myth and metaphor at all, it has only been as subjects for logical dissection and analytic dismissal.

I would not be surprised, then, to be informed by some thoughtful reader, who has patiently accompanied me through the swamps of linguistic ambiguity and the jungles of logical consequence, that something important has gotten lost along the way. Somewhere between the gremlins in the refrigerator and the rational justification of paternalism, he may well insist, I have lost sight of the seriousness of death.

What may well surprise such a reflective reader is that, in a sense, I agree with him. His point is well taken. As anyone who has ever suffered the loss of a beloved parent, an innocent child, or a cherished friend knows all too well, death is no mere logico-linguistic abstraction but a hard and poignant reality which can strike suddenly and unexpectedly at the depths of the human heart.

Nothing that I have said has been meant to deny such truths. And that I have, inevitably, left much unsaid should not be taken as evidence that I am blind to the emotional power of death or myself immune to the sorrow and grief that death can abruptly visit upon the living. And yet, after all that has been granted, I would still want once more to remind this reflective reader that this book has been, from the beginning, a study in thinking clearly about death—and that feeling, however real, is still not thinking. My project from the outset has been to explore the counsels of calm reason and not the consolations of the grieving heart.

We human beings are unique among the inhabitants of this planet in being creatures both of emotion and of reason. As feeling beings, it indeed befits us to be touched and moved by the death of one who is close to us, for such persons are precious to us and through death they are lost to us irredeemably and forever. And so, too, it is fitting that we should seek some comfort and some solace in the face of such a loss.

Yet I would insist that it befits us, too, as thinking beings, not to find our comfort and our solace only in myth and in muddle and in self-delusion. Rather, it is fitting that we search out our consolations from the standpoint of a clear and reasoned understanding of the truth, which only such rational beings as we humans uniquely are could ever achieve—or even wish to achieve.

The logical and linguistic investigations which I have undertaken here in the name of analytic philosophy have never been intended to blunt the seriousness of death as an emotional reality. They are not, that is, the stuff of which comfort and solace and consolation are made. But to the extent that what I have accomplished in this book has in fact been a step toward that clear and reasoned understanding of death which it befits our nature as rational beings to seek and to attain, I would insist that my investigations have been more than pointless word-play and sterile logic-chopping. To that extent, they pertain as well to the real affairs of the human heart. And that, I submit, is finally enough to vindicate any work of philosophy, be it "classical" or "analytic."

Notes and References

PRELUDE

1. There are a variety of good editions of Plato's *Phaedo*. A convenient one is the translation by G. M. A. Grube, published by Hackett Publishing Company (Indianapolis: 1977).

2. René Descartes, *Meditations on First Philosophy*. This work, too, is variously reprinted. The translation by D. A. Cress, Hackett Publishing Company (Indianapolis: 1979) is a handy one.

3. Immanuel Kant, *Critique of Practical Reason*. The standard translation is by T. K. Abbott, Longmans (London: 1909). The translation by L. W. Beck, University of Chicago Press (Chicago: 1949) is reprinted in the Bobbs-Merrill "Library of Liberal Arts" series and probably more accessible to the general reader. Kant's work in general is quite difficult and complex. A useable introductory survey of central Kantian themes is S. Körner's *Kant*, Penguin Books (New York: 1955).

4. Martin Heidegger, *Sein Und Zeit*. The standard English translation, under the title *Being and Time*, is by J. Macquarrie and E. Robinson, Harper & Row, Inc. (New York: 1962). The book, despite its many philosophical merits, is unfortunately opaque and cryptic in any language, and not recommended for casual reading.

5. Perhaps it always has been, but the public discussion of death has recently achieved an openness which, I suspect, is without historical parallel. The best evidence of this is the explosion of literature devoted to the subject during the past 10 to 15 years—and the enormous popular success of some of that literature. It is impossible to do justice to all of it, but a brief survey should help drive home the magnitude of the phenomenon.

Probably best known are the various works of Elisabeth Kübler-Ross on the psychology of death and dying: *On Death and Dying*, Macmillan (New York: 1969); *Questions and Answers on Death and Dying*, Macmillan (New York: 1974); *Death: The*

Final Stage of Growth, Prentice-Hall, (Englewood Cliffs, NJ: 1975); and *Living with Death and Dying,* Macmillan, (New York: 1981). Also in the same genre are P. Koestenbaum, *Is There an Answer to Death?,* Prentice-Hall (Englewood Cliffs, NJ: 1976) and the Hastings Center Report, *Death Inside Out,* edited by P. Steinfels and R. M. Veatch, Harper & Row (New York: 1975). Clinical implications are discussed in R. G. Benton, *Death and Dying: Principles and Practices in Patient Care,* Van Nostrand-Reinhold (New York: 1978). D. V. Hardt provides a good overview of this line of inquiry in *Death: The Final Frontier,* Prentice-Hall (Englewood Cliffs, NJ: 1979).

Of the "survivalist" literature, the most visible have been two books by Raymond A. Moody: *Life After Life,* Bantam Books (New York: 1975) and *Reflections on Life After Life,* Bantam (New York: 1977). Other books departing from explorations of so-called "near-death experiences" include Susy Smith, *Life is Forever: Evidence for Survival After Death,* Putnam (New York: 1974); E. S. Shneidman, *Voices of Death,* Harper & Row (New York: 1980); R. Kastenbaum (ed.), *Between Life and Death,* Springer Publishing Co. (New York: 1979); and E. Mansell Pattison, *Experience of Dying,* Prentice-Hall (Englewood Cliffs, NJ: 1977). In 1977, the Arno Press inaugurated a reprint series "The Literature of Death and Dying," dedicated to the reissue of classical works on the subject, the majority with an experiential and survivalist orientation. The moderately successful 1980 film *Resurrection,* starring Ellen Burstyn, is also worth mentioning in this connection.

In a more philosophical vein—in order of increasing speculativeness—are T. Penelhum, *Survival and Disembodied Existence,* Humanities Press (New York: 1970); J. Hick, *Death and Eternal Life,* Harper & Row (New York: 1976); and A. M. Greeley, *Death and Beyond,* Thomas More Press (Chicago: 1976).

The case of Karen Ann Quinlan, a comatose and brain-damaged woman being kept alive by means of a respirator, whose parents sought and were granted legal permission to discontinue treatment stirred up a good bit of discussion during the middle and late 1970s. See B. D. Colen, *Karen Ann Quinlan: Dying in the Age of Eternal Life,* Nash Publishing Co. (New York: 1976). Relevant issues are surveyed in T. C. Oden, *Should Treatment be Terminated?,* Harper & Row (New York: 1976); D. N. Walton, *On Defining Death,* McGill-Queen's University Press (Montreal: 1979); and the collection of essays *Killing and Letting Die* edited by B. Steinbock, Prentice-Hall (Englewood Cliffs, NJ: 1980).

Personal and cultural beliefs about death and attitudes toward death are explored in Jacques Choron's *Death and Western Thought,* Collier Books (New York: 1963) and *Modern Man and Mortality,* Harper & Row (New York: 1964) and in the essays collected by Herman Feifel under the title *The Meaning of Death,* McGraw-Hill (New York: 1959). Ernest Becker's Pulitzer Prize winning study of the fear of death from a psychoanalytic and existentialist perspective, *The Denial of Death,* The Free Press (New York: 1973) is also worth reading with regard to such attitudinal questions.

CHAPTER 0

1.   The easiest access to this topic is by way of two excellent accounts of the historical emergence and early development of the analytic movement in philosophy: J. O. Urmson's *Philosophical Analysis,* Oxford University Press (London: 1956) and G. J.

Warnock's *English Philosophy since 1900,* Oxford University Press (London: 1958). At least the first of these is available in a current American paperback edition. Both contain useful bibliographies of primary sources.

2. Probably the best overview of the later vicissitudes of the analytic movement is afforded by the essays collected in R. Rorty's *The Linguistic Turn,* University of Chicago Press (Chicago and London: 1967). Rorty's own introductory essay is an especially lucid tracing of the challenges and problems which the new movement encountered and the gambits which it evolved to attempt to deal with them.

3. I have done a bit more toward articulating my own methodological ideas in a small introductory text *The Practice of Philosophy: A Handbook for Beginners,* Prentice-Hall (Englewood Cliffs, NJ: 1978).

4. Ludwig Wittgenstein, *Philosophical Investigations,* translated by G. E. M. Anscombe, Macmillan (New York and London: 1953). Some revisions have been made in later editions. I think the most current is that issued by Basil Blackwell & Mott, Ltd. (London: 1958), but the differences concern fine points of scholarship and not substantive points of view in any case.

5. I owe this "oil" series to my colleague Paul Ziff, whose ear for such linguistic idiosyncrasies is hard to beat.

6. Formulated, I believe, by W. V. O. Quine. He, in any case, has been the contemporary philosopher who has probably most insisted on the need for identity conditions in order to legitimize the ontological status of some proposed entity. See, for example, his "Identity, Ostension, and Hypostasis," reprinted in *From a Logical Point of View,* Harvard University Press (Cambridge, MA: 1953, 1961)—available also in a Harper Torchbooks paperback edition, (New York: 1963)—and his *Word and Object,* MIT Press (Cambridge, MA: 1960). The significance of identity conditions is also usefully discussed by P. F. Strawson in the opening sections of his *Individuals,* Methuen & Co. (London: 1959) and Anchor Books (New York: 1963).

7. This point was first clearly articulated, I think, by Bishop George Berkeley during his famous critique of John Locke's conception of "matter" in the late seventeenth or early eighteenth century. Berkeley's *Three Dialogues Between Hylas and Philonous* is a charming and readable exposition of the critique. The work is variously reprinted, the Hackett Publishing Co. edition—edited by R. M. Adams, (Indianapolis: 1979)—being one handy source. In our own time, this notion of emptiness has been vividly exploited by John Wisdom in his essay "Gods," reprinted in *Logic and Language: First Series,* edited by A. G. N. Flew, Basil Blackwell (Oxford: 1963), and by Flew himself in his essay "Theology and Falsification," reprinted in *New Essays in Philosophical Theology,* edited by A. G. N. Flew and A. MacIntyre, Macmillan (New York: 1955, 1964).

8. This example is adapted from Wittgenstein's *Philosophical Investigations.*

CHAPTER 1

1. The dictionary closest to hand turned out to be *The Random House Dictionary of the English Language,* College Edition, Random House (New York: 1968), so, on those rare occasions when I cite a dictionary, that will be the one to which I am referring. Other dictionaries, however, are no more help with our questions than that one.

2. Plato, *Phaedo,* 70e–72a. (See Prelude, note (1) for a fuller citation of the work.)

3. The wet-dry family found its fullest flowering in the mediaeval picture of "perfec-tions and privations"—such "stuffs" as knowledge, power, and light being the "perfections" and their lacks or absences (ignorance, impotence, darkness) the "privations." Anselm's notorious "Ontological Proof of the Existence of God" turns on these notions, for example. Anselm points out, in essence, that God, as the most perfect being, must possess all perfections to the highest degree—and then attempts to argue that existence in reality is itself one such perfection. (One may suppose, however, that such logically parallel "perfections" as wetness, curva-ture, and bumpiness did not occur to Anselm.) And Augustine attempted to rec-oncile the existence of an omnipotent and omniscient benevolent God with the ex-istence of evil and suffering in the world by arguing that evil and suffering were mere privations—not positive "somethings" but lacks or absences—and thus could not be debited to God's moral accounts as objectionable elements of his creation. A privation being a "nothing," it cannot be the result of a positive act of creation of "somethings".

4. Failure to recognize the present tense of "is dead" as only a linguistic appearance can get one tangled up in very unpleasant puzzles and conceptual knots. For an example of these, see Douglas N. Walton's effort to come to grips with the logic of "null states" in Chapters IV and V of his *On Defining Death,* McGill-Queen's Uni-versity Press (Montreal: 1979).

5. For more details on the view of temporal discourse and ostensible reference to nominal temporal objects sketched here, see my "One Way of Understanding Time," *Philosophia,* Vol. 2, No. 4, 1972.

6. I shall return to the topic of "the moment of death" and to questions concerning "fixing the time of death" at greater length later, in Chapter 4. See especially sec-tions 4.2 and 4.8.

CHAPTER 2

1. Socrates fails to realize this in his final argument in Plato's *Phaedo.* There, Socrates identifies a soul as "the Alive in the man"—roughly, a "vital principle" instantiated in the individual person which explanatorily accounts for that person's being a liv-ing creature—and proceeds to argue that "the Alive in the man" cannot perish but must have a history as a separable entity which continues beyond that person's death. The dialogue ends shortly thereafter with Socrates' own death, and thus none of the participants ever ask the appropriate question: "So what?" It is per-haps interesting to learn that "the Alive in me" is going to survive my death—but it doesn't seem very important. For it does not follow from that fact that somehow I myself am going to survive.

2. I shall say more about the difference between talking about "minds" and talking about "souls" later, in Section 2.7 of this chapter.

3. Socrates did recognize this point. After concluding that "the Alive in a man" can-not itself die—since "opposites cannot admit their opposites" and thus, with the approach of death (the opposite of life) an "Alive" must either perish or

withdraw—Socrates went on to argue that, in addition, "the Alive in a man" also cannot itself perish, that is, simply cease to exist (although not by dying). His "argument," alas, is totally worthless. It runs: The "Alive in a man" cannot die; hence, it is undying; hence, it is immortal (like the gods); and "everyone agrees that the immortal (being akin to the gods) must also be imperishable." Whether everyone should agree, of course, is precisely one of the things at issue, however. And, indeed, they shouldn't. As we have seen, there are other ways of ceasing to exist besides dying, and an "immortal soul" could very well avail itself of one of these alternatives.

4.   This distinction parallels Strawson's between "P-predicates" and "M-predicates," drawn in his *Individuals.* ("Person-predicates" and "Material-predicates," I think, although it might be turned around: "Physical" and "Mental." Strawson's terminology here, while it has proved influential, is not the most memorable.) See note (6) of Chapter 0 for a full citation.

5.   In this discussion, I draw upon and extend the work done by my colleague D. C. Long in two excellent essays: "The Philosophical Concept of a Human Body," *Philosophical Review,* Vol. LXXIII, No. 3, 1964; and "The Bodies of Persons," *Journal of Philosophy,* Vol. LXXI, No. 10, 1974.

6.   Although Plato is confused about it. In the *Phaedo,* Socrates argues for the immortality of the soul in this sense of "soul"—as "the Alive in the (living) thing"—and then continues by simply taking it for granted that whatever thus accounts for the being alive of persons is also what accounts for the unique rational and moral competences of persons. The assumption, however, is completely gratuitous—and, in fact, probably false. Aristotle, at least, distinguishes various "grades" of souls—vegetative, animal, and rational. Aristotle's views on the soul are laid out in greatest detail in his *De Anima,* which is available in various editions and translations.

7.   Descartes pretty much single-handedly invented what we might call the "modern" notion of the mind by bundling together sensitivity, cognition, and will (volition) as "mental" faculties. You can watch him doing it in his *Meditations on First Philosophy,* cited in note (2) for the Prelude. One consequence within his own philosophy was "animal automatism"—the thesis that, for instance, dogs and cats do not have "minds" at all, but are merely "organic automata." Keith Gunderson has a good discussion of this aspect of Descartes' philosophy in *Mentality and Machines,* Doubleday Anchor (New York: 1979). For a devastating critique of this "Cartesian" concept of mind, see Richard Rorty's *Philosophy and the Mirror of Nature,* Princeton University Press (Princeton, NJ: 1979). Locke's views can be found in his *Essay Concerning Human Understanding,* the most accessible edition of which is available from Dover Press.

8.   Various historically popular positions on the "mind-body problem" are surveyed—with cartoons—in Richard Taylor's *Metaphysics,* Prentice-Hall (Englewood Cliffs, NJ: 1963, 1974). For a more extensive introductory discussion, Jerome A. Shaffer's *Philosophy of Mind,* Prentice-Hall (Englewood Cliffs, NJ: 1968), is useful.

9.   This is probably the place to say something about all those "special experiences" which are now being cited as "empirical evidence" for the existence and nature of an "afterlife" (the sorts of experiences cinematically depicted, for example, in the film *Resurrection*).

There really isn't all that much to say. One thing, alas, worth mentioning (since people do somehow manage to get muddled about it) is that none of these reported "near-death" experiences are in any literal sense experiences of a "life after death." They are not "post-death" experiences, for the simple reason that the people who had them did not die but rather lived to tell about them. None of these reports have been delivered by people who have "returned from the dead"—because death, unlike "clinical death," is the event from which, in point of logic, one doesn't "return." A clinically dead person is not a kind of dead person, and so neither are the experiences had by clinically dead persons experiences had by dead persons.

That people who have undergone heart-stoppage and resuscitation, acute anaphylactic shock, or other severe near-fatal physical traumas have often had interesting, unique, and pleasant experiences is not a claim I would be interested in quarreling with. What I would insist upon, however, is that these facts don't—and, in point of logic, couldn't possibly—show anything about "survival" or "life after death." All of these experiences are experiences had by living persons, and all of the reports of such experiences have been reports delivered by living persons. The most that such reports could ever demonstrate, then, is that living persons tend to have similar interesting, unique, and pleasant experiences in moments of near-fatal acute physical trauma.

Well, they probably do. And, what is more, we now have some biological understanding of why they do. It turns out that, at such times of acute stress and trauma, the human body produces chemicals known as "endomorphins," which are a kind of natural opiate, chemically akin (as their name suggests) to morphine. With such chemicals present in the bloodstream, it is not at all surprising that people have felt calm and joyful or have had pleasant hallucinations of bright lights and beautiful music.

A great deal has been made, too, of the cultural invariance of these near-death experiences. Christians, Jews, Hindus, and Buddhists, it has been stressed, all report the same sorts of lights and sounds and the same feelings of joy and of being welcomed. Well, again, they probably do. I certainly have no evidence to offer to the contrary. But here, again, nothing at all follows with regard to "survival" or an "afterlife." What follows from this fact of the cultural invariance of near-death experiences, of course, is that all of us—Christians, Jews, Hindus, and Buddhists alike—have the same organic biochemistry, and that our experiences at such times of "clinical death" are far more determined by that biochemistry than by our diverse cultural backgrounds.

What is really far more interesting than the fact that many people have had such vivid and pleasant experiences is the fact that so many people have tried to interpret those experiences as evidence of something for which they couldn't possibly be evidence—indeed, as evidence of something which, as we are in the process of discovering, cannot be formulated as a logically coherent hypothesis at all. All that I can do here as a practicing philosopher, however, is to note and then unravel the various logical and conceptual muddles which such attempts manifest. Explaining their prevalence, on the other hand, belongs to the sociology and psychology of persons, and not to the philosophical study of death.

10. Berkeley's critique of Locke's notion of "matter" (see note (7) for Chapter 0) runs along similar lines. At one point, Locke defends a conception of matter as

"substratum," having such mathematical properties as shape, size, position, and velocity, but lacking any other properties—in particular lacking all such sensible (i.e., sensory) qualities as color, temperature, sound, odor, flavor, and the like. What Berkeley proceeds to point out, to phrase it briefly, is that where there is form there must also be content.

A cube, for instance, must be a cube of something. That is, there must necessarily be something which fills up or occupies a cubical region of space, something which is in some way different from whatever fills up or occupies the space surrounding that cubical region and which thereby demarcates that region from its environment. It follows, concludes Berkeley, that nothing could, in point of logic, have only such mathematical properties as shape, size, and position. It would also need to have at least one more property—to demarcate its shape, size, and location within its otherwise homogeneous environment. The Lockean notion of matter as something with only mathematical properties, therefore, is itself internally incoherent.

Locke himself, indeed, offers another account of "matter" in his works—an account of an unknowable "something, I know not what" underlying sensible apperances. This notion, Berkeley points out, is not logically incoherent. It cannot even get that far. It is empty—and thus no proper candidate for logical appraisal to begin with.

CHAPTER 3

1. The first important philosophical discussion of such "body-changing" cases comes with John Locke's speculations about the possibility of "the soul of a prince entering into the body of a cobbler." See Book II, Chapter 27 of Locke's *Essay Concerning Human Understanding*.

2. It is worth noticing that in the first, "exchanging bodies," version of the story we haven't the vaguest idea of how our envisioned diabolical machine works—or even could work. Is each person's "soul" "sucked out" and pumped through the wires into the body of the other person?

    Our being at a loss here is not accidental. What it makes sense to say about the outcome of some process crucially depends upon the nature and character of that process itself. (We will, in fact, see this in some detail later in this chapter, in sections 3.15 and 3.16.) Conversely, then, the fact that we find ourselves unable to say anything at all, however speculative, about the nature and character of the process which supposedly leads to some striking outcome, while hardly conclusive evidence of confusion, should at least lead us to suspect that we may have misdescribed that ostensible outcome—or even failed coherently to describe any possible outcome at all.

3. That the underlying theory of personal identity being taken for granted is the key to resolving questions about the possibility of this or that form of "afterlife" is one of the richest and most useful insights exploited by contemporary analytic philosophy. The explorations of the notion and criteria of personal identity upon which I am about to embark recapitulate the results of several decades of fruitful work on the subject—although I admit to having added a few new twists of my own.

There are a large number of excellent books devoted, from an "analytic" perspective, to the subject of the identification of persons. One delightful place to begin a wider study of the topic is with John Perry's charming *A Dialogue on Personal Identity and Immortality*, Hackett Publishing Company (Indianapolis: 1978). Perry has also edited an excellent anthology on the topic: *Personal Identity*, UCLA Press (Los Angeles: 1975). Perry's anthology has been complemented by a second fine collection of essays, Amelie Rorty's *The Identities of Persons*, also published by the UCLA Press (Los Angeles: 1976). The two books together give a solid overview of the contemporary scene. Two important book-length studies are Sydney Shoemaker, *Self-Knowledge and Self-Identity*, Cornell University Press, (Ithaca, NY: 1963) and David Wiggins, *Identity and Spatio-Temporal Continuity*, Blackwell (Oxford: 1967). Bernard Williams' collection of his own essays, *Problems of the Self*, Cambridge University Press (London and New York: 1973), contains a number of significant papers on the subject as well.

4. Note: "are persons." The sense of the term 'body' being invoked here is 'body-1', not 'body-5'. As Antony Flew once put it, "people are what you meet." The point, of course, is that you do not meet (only) people's bodies (i.e., bodies-5).

5. This is, more or less, David Hume's famed "Bundle Theory" of the self. On this view, the self is a collection or "bundle" of "ideas and impressions" held together as a bundle by the relations of "resemblence, contiguity, and constant conjunction" obtaining among them, rather than by being related to any single temporally continuous thing. Hume's account of persons and personal identity can be found in Section I, iv, 6 of his *A Treatise on Human Nature*. The canonical edition is edited by L. A. Selby-Bigge, Clarendon Press (London: 1888, 1896), but various editions and reprintings are readily available.

6. These considerations are sufficient to show, by the way, that the process of transferring the pattern of electrical impulses from one brain to another, which we envisioned back in section 3.3, wouldn't itself be a process which transferred persons—much less "souls"—from one body to another. Any process which, per impossible, satisfied the latter description would necessarily have to be a process which preserved personal identity. What we have just seen, however, is that the process of impressing one person's pattern of transient electrical brain impulses upon another brain—new or used—precisely does not preserve such personal identity.

7. Probably the strongest contemporary defender of the indispensibility of bodily continuity for personal identity has been B. A. O. Williams. See, for example, his essay "Personal Identity and Individuation," *Proceedings of the Aristotelian Society* (1956–7) and various of the papers collected in his *Problems of the Self*.

8. Other symptoms of psychological disturbance, of course, are likely to develop in short order. A secure sense of self-identity is an essential component of "mental health." One predictable result of the sort of delusionary madness which I have been sketching, for example, is a rapidly evolving paranoia, most probably manifested in delusions of persecution.

9. As Strawson puts it, the concept of a person is "logically primitive." (See his *Individuals*, cited in note (6) for Chapter 0.) The point is that the concept of a person is not one which we derive by cobbling together other, more basic, concepts—say, the concept of a "mind" and the concept of a "body." Such concepts as those of a

"mind" and a "body" (body-5) are rather concepts which we arrive at by focusing our attention on only some of the aspects of the basic unitary concept of a person as the single logical subject of both "M-predicates" and "P-predicates," that is, both banal properties and special properties.

10. In the third of his Dialogues on personal identity and immortality (see note (3) above) John Perry arrives at the opposite result, concluding that personal identity follows the "chassis" ("shell" or body-3). His error, in essence, is to mistake the absence of any conceptual or logical connection between personal identity and brain continuity for a complete irrelevance of brain continuity to personal identity. The deeper problem which underlies this error, however, is Perry's failure to appreciate the functional component of the concept of a person—and, a fortiori, of the relevant concept of a brain. For it is not the continuity of the brain qua piece of tissue, so to speak, which is relevant to questions of personal identity but rather the continuity of the brain qua organ of cognitive competences (that is, functionally conceived). That the brain is the organ of thought, memory, and the like is, to be sure, a contingent empirical matter-of-fact and not a logical or conceptual truth. But it does not follow that it is not a logical or conceptual truth that personal identity tracks with the continuous existence of the organ of such cognitive competences—whatever it might turn out to be.

11. It is David Wiggins who deserves credit for first properly appreciating the point that different parts of the human body are differently causally implicated in the cognitive functioning of persons and thus differently relevant to questions of personal identity. See his *Identity and Spatio-Temporal Continuity*.

CHAPTER 4

1. It follows from these observations that there is no possibility of dispensing with informed judgment—for example, the disinterested judgment of competent medical personnel—in determinations of death. The point, however, is not just that there is nothing more to be measured which could serve as an automatic and decisive criterion for fixing the time of death, say, mechanically. As we shall see in a moment, the point is that the decision to be made is not a purely theoretical one at all but primarily a practical (moral or legal) one which turns, among other things, on such judgmental matters as whether or not it is worth the effort to undertake certain "heroic measures" in the particular case at hand.

2. Often misleadingly called "brain death." It is, of course, only (entire) living organisms which can literally be said to die. Individual organs simply cease to function. It is doubtless because cessation of measurable cortical activity is so frequently employed as crucial evidence of a person's death that this idiom of "brain death" has developed. We do not, after all, speak of a newly blind individual as having suffered "eye death" or of the renally disfunctional as having undergone "kidney death."

An isoelectric electroencephalogram is by no means universally relied upon as the sole criterion—or even as a criterion—for diagnosing death. It is, however, a central element of the so-called Harvard Criteria, and rapidly gaining favor among clinicians as an indicator which ought to be recognized by any adequate contemporary legal or medical definition of death. For a good survey of the current state of the diagnostic art, see Chapter 3 of Walton's *On Defining Death* cited in note (4) for Chapter 1.

3. Exactly the same point holds for "fixing the moment of life" as well. The question "When does life begin?" in fact, admits of a variety of muddles. "The moment of conception," of course, like "the moment of death," is an idealization or linguistic fiction. But even when we are well past conception and clearly have an embryo or foetus underway, it is not clear whether it would be more appropriate to classify that foetus or embryo as itself a living organism or rather as an adjunct of another living organism, the mother. The difficulty is that the biological interdependence between the mother and such an embryo or foetus resembles the biological interdependence between an organism and one of its organs as much or more as it resembles the interdependence between two autonomous organisms which are related, for example, symbiotically or as host and parasite.

This complication is reflected in the fact that the question is often framed not simply as "When does life begin?" but as "When does independent life begin?" What is theoretically relevant here is supposedly not the existence of a foetus as a determinate and identifiable entity but rather the question of its ex utero viability, its ability to survive independently outside the uterus. Unfortunately, rephrasing the question in this way does not leave us much better off. There is no more an instantaneous "moment of independent viability" than there is an instantaneous "moment of death" or "moment of conception." And whether or not a specific foetus could, at a specific time, survive ex utero depends both on the idiosyncracies of that particular foetus' individual development and upon the contingencies of the current abilities of medical technology to cope with premature birth.

In fact, the question "When does life begin?" like the question "When does life end?" is characteristically not a theoretical question at all—one which could in principle be settled by further discoveries about embryos or foetuses—but a practical, legal, or moral question about whether it would be appropriate to enact legislation permitting or prohibiting the termination of a pregnancy at certain times or under certain conditions. What is at issue, in other words, is typically not any matters of fact but rather once again the problem of settling upon defensible criteria for licensing certain morally problematic conducts. In Chapter 6, we shall see how such questions can be properly articulated and coherently discussed.

4. For a fuller discussion of many of these points, see Robert Brandom, "Freedom and Constraint by Norms," *American Philosophical Quarterly*, Vol. 16, No. 3, 1979.

5. For a dissenting view, see Paul Ziff, "The Feelings of Robots," *Analysis*, XIX, 3, 1959; reprinted in A. R. Anderson (ed.), *Minds and Machines*, Prentice-Hall (Englewood Cliffs, N.J.: 1964).

There is a vast, burgeoning, and interesting philosophical literature addressed to the question of whether a machine could in principle think—and, if so, how we could in practice tell that it was doing so. Anderson's anthology, *Minds and Machines*, is one good place to begin a further exploration of the topic; Keith Gunderson's *Mentality and Machines*, is another. Daniel Dennett's book *Brainstorms*, Bradford Books (Montgomery, VT: 1978) is a contemporary classic on the subject.

I have even contributed a few words on the matter myself: "Conversation and Intelligence," in B. DeGelder (ed.), *Knowledge and Representation,* Routledge & Kegan Paul (London: 1982); and "On Understanding the Difficulty in Understanding Understanding," in H. Parret and J. Bouveresse (eds.), *Meaning and Understanding,* Walter de Gruyter (Berlin: 1981).

6.   Analogous points hold, again, for human embryos and human foetuses. Like human corpses, embryos and foetuses are not, per se, human beings. (That is, "embryo" and "foetus" pick out natural kinds different from the natural kind "organism.") But, like human corpses, the foetuses and embryos of human persons also stand in unique and special relationships to those persons—relationships which, at least, make it appropriate to raise the question of whether or not some or all of the rights of personhood ought not be bestowed upon such embryos and foetuses as well. It is, of course, that question which is in dispute between the advocates and the opponents of relatively liberal abortion legislation, the so-called "pro-choice" and "pro-life" movements on the contemporary American political scene.

7.   These observations suggest that moral questions concerning the rights of embryos and foetuses ought to be more problematic than those concerning the rights of corpses. For, although a foetus or an embryo is no more capable of exercising those rational functions which our implicit moral theory conceptually links with the moral status of personhood than is a corpse, a human embryo or human foetus does belong to a natural kind, members of which, unlike corpses, at least have the potential to develop into rational human beings. And that, indeed, is what we find. The proper treatment of human embryos and foetuses is a matter of considerable debate; the proper treatment of human corpses is not.

CHAPTER 5

1.   The work that I do here in the area of moral philosophy, in other words, will be more "phenomenological" than analytic and a priori. That is, I shall be describing an ethical system which, I believe, already exists embodied in our moral practices, rather than recommending ethical principles for such practice on the basis, for instance, of some independent analysis of personhood or practical rationality.

2.   For an historical and philosophical examination of this classical picture, see Arthur O. Lovejoy, *The Great Chain of Being,* Harvard University Press (Cambridge, MA: 1936), reprinted by Harper Torchbooks (New York: 1960).

     The Great Chain of Being, to describe it briefly, was conceived as an explanatory system. Classically the explanations proceeded from the top downwards. The evidently teleological character of natural systems, in other words, was explained as a manifestation of rational will, as the determinate consequence of a purposive creative act of the Divine mind.

     One of the most significant revolutions in the history of science was achieved when Lamarck suggested that this explanatory order instead ought properly to be turned on its head—that is, that teleology (and, indeed, mind itself) are correctly to be explained evolutionarily, from the bottom upwards, as the emergent consequences of determinate (physical) causal processes. Whatever the merits of

Lamarck's own subsequent theorizing, it was this key idea which set the stage for and made possible the functionalist and evolutionary science of biology which we know and practice today.

3. The taxonomy of rights which I am here in the process of developing is not exactly standard, but I think that it is a useful and defensible one. The literature on rights, of course, is huge, and I do not pretend to have an adequate scholarly grasp of it nor to be able to do proper justice to it here. Two works that really should be mentioned, however, are John Stuart Mill's classic *On Liberty*—one convenient edition of which is that edited by E. Rapaport, Hackett Publishing Company (Indianapolis: 1978)—and Isaiah Berlin's *Two Concepts of Liberty,* Oxford University Press (Oxford: 1958).

4. For a thorough examination of the moral questions at stake in our treatment of animals, see the essays collected by Tom Regan and Peter Singer (eds.), *Animal Rights and Human Obligations,* Prentice-Hall (Englewood Cliffs, NJ: 1976), and Singer's own spirited defense of "animal rights" in his *Animal Liberation,* New York Review/Random House (New York: 1975).

5. This, indeed, is what the typical defender of "animal rights" characteristically overlooks. His usual focus is precisely on pleasures and pains. Noting correctly that animals do not differ essentially from us humans in those respects, however, he often goes on to conclude, erroneously, that they do not differ (importantly) from us humans in any morally relevant respects. While the resultant attitude toward animals may be commendable, such argumentation bespeaks only a too narrow view of what in fact counts as a morally relevant consideration when one is deliberating about ethical conduct.

6. While it would be folly to attempt a thorough discussion of the subject here, some remarks about the relations between the moral picture which I have briefly developed in this chapter and the main historical strands of philosophical ethics are probably in order. The most central traditional division in the study of ethics is probably that between those philosophers who hold that the moral status of an act depends upon its consequences—"consequentialists"—and those philosophers who hold that the moral status of an act depends upon its motivations —"intentionalists". Historically, the dominant consequentialist theory has been "Utilitarianism," typified by the work of Bentham and Mill, and the leading intentionalist theory has probably been some variant of the "deontological ethic" advocated by Kant.

The Utilitarian focus is on the "goods" produced by a given action —characteristically taking the form of increased pleasure or the removal of pains. This outlook is often summed up in the prescription "Act so as to produce the greatest good for the greatest number." The deontological focus, in contrast, is on the rule or (in Kant's terminology) the "maxim" which the agent is following in acting. Its outlook is perhaps best captured by Kant's famous "categorical imperative," one version of which runs, roughly: "Act so that the maxim of your action could be a law of nature for all rational beings." (See Kant's *Foundations of the Metaphysics of Morals.* The translation by Lewis White Beck for the "Library of Liberal Arts" series, Bobbs Merrill (Indianapolis: 1959), is relatively clear and readily available.)

The hypothesis naturally suggested by my own descriptive, "phenomenological," observations is that each of these schools of thought has gotten hold of one element of our actual implicit moral theory and is attempting to employ it as the basis of a complete ethical system. My observations suggest, that is, that our own implicit moral theory springs from two sources—one of which indeed yields considerations which are consequentialist, and even Utilitarian, in nature, and the other of which yields considerations which are intentionalist in character, and indeed even Kantian.

Thus, in advancing the hypothesis that the only thing of positive intrinsic value (intrinsic worth) is the exercise of moral autonomy in the deliberate and reasoned actions of a being in pursuit of what it believes to be morally right, I am in essence agreeing with Kant's claim that the only thing which is good in itself is a "good will." But in observing that the set of intrinsic values is not exhausted by considerations of intrinsic worth alone, I am also endorsing the Utilitarian point that the affective consequences of an action are surely relevant to its moral evaluation—although I am endorsing it, so to speak, in its contrapositive form, not as a prescription for right action but as a prima facie prohibition of the causing of suffering, which is, other things being equal, always as such morally wrong.

I am, in fact, convinced that the composite "bivalent" ethical theory which I have descriptively extracted from consideration of our actual moral practices can also be defended as a "correct" moral theory by (relatively) a priori arguments, but this note is certainly not the place to undertake a philosophical task of that magnitude. For the reader who is interested in pursuing the question further, however, I can recommend a couple of useful starting points: William Frankena's small book *Ethics,* Prentice-Hall (Englewood Cliffs, NJ: 1963), is an excellent introduction to the tangled complex of problems constituting moral philosophy; and R. B. Brandt's *Ethical Theory,* Prentice-Hall (Englewood Cliffs, NJ: 1959) remains the most comprehensive, and probably the best, survey and general discussion of those problems and of the significant alternative solutions to them which philosophers have historically proposed.

CHAPTER 6

1. I am speaking here, and throughout this chapter, only of what is sometimes called "active euthanasia" or "mercy killing"—the positive action of deliberately putting to death a living human being. The term 'euthanasia' is often used in a broader sense, to cover both such "mercy killing" and what is termed "passive euthanasia"—the action of allowing an already dying person to die without intervention by, for example, refraining from treatment or discontinuing treatment in a case of terminal illness. This latter terminology—which makes "mercy killing" and "letting die" both species of a single act genus—is, I think, mistaken and misleading. I shall offer my reasons for thinking so in the next chapter.

    There is a large and growing literature on euthanasia and the related ethical themes which we shall be exploring. The anthology *Ethical Issues in Death and Dying,* edited by Tom. L. Beauchamp and Seymour Perlin, Prentice-Hall, (Englewood Cliffs, NJ: 1978), is a superb collection of classical and contemporary essays on the topics of this and succeeding chapters and contains useful suggestions for further reading as well. Some other useful sources are cited in note (5) for the Prelude above.

2. Opposition to euthanasia is thus logically compatible with the advocacy of capital punishment. Interestingly enough, it is equally compatible with the advocacy of liberal and permissive abortion policies. One can, that is, morally object to euthanasia on the grounds that, as the deliberate taking of the life of an innocent person, such "mercy killing" would be a clear violation of that person's "right to life," and nevertheless consistently hold that such a "right to life" is first acquired by a human being at birth.

On this view, a human foetus is not yet a human being, and thus not yet a person but only potentially a person. The "right to life," however, is a right which only persons possess. Consequently, there will be no logical conflict between a supposed "right to life" possessed by a foetus and a mother's right—as indisputably a human being, and therefore a full-fledged person—freely to exercise her moral autonomy in choice and action.

3. The increasing technological ease of organ transplants, and the resultant growing need to find suitable organ donors, may well make such questions of expediency and arbitrariness particularly acute.

4. We see exactly this strategy pursued, for example, by opponents of permissive abortion policies. Their emphasis is always sharply on the continuousness of foetal development and the moral arbitrariness of introducing well-defined points of decision into that continuum. Opponents of abortion typically stress, too, the similarities between newborn infants and foetuses at various stages of development, pointing out, for example, that recognizable hands and feet develop fairly early in the course of pregnancy. Advocates of permissive policies, in contrast, characteristically stress the differences between foetuses and newborns, focusing attention on functional questions of ex utero viability rather than on structural points of anatomical resemblance.

5. I think that this is true, too, in the disputes over abortion, although an agreement in values can quite easily be masked by terminological differences. It is instructive to note that each side of the dispute depicts itself as the positive advocate of an acknowledged right of persons—"pro-life" versus "pro-choice"—thereby casting its opponent in the role of one who refuses to acknowledge that right. (If one is not "pro-life" or "pro-choice," then one presumably is "anti-life" or "anti-choice.")

The matter of terminology in ethical disagreements is a delicate one. The same piece of conduct, for example, will be characterized by various disputants as "infanticide," "abortion," or merely "termination of pregnancy." (Compare "murder," "mercy killing," and "euthanasia.") The most important observation to be made in this connection is that for acts too, as for things, there are various kinds of kinds. There are, that is, various ways of classfying actions. In particular, actions can be classified descriptively, and they can be classified evaluatively.

Descriptively, for example, some act may correctly be classifiable as a killing of X by Y. Evaluatively, the same action might count, for example, as an act of murder or as an act of justified self-defense. The descriptive classification leaves legal or moral questions open; the evaluative classification prejudges them or presupposes that they are already settled. Our legal system, for instance, regards some acts of killing as lawful. But it necessarily does not regard any act of murder as lawful, since murder is—by definition, as it were—unlawful killing.

In moral and legal debate, the only non-question-begging procedure, of course, is to begin with a purely descriptive characterization of the action whose legal or moral status is at issue. For the question of whether or not the action properly falls under some evaluative classification just is the question of that action's legal or moral status and cannot consistently be regarded as having been settled until the disagreement itself has been brought to some satisfactory resolution. (We shall explore all of these matters in considerably more detail in the next chapter.) Needless to say, this logically correct procedure is not universally followed among disputants whose central aim is often to achieve by rhetorical persuasion what cannot in fact be attained by cogent argumentation.

6. It seems clear that this has, in fact, become the actual state of affairs with regard to the question of abortion. That is, the moral sensibilities of a significant portion of the population have already shifted in such a way that those individuals now regard the termination of a pregnancy during its early stages not merely as morally permissible but actually as morally unproblematic. If this is indeed so, however, the "pro-life" advocates are fighting for a lost cause. The most that they could hope to accomplish would be to ensure that some legal, safe, and sterile abortions were displaced by illegal, unsafe, and septic abortions. That this is surely not an outcome which any "pro-life" advocate would call desirable suggests, then, that there may, in the end, actually be some matters of fact which the opponents of abortion are unwilling to acknowledge and accept—not facts about foetuses but facts about the settled moral convictions of vast numbers of their fellow citizens.

CHAPTER 7

1. For a helpful introduction to the theory of action, see Lawrence H. Davis, *Theory of Action,* Prentice-Hall (Englewood Cliffs, NJ: 1978).

2. I shall return to this point shortly, at length and in detail. See sections 7.10 and 7.11 of this chapter.

3. See B. D. Colen, *Karen Ann Quinlan: Dying in the Age of Eternal Life,* Nash Publishing Co. (New York: 1976) for a description of this now-famous case. Excerpts from the transcript of the court proceedings and other related materials can be found in B. Steinbock (ed.), *Killing and Letting Die,* Prentice-Hall (Englewood Cliffs, NJ: 1980) and in T. Beauchamp and S. Perlin (eds.), *Ethical Issues in Death and Dying,* cited in note (1) for Chapter 6.

4. That is to say, a case of action and a case of inaction which have the same consequences are sometimes also morally equivalent, i.e., have the same status when considered from the moral point of view. A good deal of the confusion over the difference between "mercy killing" and "letting die," however, has stemmed from the too-hasty generalization of this kind of example. We will examine the matter carefully in a few moments.

5. The same holds true for the paradigms of action and inaction which are offered in what is probably the most influential philosophical discussion of the moral symmetry or asymmetry of killing and letting die—the case of the "drowned cousins" in James Rachels' essay "Killing and Letting Die: Active and Passive Euthanasia," reprinted in both anthologies cited in note (3), Chapter 7.

    Rachels constructs two scenarios: In the first, the inheritance-greedy Smith drowns his six-year-old cousin in the bathtub and arranges things so that the death will appear accidental. In the second, the equally greedy Jones enters the bathroom with the intention of drowning his six-year-old cousin, but the cousin fortuitously slips, hits his head, and falls face down in the water; and Jones need only stand by and do nothing as the child drowns himself "accidentally."

    Both Smith's action and Jones's inaction are indeed morally reprehensible—and the account of rights and moral permissibility which I have sketched and just applied to the cases of Harold and Helene indeed arrives at precisely that conclusion. Rachels, however, takes the fact that action and inaction are morally equivalent in this case as evidence for the conclusion (roughly) that any instances of action and inaction which have isomorphic outcomes will also be morally equivalent—and that conclusion, I shall argue, simply does not follow at all.

    Rachels' mistake, to put my point in a nutshell, lies in his failure to consider the exact grounds on which Smith's conduct and Jones' conduct can respectively be judged (correctly) to be morally otiose. Instead, Rachels apparently simply takes it for granted that those grounds are identical in both cases. He appeals merely to the fact that both Smith and Jones deliberately implicate themselves causally in the death of an innocent child. What he does not do, however, is to bring that fact into contact with any explicitly formulated moral principles. Had he, in fact, attempted to formulate such principles, he would have discovered that they make essential reference, not only to those features of the two scenarios to which Rachels draws explicit attention, but to another feature of both scenarios as well—the fact that both drowned cousins were functioning rational agents prior to their deaths. And that, as we shall see, is the crucial fact which separates this pair of cases from at least some otherwise analogous paradigms of "mercy killing" and "letting die."

    Precisely the same points can be made about the paradigms of the shipwrecked sailors offered by J. Lichtenberg in her essay "The Moral Equivalence of Action and Omission," *Canadian Journal of Philosophy*, 1981. Lichtenberg, too, neglects explicitly to formulate the moral principles underlying our judgments in her paradigm cases, and consequently also falls victim to the same fallacious overhasty generalization from moral equivalence of action and inaction in some cases to moral equivalence in all cases that we find in Rachels' essay.

6. Nor should we neglect to mention the important class of positive passive legal and civil rights—conditional, for example, on one's citizenship or age or occupation—which function to constrain the conducts of such "quasi-persons" as legislatures, governmental agencies, labor unions, and corporations. Such collectivities are variously answerable to the larger society in which they are embedded, and the degree to which they fulfill the obligations correlative to such conditional positive passive rights through their "conducts" is thus a fit subject for constraint, correction, guidance, and moral or legal appraisal by that wider society (itself "acting"

collectively as an electorate, for example, or through such other "quasi-personal" agencies as the courts).

7. We can now say more precisely what it is that Rachels overlooked. Prior to their deaths, both Smith's cousin and Jones' cousin are, ex hypothesi, properly functioning rational agents, fully capable of exercising (if only immaturely) their moral autonomy in deliberation and choice. Both Smith's action and Jones' inaction, therefore, are conducts which offend against moral worth. In the cases of Alric and Bartholomew, in contrast, there is already—prior to the point of moral decision and action or inaction—a complete and irreversible loss of rational function capacities.

What Rachels fails to recognize (since he does not attempt explicitly to formulate either the ethical principles or the theory of moral value upon which our judgment in the cases of Smith and Jones is based) is that this fact makes a moral difference. It precludes certain kinds of arguments for the conclusion that action or inaction which would result in death is morally forbidden. Neither killing Alric nor allowing Bartholomew to die can correctly be shown to be an offense against moral worth. In the case of Alric, some lines of argument leading to the conclusion that action to cause Alric's death would be morally forbidden remain open. There remain in the case of Bartholomew, however, no analogous arguments which lead to the conclusion that allowing Bartholomew to die through inaction would be morally prohibited. And that is what introduces the crucial moral asymmetry between Alric's case and Bartholomew's—and thus between at least some instances of "mercy killing" and some otherwise similar instances of "letting die."

8. This observation precipitates us into the heart of the theory of action. Its consequences were first explored in depth by G. E. M. Anscombe in her pioneering work *Intention*, Cornell University Press (Ithaca, NY: 1958). Subsequent philosophical literature mapping the territory thus opened has been extensive. Myles Brand's anthology, *The Nature of Human Action*, Scott Foresman and Co. (Glenview, IL: 1971), provides a good sampling of it. For readers interested in pursuing the topic in greater depth, Alvin Goldman's *A Theory of Human Action*, Prentice-Hall (Englewood Cliffs, NJ: 1970); Arthur C. Danto's *Analytical Philosophy of Action*, Cambridge University Press (Cambridge: 1973), and Judith J. Thomson's *Acts and Other Events*, Cornell University Press (Ithaca, NY: 1977) will be especially helpful. The views which I am about to sketch here have been influenced by all of these works—although they are in full agreement with none of them.

CHAPTER 8

1. My colleague Steve Darwall drew my attention to this special danger here and suggested some of the examples which follow.

2. As I am using the term 'suicide', it should be noticed, Darcy's refusal of treatment would not, in and of itself, be an act of suicide. Like euthanasia, suicide requires a positive action, the deliberate taking of one's own life. Allowing oneself to die, then, does not count as suicide. Nor does sacrificing one's life (e.g., for a cause). The difference is acknowledged in our common idiom by the distinction between

"taking one's life" and "giving one's life." Only the former is, properly speaking, an act of suicide—although instances of self-sacrifice which risk or result in death are often, somewhat misleadingly, said to be "suicidal."

3. My argument here, it will be recognized, is Kantian. What I am claiming, in essence, is that the "maxim" upon which Elbert proposes to act cannot be consistently "universalized." (See Kant's *Foundations of the Metaphysics of Morals*, cited in note (5) for Chapter 5.) "Hobbesian" considerations addressing the quality of life in a social order in which slaves and slaveholders are in a state of "standing war" are, of course, relevant to the question of the moral legitimacy of "voluntary" enslavement, but, as I have structured the argument, they are secondary. My primary point is a logical one: Universal acceptance of the moral legitimacy of "voluntary" enslavement is inconsistent with certain facts about persons. The policy of regarding such conducts as morally permissible thus turns out to be "self-defeating," for it would inevitably come to be rejected as a policy by the very parties who supposedly appealed to it to justify their conducts in the first place.

4. The line of argument which I have taken here in defense of one sort of "paternalism" is intentionally a narrow one. I have, that is, deliberately restricted myself to purely moral considerations, and avoided any questions regarding "social costs." A more typical line of justification for paternalistic practices characteristically includes some sort of "cost-benefit analysis," intended to serve as an argument to the effect that "society" has legitimate interests which are served by interfering in the conducts of individuals "for their own good." Laws requiring the use of seat belts or the wearing of helmets by motorcyclists, for example, are often defended in part on the grounds that, although the individual motorist or cyclist endangers only himself by refusing to employ such safety devices, the resultant increased burden on public medical care facilities is a matter of legitimate societal interest which conveys a right of paternalistic interference. (For a classic discussion of paternalism, see Mill's *On Liberty*, cited in note (3) for Chapter 5 above.)

My own inclination is to find such "social" arguments in support of paternalistic policies essentially more problematic than a "purely moral" justification of the sort which I have tried here to reconstruct. In such cases as Darcy's, in any event, the question appears to be moot, for the majority of "social costs" seem to lie on the side of paternalistically intervening in her intended suicide rather than on the side of laissez faire noninterference.

5. Indeed, according to contemporary "economic" or "decision-theoretic" models, all practical rationality consists in such self-interested appraisals of the possible outcomes of envisaged actions. C. Dyke's *Philosophy of Economics*, Prentice-Hall (Englewood Cliffs, NJ: 1981) contains a good introductory discussion of the question together with some useful references.

My own appeals to the notion of "rationality" employ the term 'rational' in a fairly commonsensical way: An action is rational if there are good reasons for performing it. (In my examples, indeed, not only are there putatively good reasons for the various conducts in question but the agents themselves are in a position to offer accounts of what those reasons supposedly are. That is, in my examples, the reasons in question also function as motives.) The question, however, of whether all "good reasons" can be pressed into a single mold—"preference" or "utility" or what have you—I purposely leave open. I do not, in fact, think that they can be—but this footnote is hardly the place to argue for that thesis.

CHAPTER 9

1. For these Stoic arguments, see Lucretius, *De Rerum Natura,* 3.870ff. and 3.898ff.
2. Jonathan Swift, *Gulliver's Travels,* Part III, Chapter X. Various editions are widely available.
3. William Shakespeare, *Hamlet,* III, i, 79–80.
4. Also, of course, from Hamlet's soliloquy (III, i, 65–68). The mixing of metaphors here is pure Shakespeare and, as poetry, purely superb. To the coldly logical eye, however, it intimates—rightly as we shall see—some common conceptual conclusions lurking in the cultural background.
5. The so-called "Existentialists" (Martin Heidegger and Jean-Paul Sartre being the dominant representatives of that movement) are probably the worst offenders in this regard. For an extensive discussion with comprehensive references, see Paul Edwards' "Existentialism and Death: A Survey of Some Confusions and Absurdities," reprinted in John Donnelly (ed.), *Language, Metaphysics, and Death,* Fordham University Press (New York: 1978).
6. For a fuller examination of this notion of what something is "like," see Thomas Nagel, "What Is it Like To Be a Bat?", *Philosophical Review,* Vol. LXXXIII, 1974.
7. The discussion which follows is based upon the appraisal of "disembodied existence" offered by P. F. Strawson in his *Individuals.* (See note (6) of Chapter 0 for a full citation.)
8. Berkeley was confused about this point. He attempted to argue that the "esse" of ordinary objects was "percipi" (their existence consisted in their being perceived), in part on the grounds that one supposedly cannot conceive of, for instance, a cherry tree "unperceived and unthought of." In the very act of attempting to imagine such a cherry tree, one thinks of it oneself—and so it is not "unthought of." (See his *Three Dialogues Between Hylas and Philonous,* cited in note (7) for Chapter 0.)

    Berkeley here fails properly to acknowledge the distinction between an act of thinking and the object or content of a thought. To conceive of a cherry tree answering to his description, it is sufficient that one think of it *as* "unperceived and unthought of." The characteristic of being unthought of here belongs to the content of the thought—to what is thought of—and this fact is not contradicted by the fact (if it is a fact) that being unthought of is not itself a property of the act of thinking. To draw an analogy, I can excitedly think of a calm tiger. My act of thinking is what is excited. But it does not follow that what I think of—the calm tiger which is the object of my thought—is itself thought of as excited.
9. See A. G. N. Flew, "Can a Man Witness His Own Funeral?", *Hibbert Journal,* 1956, for a more extensive treatment of these topics (to which my own discussion is indebted).

10. The claim is defended by Ernest Becker in Chapters 2 and 3 of his *The Denial of Death*, The Free Press (New York: 1973). For reasons which I am about to offer, I do not find his defense (which runs more or less along psychoanalytic lines) to be a convincing one.

11. Jorge Luis Borges, "The Immortal," reprinted (in an excellent English translation by James E. Irby) in Borges' *Labyrinths*, New Directions Publishing Corporation (New York: 1962, 1964).

12. This last example serves as the point of departure for Bernard Williams' treatment of the risks of indefinitely prolonged life in his "The Makropulos Case: Reflections on the Tedium of Immortality," reprinted in *Problems of the Self*, cited in note (3) for Chapter 3, and also in John Donnelly's anthology, *Language, Metaphysics, and Death*, referred to in note (5) for this chapter. Williams' conclusions, however, disagree with those for which I am about to argue.

13. The parenthetical remark adverts to a dispute within the history of philosophy over, very roughly, whether happiness is the sort of thing which can coherently figure in one's practical reasoning as a goal, aim, or end of action. Aristotle is probably the chief defender of an affirmative answer to this question (see the treatment of "eudaemonia" in his *Nichomachean Ethics*), and Kant probably the chief opponent (see the remarks on happiness in his *Foundations of the Metaphysics of Morals*). For what we are up to here, however, we can safely bypass this fine point in the philosophy of action and value.

14. This optimistic point of view is, as one might expect, embraced by a number of writers of science fiction. Perhaps its most successful advocate is Robert Heinlein, whose recurrent "immortal" character, Lazarus Long, (see, for instance, Heinlein's novel *Time Enough for Love*) has a lust and savor for life which is undiminished by centuries of living.

15. A good introduction to philosophical epistemology and the problem of skepticism can be found in R. M. Chisholm, *Theory of Knowledge*, Prentice-Hall (Englewood Cliffs, NJ: 1966). *The Foundations of Knowledge*, a collection of essays edited by Charles Landesman, Prentice-Hall (Englewood Cliffs, NJ: 1970), contains a number of important and useful discussions of the topic as well.

16. The metaphor, we recall—and the picture which I am about to develop from it as well—are Heidegger's. (His *Being and Time* is cited in note (4) for the Prelude.) For an extended (unsympathetic) appraisal of Heidegger's work in this connection, see Paul Edwards' *Heidegger on Death: A Critical Evaluation*, MONIST Monograph #1, The Hegler Institute (LaSalle, IL: 1979).

17. This line of thought gives rise to the notorious skeptical "problem of other minds," a detailed formulation of which can be found in the Introduction to *The Philosophy of Mind*, edited by Vere C. Chappell, Prentice-Hall (Englewood Cliffs, NJ: 1962). Ludwig Wittgenstein's response to the problem, as presented in his *Philosophical Investigations* (see note (4) for Chapter 0), has proved important and influential. For further exploration, see also Norman Malcolm's review "Wittgenstein's *Philosophical Investigations*" in *Philosophical Review*, Vol. LXIII, 1954 (and variously reprinted), and the discussion in Richard Rorty's *Philosophy and the Mirror of Nature*, cited in note (7) for Chapter 2. An insatiable reader may also wish to consult my essays "The Concept of Linguistic Correctness," *Philosophical Studies*, Vol. 30, 1976, and "Speaking Lions," *Canadian Journal of Philosophy*, Vol. VII, No. 1, 1977.

18. We ought not leave this discussion without a few remarks about the "aloneness" of death—another topic over which various Existentialist philosophers have expended much ink. The claim that "all men die alone" has both an ordinary and a "philosophical" sense. In its ordinary sense, unsurprisingly enough, the claim is false. Some people indeed die alone; but others die in crowded hospital wards or at rock music concerts or on busy public streets. In its "philosophical" sense, however, the claim again suggests that there is something especially "private" about death.

There isn't, of course. Just as my own death will not be a "special" or "private" experience, so, too, it will not be a "special" or "private" achievement. "I must die my own death alone" should rather be compared with "I must suffer my own headaches alone." The reason that no one else can suffer my headaches is not the mysterious one that I have a "special" or "private" access to those headaches which, so to speak, happen to be mine but rather the trivial one that 'my headaches' just means 'the headaches from which I suffer'. The headaches from which someone else suffers are not my headaches but his or her headaches.

Similarly, it is only in this trivial sense that my death is something which I must face alone—not for the mysterious reason that I have a "special" or "privileged" relationship to some death which, so to speak, also happens to be mine, but for the tedious reason that, if I wasn't the person who died, it wouldn't be my death which had occurred. 'My death', in this context, just means 'the event of my dying'.

To the extent that "Every man must die alone" says something true, then, it says something trivially true. What it says, roughly, is that dying is not a collective activity like playing baseball or making love. "Every man must die alone," in other words, is a remark rather like "Every man must play solitare alone." It does not reveal a "deep metaphysical necessity." It reflects a boring linguistic truth: We don't call a game 'solitare' if it's played by more than one player—and (just as we don't call a headache 'mine' if it isn't my head that aches), we don't call a death 'mine' if someone other than me is the person who dies.